CHARGING UP SAN JUAN HILL

WITNESS TO HISTORY

Peter Charles Hoffer and Williamjames Hull Hoffer, Series Editors

Williamjames Hull Hoffer, *The Caning of Charles Sumner: Honor, Idealism, and the Origins of the Civil War*

Tim Lehman, *Bloodshed at Little Bighorn: Sitting Bull, Custer, and the Destinies of Nations*

Daniel R. Mandell, *King Philip's War: Colonial Expansion, Native Resistance, and the End of Indian Sovereignty*

Erik R. Seeman, *The Huron-Wendat Feast of the Dead: Indian-European Encounters in Early North America*

Peter Charles Hoffer, *When Benjamin Franklin Met the Reverend Whitefield: Enlightenment, Revival, and the Power of the Printed Word*

William Thomas Allison, *My Lai: An American Atrocity in the Vietnam War*

Peter Charles Hoffer, *Prelude to Revolution: The Salem Gunpowder Raid of 1775*

Michael Dennis, *Blood on Steel: Chicago Steelworkers and the Strike of 1937*

Benjamin F. Alexander, *Coxey's Army: Popular Protest in the Gilded Age*

John R. Van Atta, *Wolf by the Ears: The Missouri Crisis, 1819–1821*

Donald R. Hickey, *Glorious Victory: Andrew Jackson and the Battle of New Orleans*

Sean Condon, *Shays's Rebellion: Authority and Distress in Post-Revolutionary America*

John C. McManus, *Hell before Their Very Eyes: American Soldiers Liberate Concentration Camps in Germany, April 1945*

Lorri Glover, *The Fate of the Revolution: Virginians Debate the Constitution*

Terri Diane Halperin, *The Alien and Sedition Acts of 1798: Testing the Constitution*

Robert A. Pratt, *Selma's Bloody Sunday: Protest, Voting Rights, and the Struggle for Racial Equality*

Peter Charles Hoffer, *John Quincy Adams and the Gag Rule: 1835–1850*

Childers, Christopher, *The Webster-Hayne Debate: Defining Nationhood in the Early American Republic*

Charging Up San Juan Hill

THEODORE ROOSEVELT
and the MAKING of IMPERIAL AMERICA

JOHN R. VAN ATTA
BRUNSWICK SCHOOL
GREENWICH, CONNECTICUT

Johns Hopkins University Press | *Baltimore*

© 2018 Johns Hopkins University Press
All rights reserved. Published 2018
Printed in the United States of America on acid-free paper
9 8 7 6 5 4 3 2 1

Johns Hopkins University Press
2715 North Charles Street
Baltimore, Maryland 21218-4363
www.press.jhu.edu

Library of Congress Cataloging-in-Publication Data

Names: Van Atta, John Robert, author.
Title: Charging up San Juan Hill : Theodore Roosevelt and the making of
   imperial America / John R. Van Atta.
Description: Baltimore : Johns Hopkins University Press, 2018. | Series:
   Witness to history | Includes bibliographical references and index.
Identifiers: LCCN 2017046657| ISBN 9781421425863 (hardcover : alk. paper) |
   ISBN 9781421425870 (pbk. : alk. paper) | ISBN 9781421425887 (electronic) |
   ISBN 1421425866 (hardcover : alk. paper) | ISBN 1421425874 (pbk. : alk.
   paper) | ISBN 1421425882 (electronic)
Subjects: LCSH: Roosevelt, Theodore, 1858–1919—Military leadership. | United
   States. Army. Volunteer Cavalry, 1st. | San Juan Hill, Battle of, Cuba,
   1898. | Spanish-American War, 1898—Campaigns—Cuba.
Classification: LCC E757 .V36 2018 | DDC 973.91/1092—dc23
LC record available at https://lccn.loc.gov/2017046657

A catalog record for this book is available from the British Library.

*Special discounts are available for bulk purchases of this book. For more information,
please contact Special Sales at 410-516-6936 or specialsales@press.jhu.edu.*

Johns Hopkins University Press uses environmentally friendly book materials,
including recycled text paper that is composed of at least 30 percent post-consumer
waste, whenever possible.

For the two Lucys, as usual

CONTENTS

PROLOGUE: Old Values, New Challenges   1

1   Legacies   9

2   Jingo Doctrines   32

3   Teddy's Terrors   62

4   Crowded Hour   88

5   New Empire   121

EPILOGUE: Eclipse of Old Heroes   159

Acknowledgments   167
Notes   169
Essay on Sources   193
Index   201

CHARGING UP SAN JUAN HILL

PROLOGUE
Old Values, New Challenges

BELOW A CUBAN SUN SO HOT THAT IT STUNG THEIR EYES, the troopers hunkered low at the base of Kettle Hill, facing the San Juan Heights. Spanish Mauser bullets zipped overhead, while enemy artillery shells landed all around them. Already that morning, they had lost some of their number even before the main action started. During those moments on July 1, 1898, more than five hundred Rough Riders, converted from cavalry into infantry, nervously pondered the uphill charge they had to make, perhaps only minutes away.

Flanking maneuvers offered no chance of capturing the heights; the only option was direct attack. Driving Spanish forces from the high ground meant control of Santiago and, soon enough, US victory in the war. No one doubted that enemy fire would claim a heavy toll, as it had only days before at Las Guásimas, but these unusual citizen-soldiers and their unlikely commander, the 39-year-old Col. Theodore Roosevelt—TR—had volunteered for exactly this kind of mission, hoping to demonstrate their manhood and commitment to civic values.

Finally, at about 1:00 p.m. the order came from the rear to move forward. Observers at a distance would soon spot the skirmish lines of blue-uniformed infantrymen and cavalry troopers beginning their slow, deliberate ascent toward the Spanish trenches and blockhouses on the hillcrests. The Rough Riders, for their part, were to initiate their attack up Kettle Hill, named for the sugar-processing apparatus left abandoned on top. Nearly overcome with excitement, Roosevelt raced for his chestnut gelding, Little Texas, one of the few horses present, and ordered his men to follow. The officers conveyed the order up and down the line. Thus began "my 'crowded hour,'" TR later recounted.[1]

That was a curious phrase. In thus referring to the critical moment of his life, Roosevelt may have been thinking of a stanza from Thomas Osbert Mordaunt's "The Call":

> Sound, sound the clarion, fill the fife,
> Throughout the sensual world proclaim,
> One crowded hour of glorious life
> Is worth an age without a name.

Mordaunt composed the poem when he served in the British army during the Seven Years' War of 1756–1763. It touched chords of memory that ran deep in the Anglo-American political tradition, evoking past sacrifices in the name of freedom against oppressive enemies:

> When first you show'd me at your feet
> Pale liberty, religion tied,
> I flew to shut the glorious gate
> Of freedom on a tyrant's pride.[2]

In later years, as former troopers told and retold the story of July 1, 1898, they still marveled that their colonel had lived through that "crowded" moment, charging right into a lethal "hail storm" of Spanish bullets. That he did survive seemed almost providential, a miracle of modern warfare. "He is the bravest man I ever saw," said Rough Rider Private Grant Travis, aged 36, a former schoolteacher from Aztec, New Mexico. Many others agreed: courage almost to the point of recklessness.[3]

The Rough Riders' advance up Kettle Hill succeeded that day, despite heavy losses, and so did a similar attack on another prominence in the San Juan Heights. Reporting for the *New York Herald*, Richard Harding Davis conflated the fighting of July 1 under one name, making Roosevelt the "Hero of San Juan Hill." That reputation launched him on a trajectory of fame that would lead, in little more than three years, to the presidency of the United States—another miracle, one of modern politics. The events on that single day thus became a crucial turning point in US history, one that survivors held themselves privileged to have witnessed. Still more, the "Battle of San Juan Hill"—along with the example of Roosevelt and his Rough Riders—opens a window onto an important part of American culture at that time.

Most of the story in the pages that follow—a tale of two miracles—concentrates on TR and his famous 1898 regiment, along with the immediate political aftermath of the Spanish-American War. But the overarching problem it addresses is the cultural shift toward an *overseas* empire by a republican nation whose original political identity had been forged in revolutionary defiance of imperial power. How could that happen? Part of the answer goes back to the very start of the republic, involving concepts of nationality and precepts of character present then, as well as later. By the late nineteenth century, the preservation—or, more accurately, modification—of key early values of civic virtue, personal sacrifice, and public service proved increasingly vital in an era of jarring social changes, capitalist excess, lingering sectional tensions between North and South, racial readjustment, and softening manhood. By exploiting his renown as a Rough Rider hero, TR the politician played a unique role in that modification, helping to reformulate not just American imperial destiny but also dominant popular belief at home.

Since 1776, political and religious thinkers in America had always coped with a psychic contradiction rooted at the very heart of their experiment in governmental freedom: the worry that American citizens, liberated from constraints, would become increasingly corrupt, lawless, self-centered, and fixated on luxury. In that event, they would lose the vital force that held them together—that is, their sense of commitment to one another, their devotion to the common good. That possibility loomed as white Americans during the nineteenth century expanded farther and farther westward, pushing not only the geographical but also the cultural meaning of their settlers' empire. Yet the very process of expansion toward the western limits of the continent had always seemed therapeutic and restorative as well. The architects of the early nation—and later public leaders including Roosevelt—understood republics to be fragile and that republican governance required attention to the more general issue of the structure and character of society. Republican societies, being vulnerable to decay from within, seldom survived long without somehow regenerating core virtues that replenished the hardiness and moral strength of their people. The West had seemed to provide a special venue for that process, and now the imperialists of 1898 believed that further expansion outward, beyond continental boundaries, could do the same.[4]

That vernacular of regeneration, varying from voice to voice and shifting in form to fit changing circumstances, echoed much deeper into the nineteenth century than historians often realize. In matters of governance, it affected both domestic and foreign policy making. Without doubt, it influenced Americans' impressions, beliefs, and hopes for the future in the decades prior to the Civil War, especially in the North. Interpreting John Brown's 1859 raid on Harpers Ferry, for example, a writer for *Atlantic Monthly* declared in March 1860 that "the lesson of manliness, uprightness, and courage, which his life teaches, is to be learned by us, not merely as lovers of liberty, not as opponents of slavery, but as men who need more manliness, more uprightness, more courage and simplicity in our common lives." Abraham Lincoln, pondering whom to choose for his cabinet prior to his inauguration in 1861, reportedly said "that while the population of the country had immensely increased, really great men were scarcer than they used to be." Similar sentiments appeared repeatedly in the words, both public and private, of Theodore Roosevelt and other advocates of imperial expansion.[5]

Even the ending of slavery would later seem to many late-nineteenth-century observers, Roosevelt included, just one historical moment in the ongoing struggle to identify and preserve—to preserve by applying to new challenges—those same basic traits of strong moral character. In the 1890s, TR stated the argument in somewhat different terms, of course, but still in language not so distant from the early-nineteenth-century emphasis on public virtue. Although he spoke of roles for both sexes, Roosevelt's primary gender-based concern, like that of many others, focused on American manhood—the declining strength of male leaders in society, especially the privileged elite that had once bred so many of those leaders. Public views of the *cultural* as well as the military importance of the Rough Riders fit in a much broader context of American experience, extending into not only politics but also the music, art, advertising, entertainment, and popular literature of the period. Even some of the earliest American psychologists joined in, citing the aggressive play of young boys as they acted out—or, as G. Stanley Hall put it, "recapitulated"—the tales of soldiering back in the days of the American Revolution or the Civil War.[6]

As a politician of large vision as well as personal ambition, Roosevelt keenly observed the big picture of events and circumstances of his time. Yet as a prolific historian and biographer, he also knew the ideological currents of the early republic. Not that he longed for a rustic past of the Jeffersonian order; he was not that kind of republican. But a strongly nationalist historical perspective, rooted in earlier experience, heavily influenced his view of America in the 1890s. He believed that Americans of his generation had an obligation to live up to the ideals and, if possible, surpass the accomplishments of their forebears. In a republic, private sacrifices must be made for the public good. The revolutionary and Civil War–era leaders he admired most—George Washington, Alexander Hamilton, Abraham Lincoln—had known, however, that public spiritedness among citizens came only with difficulty. They, too, in their times, had worried about the natural loyalty of ordinary Americans. They, too, sometimes looked to the capacity of federal power to anchor the passions of the electorate in national causes. For them, too, devotion to the common good, synonymous with civic virtue, became most important in times of warfare or preparation for war. And like them, Roosevelt wanted to build a stronger nation. Although a man of a much different time, he saw himself as cut from similar cloth.[7]

Apart from just nation-building, however, Roosevelt resembled Alexander Hamilton, for one, in believing that the United States had been an "empire" from the beginning. It puzzled him that anyone could think otherwise. Americans had always been expansionistic. Their country had started out with a land domain that stretched to the Mississippi; its hardy frontier settlers, men and women alike, had surged still farther westward, pushing less "fit" native peoples out of their way; its diplomats had placed additional territory within the nation's increasingly distant grasp; its armies had defeated Mexico in a war of conquest that had secured much of the far West under US control. In matters of American westward expansion, the ends always somehow justified the means. In his four-volume magnum opus, *The Winning of the West*, TR embraced both the concept and the consequences of "Manifest Destiny." As he saw it, expansion was historically ordained, the birthright of a culturally "superior" Anglo-Saxon people. To him, there were no serious moral differences between the United States forcibly occupying the continent and its acquisition of overseas possessions in his own time. Not only destiny but American national interest required it. Even so, he always preferred the word "expansion" to the more aggressive connotations of "imperial" or "imperialistic."[8]

Just prior to the Spanish-American War of 1898, Roosevelt had served in Washington as assistant secretary of the navy. During that time, his early developing views on transforming the United States from an expanding continental republic into a transoceanic empire had begun to crystalize. To some extent, this imperial vision emerged from an inflected Darwinian notion of struggle for fitness not only among different peoples but also among nations. Even before, however, Roosevelt's reputation for "jingoism"—that is, his extreme, warlike expression of patriotism—had stood well established in Washington circles, and he used his position in President William McKinley's administration to advance those views. "All the great masterful races have been fighting races," he announced at the Naval War College in Newport, Rhode Island, on June 2, 1897, "and the minute that a race loses the hard fighting virtues, then, no matter what else it may retain, no matter how skilled in commerce and finance, in science or art, it has lost its proud right to stand as the equal of the best." Material prosperity, thrift, energy, and business enterprise—all this was well and good, but "we know that even these are of no avail without the civic and social virtues."

He made that speech to naval officers at a moment when tensions over Cuba were beginning to reach fever proportions. He cited the conviction, poise, and iron will of his early republic heroes, Washington and Lincoln in particular. "It is on men such as these, and not on the advocates of peace at any price," Roosevelt declared, "that we must rely in every crisis which deeply touches the true greatness and true honor of the Republic." Still, apart from leadership in the past, he assured that America could still boast "not a few men of means . . . who are always ready to balance a temporary interruption of money-making, or a temporary financial and commercial disaster, against the self-sacrifice necessary in upholding the honor of the nation and the glory of the flag." When war with Spain broke out in April 1898, TR would waste no time resigning from the Navy Department in order to practice in person the military responsibility that he advocated so strongly for others.[9]

Because of such impulsive behavior and the aggressive patriotism that inspired it—and also because of his now-archaic racial and ethnic notions, his preachy style, and his over-the-top ebullience of personality—Roosevelt might be hard for most Americans nowadays to understand. Certainly his imperialism has not sat well among modern scholars, especially those who lament the repeated manifestations of US aggression since TR's era. Seldom have America's wars of intervention gone as well as expected. Yet to dismiss

Roosevelt as emotionally stunted, as a crazed militarist, or as a flattened, cartoonlike figure, adds little historical understanding of the man or his actions. If, however, we regard him in a longer historical view of republican nation-building, frontier expansion, and empire development—America's history as *he* saw it—then TR's jingoistic attitude and imperial vision for the United States can appear today as less driven by irrational impulses.[10]

The military story of TR and the Rough Riders is best understood as emanating from broad dictates of culture and society as well as from more common considerations of weapons, strategy, leadership, economic power, and national interest. Serving cultural and societal as well as military purposes of that time, the conception, formation, and public image of Roosevelt's famous First Volunteer Cavalry Regiment—the Rough Riders—all related much more closely to questions of nation- or empire-building than many modern writers have noted. His experience in Cuba confirmed Roosevelt as a popular force in American life before he became a political one. Without that experience, he would never have reached a position to become president and, for that matter, would likely have gone down as only a minor figure in American history, unknown to most people living now.[11]

This book spans the brief time of America's most intensive war fever, 1897–1898, while also tracking Roosevelt's rise to the presidency, 1898–1901. It presents TR primarily as a sensitive reflector of cultural currents that ran through him and motivated his own major choices in the late 1890s, especially his personal decision to fight in Cuba during the Spanish-American War. His urge to lead by exhibiting "manly" courage, for example, mirrored the sentiments of other prominent thinkers and writers of the Civil War and post–Civil War generations. Some young northern intellectuals who had served in that war emerged from the experience feeling that their "hearts were touched by fire," as one of them, Oliver Wendell Holmes Jr., later phrased it. Still others who had missed the war themselves reached similar conclusions about its effect on American culture and came to think of military virtues—discipline, honor, service, devotion to duty, self-sacrifice—as necessary for cultural health. On that point, white northerners and southerners could agree even while still quarreling over other things. A nation that grew flabby morally, intellectually, and militarily would face slow but sure disintegration, like that of ancient Rome, and in the 1890s many Americans asked whether averting that fate could still be possible. Roosevelt answered "yes," but not without a fundamental reinforcing of older ideals to meet the social problems of his time.[12]

In short, the global expansion of American influence—indeed, the building of an empire outward from a strengthened core of shared values at home—connected to the broader question of cultural sustainability as much as it did to the increasing of trade, political power, and military might. It was a question as old as the republic itself.

1

Legacies

IN AN ARCHIVAL COLLECTION AT HARVARD, there is a surprising photograph of 6-year-old Theodore Roosevelt and his younger brother Elliott, both perched at a second-floor window in their grandfather's New York City mansion, watching Abraham Lincoln's funeral procession as it passed below, through Union Square, on April 24, 1865. Apart from the gloom of the occasion, it thrilled "Teedie" to see the soldier-heroes on parade. At one point, as the Invalid Corps of maimed federal troops marched by, tiny Edith Carow, young Theodore's childhood friend and future wife, became frightened at the sight of the crippled men. Disgusted, little Theodore promptly locked her in a nearby closet so that her reaction would not disturb his observation of the honored veterans who had made it home, their empty sleeves and reduced trouser legs testifying to brave sacrifices on behalf of a renewed republic.[1]

And indeed, the republic had been *renewed*, not merely preserved. The United States that the martyred president, his Republican Party, and the federal army had "saved" was no longer the *old* Union. Even so, the same old qualities of character, public and private, were to fortify the *new*—perhaps all the more so. "The Revolution freed us from England," said African American minister R. C. Ransom in 1898, but the Civil War had "freed us from ourselves; freed north and south; freed master as well as slave, and our baptism of blood and fire has left us purified." The "new birth of freedom" that Lincoln referred to in the 1863 Gettysburg Address went far beyond the prewar structure of compromises, accommodations, and concessions for slaveholders in the South. By that point, little choice remained but to complete the bloodiest of all American wars. Northern military might, in the name of freedom nationally, at last had settled the great sectional question of slavery in America. The men in blue uniform who had survived that war could carry with them through the remainder of their lives the satisfaction of knowing that their sacrifices had meant something and that their souls had been tested.[2]

At the beginning of the nineteenth century, Americans had lived mostly east of the Appalachians, moved in a 2-mile-an-hour world, worked by the preindustrial rhythms of nature, illuminated their homes by candles or whale oil, heard that Thomas Jefferson had been chosen president, and scarcely knew the western reaches of their own continent. By the century's end, the nation stretched to the Pacific, steam engines powered ships and propelled land travelers along far-flung bands of steel, telegraph lines crisscrossed the landscape, electric streetcars rattled down big city streets, office telephones jangled, and luminous bulbs shattered the darkness.

In 1898, William McKinley, a Republican and Union veteran, sat in the White House. Census officials said that the "frontier" no longer existed. The once-proud Indian tribes who had roamed those regions now huddled on bleak reservations. White northerners and southerners, though still bitter from the war, slowly rediscovered the common heritage they still shared, while black Americans settled into an undeserved status as second-class citizens. Urban ghettoes teemed with "new immigrants," largely Catholics and Jews, who defied the stilted Anglo-Saxon concept of what "civilized" meant. Labor violence had escalated, as workers demanded fair treatment and a decent living. An increasingly frenetic, industrial economy, now recovering from depression in 1893, generated riches and a pursuit of wealth scarcely imagined a hundred years before. Meanwhile, America's social critics, speaking for those left out of the financial bonanza, viewed pompous assurances of progress as ringing hollow; to them, it was only a "gilded age."

The year 1898 had dawned with Americans expecting military intervention in Cuba against the once-extensive New World empire of Spain. The now 39-year-old Roosevelt welcomed such a war, ending four centuries of Spanish tyranny—part of a "world movement," he wrote hopefully, to liberate and enlighten the benighted. The United States would replace Spain with a qualitatively superior empire, he thought, while also regenerating at home the social values that seemed to have decayed since the Civil War. That common cause and its unifying side effects might lift the spirit, character, and public responsibility of Americans themselves, distracting from crises at home and ushering in a new era of national glory.[3]

Lessons of Citizenship

Born into the wealthy New York City elite, young TR—"Teedie," his family called him—grew up listening to stories of Civil War heroics on both sides. His father, Theodore Sr., represented a long-established clan of New York merchants and bankers. Twenty-nine years old when the Civil War broke out, the elder Roosevelt took the privileged-class option of hiring a substitute, regarded then as acceptable for one of his social prominence. By contrast, young Theodore's mother, Martha Bulloch Roosevelt, hailed from an aristocratic Georgia family and privately sympathized with the South. Some of her relatives fought for the Confederacy. The fact that Theodore Sr.'s wife and in-laws stood on the opposing side would have made it almost unthinkable for him to take up arms for the Union even had he been so inclined. Still, that decision might have been the only one of his father's that ever registered as a disappointment to young Theodore, who later regarded a citizen's willingness to fight as a hallmark of manhood. In all other ways, the elder Roosevelt, a moral exemplar who inspired many by his charitable work in New York, modeled the public virtue that his eldest son would hope to emulate.[4]

In a household thus divided between North and South, the little boy gravitated to the pro-Union view. An aunt witnessed him one time punctuating his bedtime prayers with a hope that Providence might "grind the southern troops to powder." Over the years to follow, the younger Theodore worked to overcome physical infirmities tied to his near-fatal struggle with childhood asthma and with the trauma of his father's unexpected death, in 1878, at age 46. TR married soon after graduating from Harvard College in 1880, won election to the New York Assembly the following year, and published his first book, *The Naval War of 1812*, a year after that. But then his whole world came crashing down with the tragic loss of his mother and his first wife, Alice

Hathaway Lee, on the very same day in February 1884, the former from typhoid fever, the latter from kidney failure after childbirth. For a time, he thought there remained little reason to live.

That cruel double blow sent him away from New York state politics and in search of emotional reconstruction as a rancher in the distant Badlands of Dakota Territory. "It was a land of vast silent spaces, of lonely rivers, and of plains where the wild game stared at the passing horseman," he later wrote. "It was a land of scattered ranches, of herds of long-horned cattle, and of reckless riders who unmoved looked in the eyes of life or of death." Roosevelt reinvented himself in this alternative American society of rugged cowboy types, as popularized in the novels and artwork of his friends Owen Wister and Frederic Remington. He looked with admiration on the men who worked for him on his cattle ranch in Medora, finding them to be the best examples of manly virtue he had ever come across. They were "hardworking, laboring men," he told his sister Anna, "Americans through and through." In the company of these tough westerners, he experienced the self-redefinition he had gone west to find. His time with the Rough Riders, years later, would have the same effect on him.[5]

But Roosevelt's ideas on the importance of citizenship had developed already before that. They had been planted by the civic legacy of the Civil War, his father's influence, and the academic lessons of Harvard. He never refrained from expounding on the subject of a citizen's duties. Asked in 1886 to speak at a Fourth of July gathering in Dakota, the audacious 28-year-old easterner prescribed the audience's civic task as if he were a founding father himself: "We must remember that the Republic can only be kept pure by the individual purity of its members; and that if it becomes once thoroughly corrupted, it will surely cease to exist." For a people to rule themselves, he declared, was to take on "the responsibilities of sovereigns, not of subjects."[6]

Over the next ten years, he would return to the East, remarry, and resume a career in public service—first as a member of the federal civil service board in Washington and later as New York City police commissioner. He would also publish all four volumes of his principal work of history, *The Winning of the West*. Meanwhile, his views on the obligations of a male citizen, as he refined them further, went in a martial direction, blending citizenship with soldiering. In 1893, addressing the Liberal Club of Buffalo, New York, he declared that "no amount of attention to civic duties will save a nation if the domestic life is undetermined, or there is lack of the rude military virtues which alone

Theodore Roosevelt in his late twenties, during his time in the Dakota Territory, about 1886. Following the death of his first wife in 1884, Roosevelt went west, became a full-time rancher, and reinvented himself among the rugged cowboy types he came to know. Library of Congress, LC-USZ62-91139

can assure a country's position in the world." More of America's "good citizens" should go into politics, he instructed, and do so in the same spirit "in which their fathers went into the Federal armies."[7]

Thus TR's experience in the West, while vital to his growth, only supplemented and made stronger the traits of mind, temperament, and character already engrained in him from early age. One writer characterizes young TR as "a child of the Civil War," and that accounts for some of his motivation in 1898. His generation had not fought a war, and now it might produce its own round of national heroes. Younger men typically seek ways to measure up to their fathers. But that element of Roosevelt's consciousness combined early on with a hard-wired notion that American males, especially privileged ones, must prove fitness under adversity. Their doing so might prevent the cultural decay that had befallen earlier civilizations. Some of the Civil War veterans whom he knew personally had said the same.[8]

Manhood

The Confederate minié ball sliced painfully through the left side of his chest and lodged somewhere near the surface of his right side. First Sgt. Henry J. Smith, who saw him fall, quickly carried the bleeding officer to the rear, ripped open his tunic, and somehow managed to squeeze the bullet back out through the entrance hole. Smith then presented the mangled piece of soft lead to the barely conscious, 20-year-old first lieutenant, Oliver Wendell Holmes Jr.

By that moment in Holmes's life—sometime after 8:00 p.m. on October 21, 1861—roughly half of the Union attacking force of 1,700 men had been injured, captured, or killed in fighting that took place just across the Potomac River on the Virginia side, a clash later known as the battle of Ball's Bluff. "The fire of the rebels was . . . something terrible," scribbled Union captain Casper Crowninshield the following day, "I never saw such a sight and God grant I may never see another." Of the twenty-two officers of Holmes's regiment, the Massachusetts Twentieth, only nine came through the battle unscathed. An examining physician later found that Holmes had survived by a trajectory of a fraction of an inch, the bullet just missing his lungs and heart. The wound in his breast, plugged with lint, healed soon enough without infection.[9]

Such were the stories that young Theodore Roosevelt loved. He never tired of them, nor did his admiration of former Union soldiers ever fade. To him, they epitomized the heroic qualities and deeds that needed to be replicated by his own generation. The Civil War would alter America in many ways and linger in memory for a long time. As Mark Twain and Charles Dudley Warner later said, the war and its aftermath had "uprooted institutions that were centuries old, changed the politics of a people, transformed the social life of half the country, and wrought so profoundly upon the entire national character that the influence cannot be measured short of two or three generations." When his chance came in 1902 to fill a vacancy on the US Supreme Court, President Roosevelt would select Holmes partly because he symbolized the "strenuous manhood" of that earlier era.[10]

Or so it later seemed. That battle in 1861 would turn out to be another humiliating defeat for the Federal Army of the Potomac, then commanded by the overly cautious Maj. Gen. George B. McClellan. For young Holmes, it would register as the first of several close calls in the war. He would serve for a total of three years in the Union army, facing combat during the first two of them, including McClellan's Peninsula campaign and the Battle of Antietam. Twice more Holmes would be wounded, once survive a life-threatening bout with dysentery, and finally complete the third year of his enlistment as an aide to generals Horatio G. Wright and John Sedgwick of the Sixth Corps. "It's odd how indifferent one gets to the sight of death," he wrote to his mother late in 1862. Six feet, three inches tall and skinny, at just 136 pounds, Holmes little resembled the model warrior, but he maintained a soldierly bearing and in later life would often speak in military metaphors. He cultivated enormous curling mustaches, a soldier's fashion of that day. On September 17 of every year for the rest of his life, he ceremoniously raised a glass of wine in tribute to friends who had fallen at the Battle of Antietam on that date in 1862—and where he had taken a bullet in the neck, again nearly killing him.[11]

During his final winter in the army, 1863–1864, Holmes found some time to reflect on the bitter experience of military conflict. Such carnage, he could only conclude, betokened the grim, impersonal, history-shaping process of materialist evolution—the constant struggle for supremacy among conflicting nations, races, and ideas. Finally, during the Virginia campaign of late spring 1864, he had seen enough. "Many a man has gone crazy since this campaign began from the terrible pressure on mind & body," he wrote. The constant anxiety for survival "demoralizes me as it does any nervous man—and now I honestly think the duty of fighting has ceased for me." As a commissioned officer, it was his privilege to resign, and, refusing promotion, he did so.[12]

Holmes qualified as a New England blueblood. He was born in Boston, Massachusetts, on March 8, 1841. His father was the famous physician, essayist, and poet Oliver Wendell Holmes Sr.; his mother, Amelia Lee (Jackson) Holmes, was a prominent figure in Boston society and promoter of charitable causes. If the elder Holmes, a transcendentalist and friend of Ralph Waldo Emerson, represented the flowering of American letters, Amelia exemplified the republican woman of conscience, animated by civic responsibility. It was she who most guided her son's values and early choices, fixing in him a Christian moral compass that his Harvard College reading in Malthus and Darwin, along with his wartime experience, would leave in shambles. He would espouse agnosticism in later life. Believing the performance of one's moral duty to be the loftiest expression of human evolution, he decided in spring 1861 to join the Twentieth Massachusetts Volunteer Infantry, nicknamed the "Harvard Regiment" because it included scions of the northeastern elite. But

Ball's Bluff gave Holmes and the Twentieth a baptism of fire they would never forget.[13]

Twenty years would pass before Holmes started to speak publicly on the cultural meaning of the war, as he saw it. After his army service, he returned to study law at Harvard, married, established a commercial practice in Boston, taught budding lawyers at the law school, received appointment to the Supreme Judicial Court of Massachusetts, and published an iconic work in American legal scholarship, *The Common Law* (1881). In that book, which became a cornerstone text of modern sociological jurisprudence, he famously declared: "The life of the law has not been logic, but experience." For sure, he knew the power, if not the logic, of grim experience.

If Holmes experienced symptoms of what today we identify as post-traumatic stress, he did not show it much—nor did others of that time. One reason might have been that Civil War veterans were celebrated citizens in the postwar decades, seen as modeling the qualities of honor, sacrifice, and manly character—in all, a traditional ideal of civic virtue—that most Americans, in both North and South, still admired. People liked to recognize the old soldiers on important public occasions, and politicians, including TR, seldom missed the opportunity. Henry L. Stoddard, a political commentator of the 1870s and 1880s, quipped that official gatherings of those years always featured at least one war survivor conspicuously stationed on the speaker's platform. Many federal army veterans angled for patronage appointments or sought election to office; indeed, all the presidents from Ulysses S. Grant to William McKinley, with the exception of the Democrat Grover Cleveland, had worn Union blue. On the rebel side, of course, the former soldiers symbolized the noble fight for the "lost cause" of southern rights. For Civil War veterans to have appeared psychologically damaged would not have fit their heroic image. Thus to younger men of Roosevelt's generation, the experience of war could easily have looked more ennobling than impairing.[14]

Duties of celebrity aside, what sense did it make to have risked, or sacrificed, one's life in war? Holmes asked that question in a Memorial Day address on May 30, 1884. The place was Keene, New Hampshire; the group, a chapter of the Grand Army of the Republic, Union army veterans, now middle-aged. Holmes's answer applied as well for those on the Confederate side. "To fight out a war, you must believe something and want something with all your might. . . . [Y]ou must be willing to commit yourself to a course, perhaps a long and hard one, without being able to foresee exactly where you will come out." To live fully meant accepting risk, to embrace "action and passion," on peril not of dying but of "being judged not to have lived." He thought not only of the soldiers who had perished but of their widows left behind, some of them also sitting in the audience: "those still living whose sex forbade them to offer their lives, but who gave instead their happiness." For Holmes, it became a mark of pride to have served and suffered. The generation that had conducted the war had been "set apart by its experience," and its "great good fortune," as the passing of time now made clear, was that "in our youth our hearts were touched with fire."[15]

By the thirtieth anniversary of Appomattox, in 1895, many of the surviving men in blue who had celebrated Union victory—and those in gray who had not—could reflect back upon fulfilled lives. By then, they could observe days of relative sectional reconciliation between white northerners and southerners. Many witnesses in that period commented on the increasing observance of Memorial Day in both North and South, with veterans' memories on both sides adhering more and more to the same ideal of martial heroism. Horrible recollections of crisis and battles and death and mourning had gradually faded. But the Civil War generation, now middle-aged, also had lived to see a time of commercial excess, political mediocrity, and cultural softness compared to their experience of war.[16]

Memorial Day of 1895 again inspired Holmes, now aged 54, to philosophical musing, this time before the graduating class at Harvard, the sons of his own fire-hardened generation. They packed into Sanders Theater in Memorial Hall, a massive Victorian Gothic structure built in the 1870s to honor the college's departed heroes, including Robert Gould Shaw and Charles Russell Lowell. These college seniors had grown up in an era of peace and comparative ease. War had fallen "out of fashion," Holmes observed, "and the man who commands attention of his fellows is the man of wealth." That troubled him, as it did others, like Roosevelt, who worried for the future of the republic. Therefore, the occasion required a different message from what the younger listeners might have expected. "I believe that the struggle for life is the order of the world, at which it is vain to repine," Holmes insisted, and human "destiny" was not comfort but "battle," and "the faith is true and adorable which leads a soldier to throw away his life in obedience to a blindly accepted duty, in a cause which he little understands, in a plan of campaign of which he has little notion, under tactics of which he does not see the use." In America of the mid-1890s, a "snug, over-safe corner of the world," young men should prepare for danger, he instructed. Such was the schooling needed "in this time of individualist negations, . . . revolting at discipline, loving flesh-pots, and denying that anything is worthy of reverence—in order that we may remember all that buffoons forget."[17]

Many young men did not forget Holmes's words, however. Widely reprinted, the 1895 address circulated through the Northeast. "By Jove, that speech of Holmes' was fine," Theodore Roosevelt gushed to his lifelong friend and confidant Henry Cabot Lodge, a fellow Harvard graduate and now a US senator from Massachusetts. TR added that pacifists around the country should "learn it by heart" and "repeat it forwards and backwards."[18]

Holmes's voice was not a lonely one crying in a cultural wilderness. Joshua Lawrence Chamberlain, renowned for holding Little Round Top at Gettysburg and shot six times during the war, also championed warfare for fostering of courage and personal discipline, resilience and devotion to others. Horace Porter, a West Point graduate who as a lieutenant colonel had served as aide-de-camp to generals Ulysses S. Grant and William T. Sherman during the war, lamented the ebbing of martial qualities in America's young men of the 1880s. He cited the "unambitious, namby-pamby life, surrounded by all the safeguards of civilization." The cure would be the danger of taking "his life in his hands," the pressure of having to "assert his rights . . . with deadly weapons," knowing he "will be drummed out of the community if once . . . caught showing the white feather." In 1890, Henry Lee Higginson, wealthy entrepreneur, philanthropist, and another former Union soldier, dedicated "Soldiers Field" at Harvard to six former classmates who had fought and died. "Don't grow rich; you'll find it much more difficult to be a useful citizen," Higginson said. "The useful citizen holds his time . . . and his life always ready at the hint of his country." Lodge procured a copy of Higginson's speech and sent it to Roosevelt, knowing how TR shared that sentiment exactly.[19]

Still others who missed wartime service addressed comparable themes. Brooks Adams, in his 1896 book *The Law of Civilization and Decay*, argued that the pursuit of wealth in an overly commercialized society would eventually weaken the privileged classes: "the imagination fades, and the emotional, the martial, and the artistic types of manhood decay." When a "highly centralized" culture disintegrated under economic competition, "it is because the energy of the race has been exhausted." Look at ancient Rome, Adams advised, echoing the earlier work of historian Edward Gibbon: eventually the "race of soldiers vanished," the farms where they had once flourished "left desolate," the minds of later Romans lacking the "martial" and "amatory [sexual] instincts." American expansionists would have taken interest in another of Adams's contentions: "All the [historical] evidence points to the conclusion that the infusion of vitality which Rome ever drew from territories beyond her borders, was the cause both of her strength and of her longevity." Roosevelt, reading the book in 1896, disliked Adams's pessimism, commenting more optimistically that "as long as the birth rate exceeds the death rate, and as long as the people of a nation will fight, and show some capacity of self-restraint and self-guidance in political affairs, it is idle to compare that nation with the dying empire which fell because there sprang from its loins no children to defend it against the barbarians." Reviewing the book in *Forum* magazine, Roosevelt felt that Adams went "beyond what he can prove" when he asserted "that the martial type necessarily decays as civilization progresses." Soon enough, however, TR would prove the endurance of the "martial type" via his Rough Riders.[20]

Demographic trends also help to explain the late-nineteenth-century anxiety about young Americans of Roosevelt's time. The birth rate for white Anglo-Saxon families had declined precipitously during that period—disturbing news to those who thought civilization depended on that particular group. White Americans would give birth to 124 children per 1,000 women aged between 15 and 44 in 1900, in contrast to 278 per 1,000 a century earlier. The average number of children in families would decline to 3.42 in 1910, compared to about 5 in 1800. As one writer for the *North American Review* noted in 1895, "the cost and care of bringing up a child properly have become so great that there is an increasing sentiment in favor of small families." The changes most affected middle-to-upper-class whites living in urban areas, while family sizes for rural whites, immigrants, and blacks remained significantly higher. More and more urban boys had never known such agricultural chores as tending crops, feeding animals, spreading manure, and fixing fences. Writer and outdoorsman Ernest Thompson Seton, who believed that urban life had eroded the traditional virtues of Americans, wrote, "We know money grubbing, machine politics, degrading sports, cigarettes, . . . false ideals, moral laxity and lessening church power, in a word '*City rot*' has worked evil in the nation."[21]

Such "modernization" threatened to take a toll psychologically as well as morally. The pervasive malady said to afflict "overcivilized" white adult males went by the term "neurasthenia," defined medically in 1881 as "nervelessness" or "a lack of nerve force." It was male weakness explained in physiological and environmental terms instead of just moralistic ones. Starting around 1870, physicians considered neurasthenia a health problem of near epidemic proportions, sapping men's "manliness." Presumed symptoms varied from headaches and chronic fatigue to depression and impotence. The condition supposedly resulted from overuse of the intellect and neglect of physical activity. Further, the neurasthenic affliction was not limited to males. Some physicians of the era said that women fell victim from excessive mental strain, resulting also in a loss of reproductive potential.[22]

The "physical culture" movement of the late nineteenth century seemed to offer one remedy. And so would the example of the "dudes"—the eastern college men—who became famous as Rough Riders, converting athletic prowess into military capability. The movement's promoters ranged from the rational to the nutty. Bernarr Macfadden, a man of bizarre notions whose book *The Virile Powers of Superb Manhood* (1900) made a stir when it appeared, might register today as the nuttiest. At the same time, many schools, guided by Diocletian Lewis's *New Gymnastics for Men, Women, and Children* (1862), had instituted calisthenics programs and would further expand their athletic offerings after the Spanish-American War. A variety of specialized devices, from beanbags and bowling pins to pulley weights and rowing machines, served the purpose. At Harvard, Dudley A. Sargent became one of the first professors of physical education, and Roosevelt knew Sargent's course. Where rivers and lakes permitted, sculling was all the rage. Golf, boxing, bicycling, riding, hiking, and camping each contributed to a sports revolution to rout lethargy and make men "manly." Among school sports, football held special appeal because of its analogue to warfare, pitting one team against another in conquest or defense of territory and encouraging a lust for battle. "Physical culturists" of all stripes, including the YMCA-inspired "muscular Christians," agreed that athletic endeavor not only prevented debilitating neurasthenia but also girded young men against the unsavory temptations of saloons, gambling tables, and bordellos. Roosevelt had witnessed that kind of decadence too, during his tenure as New York City police commissioner from 1895 to 1897.[23]

The Boy Scout movement, imported to America from Britain, also combined physical strengthening and moral uprightness for young men. No one promoted those values more than the scouts' English founder, Lord Robert Baden-Powell: "We badly need some training for our lads if we are to keep up [the] manliness of our race instead of lapsing into a nation of soft, sloppy, cigarette suckers." Would the pampered urban life of the professional and business classes endanger male fitness and render them unprepared for war? As naval historian Alfred Thayer Mahan said, war might be seen not only as a "necessary evil" but "a remedy for greater evils, especially moral evils." Roosevelt, though faulted for romanticizing war, echoed that concern as well.[24]

In all of this, one finds ethno-cultural, racial, and gender-based assumptions that would disturb many Americans of today. Xenophobia and discrimination against blacks often accompanied the emphasis on patriotic manhood. As the proportion of Anglo-Saxons in the American population declined in the early part of the century, the insecurities of that group multiplied. Bigotry swept America in the 1890s, springing partly from economic crisis—the depression in 1893—and partly from deeply rooted belief. What had been true in early New England remained true: any perceived decay of standards, manners, and morals got blamed on strangers. And to cure social disorders, the usual "solution" was to revive old-fashioned values.[25]

Especially suspect were the "new immigrants" from Eastern and Southern Europe, in addition to the continuing influx of the Irish. These immigrants identified mostly as Catholics and Jews, working class, sometimes politically radical, and usually drawn to cities, where they gathered in certain areas of town. Regarding African Americans, it was a more familiar story. Most American whites took it as given that blacks were racially inferior, and the work of scientists and scholars seldom challenged that perspective. The conventional notion of ideal manhood excluded as many as it embraced. American "heroes" did not just *happen* to be white, Anglo-Saxon, and Protestant. When middle- and upper-class whites thought of the strong men their sons might become, the models they chose resembled themselves racially, ethnically, and religiously.[26]

Mission

"My plea is not save America for America's sake," Congregationalist pastor Josiah Strong avowed in 1885, "but, save America for the world's sake." At first, that might sound no different from the implorations that Protestant Americans had heard from church pulpits since the days of Massachusetts Puritan colonist John Winthrop and his "Model of Christian Charity." The ongoing mission of New World Christians had been to establish inspirational models for the rest of mankind. The difference is that Strong wanted to preserve—by expanding—a heritage already well established by his time, one that he thought tottered on the brink of dissolution unless believers joined together now in shoring it up.[27]

Throughout his adult life, Theodore Roosevelt also would fill the role of "crusader militant." He and Strong knew each other but not closely. Yet the two men shared a range of fundamental beliefs, including societal prejudices, and would influence their respective communities of followers in similar ways. Under his father's pervasive influence, Roosevelt had been raised to believe that strong moral character defined a good man and a good woman, just as much as did physical hardiness and personal courage.

By 1898, Strong had become perhaps the most influential religious leader in the United States. For many, he was *the* compelling voice of the Social Gospel. His best-known book, *Our Country: Its Possible Future and Its Present Crisis*, which appeared in 1885, would rank alongside Washington Gladden's *Applied Christianity* (1886) and Walter Rauschenbusch's *Christianity and the Social Crisis* (1907) as a defining text of a movement that could in some ways be viewed as America's "Third Great Awakening." By the time of Strong's death, in 1916, *Our Country* had sold upward of 176,000 copies. In addition, hundreds of newspapers, magazines, and journals had printed excerpts from the book and from related essays that Strong composed during his most prolific years as an author.[28]

Does Strong really belong among the "prophets" of imperial expansion? In fact, he *does*, especially if we define American expansionism of the 1890s in cultural terms as well as economic, political, and military ones. Various expressions of the imperial impulse operated at the same time, as they did in Roosevelt's mind. He and Strong corresponded occasionally, and it was TR who in 1900 would introduce the minister to Mahan, sparking a relationship that would sway some of Strong's later works.[29]

Strong's piercing gaze and luxuriant beard, with massive upturned mustaches like Holmes's, furnished him with a distinctive appearance that complemented his zealous personality. Born in Naperville, Illinois, in 1847, he had lived from age five to adulthood in Hudson, Ohio, a pre–Civil War hotbed of abolitionism and home for a time of the radical antislavery martyr John Brown. There, he attended Western Reserve College en route to further study at Lane Theological Seminary in Cincinnati, the institution that Rev. Lyman Beecher had shaped from 1832 to 1850 as a breeding ground for antebellum social reform. Like Beecher, Strong would become obsessed with America's frontier West as the environmental key to the moral regeneration of the republic. In 1881, Strong became secretary of the Ohio Home Missionary Society, the position that would launch him on a career of missionary advocacy and evangelical service. He undertook the writing of *Our Country* primarily to encourage missionary activity in the western parts of the nation, insisting on a soldier-like commitment from educated young men and women of the Northeast.[30]

Strong's notion of Anglo-Saxon superiority anchored his fundamental beliefs. He interpreted anything that theoretically conflicted with that perspective—the "new" immigrants, Catholics, Mormons, saloons, tobacco, large cities, socialism, concentrations of excessive wealth, obsession with luxury, and self-indulgence—as a problem that not only threatened civic virtue but also impeded the moralistic nation-building he envisioned. Rapid population growth in American cities, he thought, especially threatened the moral foundations of the republic. The Anglo-Saxon heritage, as exemplified first by Great Britain and now the United States, had made the two greatest ideological contributions to world civilization: the "fire of liberty" and what he called "pure *spiritual* Christianity." Strong indicated little regard for indigenous non-white cultures of any kind—not surprising, in that early cultural anthropologists, such as Franz Boas and his younger disciples, had yet to make much of a dent on public consciousness. Nor, of course, did such talk of Anglo-Saxon supremacy impress everyone at home. As an Irish writer observed in the *New York Journal*, "Those who speak of this Anglo-Saxon nation misrepresent and insult 90 per cent of the American people who are no more Anglo-Saxons than they are Hindoos." Writers like Strong left out "the patriotic old-time element, who have no banking nor mercantile ties with England and no large fortunes to swap off for their daughters."[31]

In parallel with similar efforts in Great Britain, American Protestant missionary activity swelled in the late nineteenth century, not only within the United States but also in far-off lands, borne on the wings of expanding world commerce. The YMCA's Student Volunteer Movement, forming in the late 1880s under Dwight L. Moody's evangelical aegis in Northfield, Massachusetts, exemplified the crusading spirit of improvement and attracted enthusiasts from some two hundred colleges. "Don't stay in this country theorizing, when a hundred thousand heathens a day are dying without hope because we are not there teaching the Gospel to them," drilled one movement official, mainly referring to the Far East. Strong went a step further, however, with ominous implications for anti-imperialists, who believed that the Pacific shores marked the natural—and safe—limits of American expansion. Anglo-Saxons possessed an instinctive "genius for colonizing," he declared, as demonstrated already by the "westward sweep of successive generations across the continent."[32]

That half-mythologized notion of the West pervaded the American consciousness through much of the nineteenth and early twentieth centuries. So when the US Census Bureau officially declared the frontier to be "closed" in 1890, it seemed that something essential in American life was coming to an end. The "disappearance" of the frontier, however much romanticized, damaged Americans' sense of identity, leaving them without the traditional challenge of territorial expansion.

That vague sense of loss underlay much of the Chicago World's Fair of 1893—the World's Columbian Exposition, in honor of Christopher Columbus. The fairgrounds featured a vast "White City," all just a façade constructed from plaster and wood, illuminated dramatically at night with massive floodlights and fireworks displays. This artificial extravaganza celebrated the march of civilization—primarily *American* civilization—which included the taming of "savage" peoples, mind-boggling advances of technology, an ongoing national recovery from the Civil War, and, perhaps most importantly, "Manifest Destiny" and the westward course of empire. Tucked in a secluded, man-made lagoon in the center of the "White City" was a "Hunter's Cabin," redolent of Daniel Boone and Davy Crockett, stocked with rifles that once supposedly had belonged to those two. The funding for the cabin project came from the Boone and Crockett Club of New York City, a hunter and conservationist organization that Theodore Roosevelt had established at Manhattan's University Club in 1887. Its membership listed a small who's-who of upper-class eastern "men of social standing," including TR's close friends Henry Cabot Lodge, Owen Wister, Winthrop Chanler, and Gifford Pinchot. It also featured the historian Francis Parkman, Gen. William T. Sherman, and future American diplomats Elihu Root and Henry L. Stimson, along with the premier New York financier of the age, J. P. Morgan. All along, many of the great myths of the West, together with Strong's notion of redeeming the frontier, sprang from *eastern* imaginations.[33]

The 1893 meeting of the American Historical Association in Chicago coincided with the World's Columbian Exposition. There, a 32-year-old, Johns Hopkins–trained historian, Frederick Jackson Turner, would articulate the supposed "loss" of the frontier better than anyone. A presentation he gave at the meeting, though sparsely attended at the time, unveiled what soon would become known as his "frontier thesis," detailing the historical impact of the West on the sustaining of democracy in the United States. "American social development has been continually beginning over again on the frontier," he declared. "This perennial rebirth, this fluidity of American life, this expansion westward with its new opportunities, its continuous touch with the simplicity of primitive society, furnish the forces dominating American character," said Turner. In this advance, the frontier was the "outer edge of the wave," a convergence of "savagery and civilization." So, in theory, that frontier heritage had produced the kinds of men and women that TR thought he had encountered in the West: better citizens, stronger, more individual, and exceptional. To lose that environment—and those qualities in Americans—caused some to worry as to the future of the nation.[34]

Roosevelt's view of the West mostly dovetailed with Turner's. As he prepared his third volume of The Winning of the West, in February 1894, TR wrote to Turner: "I think you have struck some first class ideas, and have put into definite shape a good deal of thought which has been floating around rather loosely." Today, the work of both would be viewed as too little documented and narrow in scope, lacking in multicultural awareness, unsympathetic toward Native Americans, sexist regarding women's contributions, and racist in being white-focused. But both men—along with Strong—still addressed a pressing question of *their* time: If not in the West, then where might Americans regenerate their vital energies? To Roosevelt, the answer seemed obvious. The frontier for Americans had not vanished but shifted elsewhere. War and transoceanic expansion would now answer their need.[35]

Mahan

If there was one thing he abhorred, it was sea duty—odd in someone trained for that occupation. Alfred Thayer Mahan hailed from a family in which strict obedience to authority, ardent Episcopalianism, and army heroics, *not* naval ones, constituted proofs of one's character. His father, Dennis Hart Mahan, who taught military engineering at West Point, and his mother, Mary Helena Okill, ran an oppressively stern household, the kind that drives some children to rebel and others to internalize discipline. With young Mahan, as with young Theodore Roosevelt, it turned out more the latter. Both men would come to believe that too many Americans practiced too little self-discipline in their lives.

Mahan eventually attended the US Naval Academy at Annapolis but hated it, finding the 1850s curriculum insufficiently academic. Still, he graduated second in his 1859 class of midshipmen. Arrogant, vain, and pompous, he more often than not repelled personal acquaintances. His Civil War service amounted to little more than the tedium of blockade assignments, while chronic seasickness and fear of the ocean subverted any potential he had as an operational officer. Besides, he had established no reputation for competence on the water; boats under his command had a strange way of colliding with other vessels and, sometimes, immobile structures. Tall, thin, and lavishly bearded, he wrestled all his life with an alcoholic habit that he had acquired to medicate chronic intense headaches—or possibly neuralgia, for which no other effective relief existed. Mahan achieved the rank of captain in 1885 but never rose beyond that during a thirty-seven-year stint in active service.

Yet he stands today as one of the most revered naval figures in American history—as an author, not a sailor. If the pen is mightier than the sword, Mahan showed that combining the two could be mightier still. Like so much else about him, this career as a naval writer and theorist also began unpredictably. While stationed at the Brooklyn Navy Yard in 1883, Mahan received out of the blue an offer from Charles Scribner's Sons to write a book for their new series on the naval history of the Civil War. Leaping at the chance, he finished the volume, *The Gulf and Inland Waters*, in less than five months. The work foreshadowed none of the strategic insight that would later make him famous, but it drew the attention of Stephen B. Luce of the US Naval War College in Newport, Rhode Island. Luce hired Mahan to teach naval history, which led in 1890 to publication of his classroom lectures as *The Influence of Sea Power upon History, 1660–1783*, a now-classic text. He followed that in 1892 with *The Influence of Sea Power upon the French Revolution and Empire, 1793–1812*.[36]

In both works, Mahan argued that strong nations had to build powerful navies, if not so much to spearhead imperial expansion, as in the modern cases of Great Britain, France, and Spain, then at least to protect widening commercial interests. The two *Influence* books electrified the foreign policy community in the United States, especially the younger expansionists whose attention focused on the European powers then contesting for hegemony in Africa, East Asia, and the Pacific. Roosevelt, though busy working as a civil service commissioner in Washington, spent two days in May 1890 poring over *The Influence of Sea Power upon History*. "I think it is very much the clearest and most instructive general work of the kind with which I am acquainted," Roosevelt wrote Mahan. He wished the book "could be placed where it would be read by the navy's foes, especially in congress." In public, TR used the book to promote his own belief in the need for a naval build-up. "A squadron of heavy battle-ships, able to sail out and attack the enemy's vessels as they approached . . . would effectually guard a thousand miles of coast," he contended in his review of the book for *Atlantic Monthly*. The two men quickly struck up a close personal friendship that would last over a decade until their equally prodigious egos started to conflict.[37]

At first, American overseas expansion of the late 1800s would compete with but did not replicate the global imperialism of that time. Before that, Manifest Destiny qualified as empire-building, but it had not required naval force. Great Britain and its European rivals had by 1880 expanded their colonial possessions to the point of controlling roughly two-thirds of the world's habitable regions, and by the late 1890s, that domination included the vast majority of the so-called dark continent of Africa, along with extensive commercial operations in Asia, especially China. To enforce their grasp, Europeans relied on a technological war-making capability that less industrialized peoples could not contest, forcing not only a spread of governmental hegemony but of cultural influence as well. As Mahan judged, European empires, especially the British, had achieved ethnic as well as a political conquest and, in doing so, had considerably advanced world civilization.[38]

Sparking American expansionism in part, the volume of US overseas exports had begun to explode even before the Panic of 1893, and between 1895 and the start of World War I, the value of this outpouring would rise 240 percent, from $800 million to $2.3 billion. That amount would include a 500 percent increase in the world demand for American manufactured goods. Agricultural producers, too, had come to depend on foreign markets, with some 20 percent of their harvests being sold abroad in that period. American business investments overseas also had started to boom and would quadruple between 1897 and 1914, from some $634 million to about $2.6 billion.[39]

The threat to the Pacific part of this US commerce had grown real enough by the 1890s. Germany and Japan coveted those profits, and the imperial-minded regimes of both wanted naval bases to extend their reach. Spain, by

Alfred Thayer Mahan, about 1910. The premier American naval strategist of his time, Mahan advocated the "Large Policy" that influenced other proponents of enhanced US naval power and imperial expansion, including his friend Roosevelt. Library of Congress, LC-DIG-ggbain-17956

contrast, was now the most vulnerable of international competitors. If the United States were to extend its reach overseas, it would have to do so—most likely at Spain's expense—before other more powerful foes beat them to it.

For the United States in 1890, Mahan argued for constructing modern steel-armored steamships, establishing coaling stations in strategic locations, defining—and expanding—perimeters of coastal defense, fortifying US interests in the Caribbean and the Pacific as far as Hawaii, and building a canal through Central America to facilitate movement of American naval forces between both oceans. In this program for the United States, and in his commentary on its cultural benefits at home, Mahan reflected ideas already pervasive more than he hit upon original lines of thought. Even so, eager naval advocates of the 1890s, like Roosevelt, credited Mahan as a pivotal influence on America's new imperial directions.[40]

In a series of shorter writings that followed the *Influence* books, Mahan articulated this new course of expansion while attacking isolationists. America must turn "eyes outward, instead of inward only," he declared in the December 1890 issue of *Atlantic Monthly*. The motto that Louis XIV ordered inscribed on seventeenth-century French cannons, *Ultima ratio regum* (the "last argument of kings"—that is, readiness for war), "is not without its message to republics," he counseled. No foreign policy of "passive self-defence" of America's sea frontiers could suffice in a world increasingly caught up in "struggle and vicissitude." American westward expansion had taught that lesson already, Mahan believed. The newly settled people of the Pacific states, men and women of more "aggressive spirit" than many of the East, could best appreciate the threat of transoceanic European colonies to the west of them and of "the advancing civilization of Japan." Three specific recommendations followed: first, increased protection of chief harbors, by fortifications on both oceans and coastal defense vessels; second, a naval force "of offensive power, which alone enables a country to extend its influence outward"; and third, prevention of any foreign state from acquiring "a coaling position within three thousand miles of San Francisco," a distance encompassing the Hawaiian and Galapagos islands and the coast of Central America. In all of this, breaking from outdated Jeffersonian practice, Mahan also urged a more "cordial understanding" between the United States and Great Britain. Both had pursued their interests while also, more than others, being "controlled by a sense of law and justice, drawn from the same sources, and deep-rooted in their instincts."[41]

Many members of Congress had already awakened to the need for a larger, modernized navy. Mahan's work gave them further impetus. After assuming the presidency in 1889, Benjamin Harrison started ramping up US naval forces. Secretary of the Navy Benjamin F. Tracy lobbied the Republican-dominated Fifty-First Congress for greater military support of America's growing international commerce, a "blue water navy" for offensive operations rather than just coastal defense, replacing the obsolete ships left over from the Civil War. Lawmakers responded in 1890 by passing the Navy Bill, which authorized construction of three new battleships, the USS *Indiana*, the USS *Massachusetts*, and the USS *Oregon*, along with an appropriation for the USS *Iowa* two years later. All four would see Spanish-American War action in the blockading of Santiago—critical in preventing the escape of Spanish vessels after the "Battle of San Juan Hill."[42]

Nations that sat back and ignored their defenses would face dissolution, Mahan thought, just as comparative religion taught that "creeds which reject missionary enterprise are foredoomed to decay." This rule of survival applied for republics, fragile enough by nature, as much as for societies controlled by monarchs and emperors. "In our infancy we bordered upon the Atlantic only; our youth carried our boundary to the Gulf of Mexico; to-day maturity sees us upon the Pacific," he wrote in the March 1893 number of *Forum*. "Have we no right ... to progress farther in any direction?" Echoing writers like Josiah Strong, he asked rhetorically whether world civilization could have profited more had Englishmen, nearly three centuries before, "heeded the cautious hesitancy that now bids us reject every advance beyond our shorelines!" Again citing early republic antecedents, he lamented two years later in *Harper's* that while many Americans quoted President Washington's 1796 warning against entangling alliances, they "too readily forget his teaching about preparation for war."[43]

Mahan easily won over proponents of the expansionist "Large Policy," like TR and Lodge, because they already agreed with every strategic recommendation he advanced. But the lure of his writings went beyond just that. He also warned of the waning "spiritual element" of American civilization—the soft, materialistic, self-indulgent values that seemed to be eroding an older, shared commitment to the common good. Had "public conviction"—a "very different thing from popular impression," he instructed—depreciated to nothing but "sounding brass and a tinkling cymbal"? To yield, "without contention," a belief in moral rightness could only entail a "deterioration of character." If the phrase "death before dishonor" had been "abused infamously," as in the war between the North and South, it nonetheless contained "a vital truth," as northerners and southerners alike could agree. Any "soldier" could not "but resent the implication that he is unable or unwilling to meet force with force." Self-surrender, courage, and manhood, Mahan insisted, remained the hallmarks of western civilization, just as respect for constituted authority "is urgently needed in these days when lawlessness is erected into a religion." If Americans now cared most for material wealth, "I know not what we have to offer to save ourselves or others," he preached. Nothing loomed more ominous "for the future of our race than that tendency, vociferous at present, which refuses to recognize [value] in the profession of arms."[44]

Imperialism differs from one historical case to another, but in nearly all it has reflected deeply ingrained values at an ideological core. In the American experience, the same has been true of the opposition to imperial expansion as well. For better or worse, the United States had operated as both a republic and an empire since its revolutionary origin. For their part, Roosevelt and other like-minded intellectuals, politicians, and military leaders of the late nineteenth century saw the power of the nation as largely internal: its citizens' strength of character and their commitment to traditional ideals of public virtue. Externally, too, the competitive pressure on the United States to expand outward, beyond its continental boundaries, mounted steadily. The major European nations, empowered by science and industry, modern weaponry and technology, organization and administrative efficiency, had advanced into the Far East, Africa, and elsewhere. By comparison, the American republic lagged far behind.[45]

The "new" imperialism of this period contrasted with earlier European colonialism, pitting "superior" against "backward" peoples, establishing white over nonwhite—all toward a presumed "progress" of civilizations generally. Social Darwinism, whose proponents argued that human relations as well as laws of nature mandated a constant struggle, dictated that nations, too, must either conquer or decline. For the United States in 1898, this meant not only hegemony over Hawaii and control of other mid-Pacific islands but also a canal through Central America and full control of the Caribbean sea lanes approaching it. As Mahan wrote before the war with Spain, American defense required more than just controlling the continent. It called for "defence of our just national interests, whatever they be and wherever they are"—hence the argument for an enhanced navy. But the expansionist vision did not yet include the Philippine Islands, which Spain held, or any other possessions in the far Pacific.[46]

As part of what it did include, however, warfare, and not just preparation for it, represented a key element. If fighting was needed to elevate the character of any dominating people, then periodic bloodlettings became necessary to keep nations fit and alert. Or so said the "jingos" of that time.

2

Jingo Doctrines

UNDER A CANOPY OF LINGERING POWDER SMOKE, the long past "spirit of '76 and '61" moved through the crowd at New York's Madison Square Garden on the evening of March 14, 1898. The military, bicycle, and athletic exhibition sponsored by the Military Athletic League of America opened with the band's inspiring rendition of the "Star Spangled Banner," not yet the official national anthem. It closed with the jarring din of Capt. David Wilson's battery of Gatling guns. Patriotic exuberance surged throughout the building. "Nothing could show more clearly the deep-seated love of country engrafted in the hearts of the American public by recent important events," the *New York American* reported.

The highlight of the evening proved to be an exhibition by members of the Sixth US Cavalry, a display of "rough" and "acrobatic" riding on bareback. "The men rode with the abandon of cowboys, leaping from ground to horse, forward, backward and sideways with an ease and finish, which only a well-trained athlete could have accomplished," said one onlooker. Their presentation "would have put Buffalo Bill's rough riders to shame if they had been fortunate enough to witness it," remarked another. Much of the crowd went home feeling somehow reassured that Uncle Sam's men in uniform could meet the military challenge that now loomed: "Now let the Dons come on; we are ready for them."[1]

As historian Kristin Hoganson has noted, without cultural analysis, including study of their ideological roots, it is difficult to explain how the Spanish-American War and the subsequent US counterinsurgency in the Philippines could have happened. These were "wars of choice," not necessity, costing roughly the same number of American lives—over four thousand—as the 2003–2009 war in Iraq. To this question of causality, military historians often apply the rationality test, trying to identify some kind of discernible, or "necessary," result that appears unlikely to have occurred other than by violent means. By such strictly "rational" criteria, the decision of the United States to fight Spain in 1898 makes only limited sense. American territory had not been invaded, its vital economic interests not endangered; westward expansion had satisfied the need for living space; no political exigencies for war, as in 1861, could justify it; Spain had grown too weak, militarily and economically, to pose an international threat; and US imperial interests at the time did not require taking Cuba and the Philippines from Spain.

So why did the McKinley administration and Congress decide on a course for war in April 1898? And why were so many Americans, including Theodore Roosevelt, so eager to participate in that war? The answers, again, reside in the early American republic and, in later years, the mysterious intertwining of experience and myth that became the stuff of popular belief.[2]

The "Cowboy" West

If jingoism for the sake of traditional ideals had become the prevalent mood by the start of 1898, it was not so everywhere or with everybody. But when the battleship *Maine* suddenly exploded in Havana harbor on February 15, 1898, public clamor for war against Spain escalated beyond control. While pro-war voices like Henry Cabot Lodge, Alfred Thayer Mahan, and Theodore Roosevelt had sought to influence opinions in Washington and around the country, the *Maine* disaster suddenly made their argument easily understandable to ordinary Americans. It was as if the country had been challenged in public to a gunfight, and as any cowboy worth his salt knew, no man of honor could just turn and walk away.

In the late nineteenth century, many popular notions of American identity came from mythological concepts of the American West. That half-imagined

"West" reflected far less the frontier that academics like Turner had concocted and much more the once-vibrant, rough-riding, gunfighting milieu of Buffalo Bill, Owen Wister, and Frederic Remington. In his own writing about western experience, Roosevelt emphasized the need for the urban higher classes to throw off their sedentary malaise and nervous disorders and to recover the manly, adventuresome spirit of frontier conquest that he, too, thought had once defined Americans. On that subject, no other figure of the time would bridge the academic and the popular, the real and the mythical, better than Roosevelt did. And in his jingoistic formula, the Rough Riders could become in the popular mind a pure assertion of "American spirit" in the months following the *Maine* disaster.

How did the real-life West get transmuted into the widely appealing elements of imagination and popular myth, much of it originating in the East? The answer is, of course, complicated and multidimensional, but part of it lies in the "dime novels" of the late nineteenth century, the cheap pulp literature that appealed to more and more ordinary Americans by the mid-to-late 1800s. Although only a part of the era's vast output of lurid fantasy stories, titles such as "Black Hat Jack," "Crack Skull Bob," "Buckskin Sam the Scalp-Hunter," "Ted Strong and the Last of the Herd," "Malaeska: the Indian Wife of the White Hunter," and "The Woman Trapper: Arkansas Sal and the Apaches" became the lowbrow fare of choice all over the country—cowboys and Indians, good guys versus bad guys, tough men and tough women alike.[3]

Another part involves the Wild West shows of that era, an entertainment phenomenon of the late 1800s. Since most Americans could not go out west themselves, popular entertainers would bring the "Wild West" to them. The state of the art, established in 1883, was "Buffalo Bill's Wild West," which became in 1893 "Buffalo Bill's Wild West and Congress of Rough Riders of the World." William F. Cody—known as "Buffalo Bill"—had been at different times an army scout, Pony Express rider, wagon train driver, buffalo hunter for the Kansas Pacific Railroad, fur trapper, gold prospector, and a rancher before he became a showman. His Wild West Show and its imitators employed horse culture groups from all over the world, but primarily they featured American cowboys, Indians, and former soldiers, including many who had actually participated in the real-life events reenacted before eager audiences. In the Buffalo Bill version, the performance finale was always some kind of an Indian attack on white settlers, stagecoaches, or wagon trains, with Bill himself and his entourage of brave white rescuers riding in to save the day.

Poster for Buffalo Bill's Wild West and Congress of Rough Riders of the World. Wild West shows of the late nineteenth century, especially that of "Buffalo Bill" (William Cody), became a popular entertainment craze. For Americans who could not go out west for real, such extravaganzas brought the mythical "West" to them. Library of Congress, LC-DIG-ds-08325

The whole idea was to glamorize the West, to celebrate white westward expansion, and emphasize the high character and cultural values of white cowboys, soldiers, and settlers who had conquered and "civilized" distant lands. All of this, too, would later carry over into other areas of popular culture and mass entertainment: the publishing, film, and television industries in decades to come. Wild West shows became wildly popular in the United States and even in Europe. Within its first two years, some 10 million people saw Cody's show. In 1899 alone, Buffalo Bill's Wild West Show covered more than 11,000 miles in two hundred days—341 performances in 132 cities and towns all over the country.[4]

More serious western literature had begun hitting the market as well, fostering the image of far westerners as a breed apart. As Mark Twain had written in *Roughing It*, an 1872 account of his own travels through the Utah Territory and Nevada, it was a "driving, vigorous, restless" population of young men—"not simpering, dainty, kid-gloved weaklings, but stalwart, muscular, dauntless young braves, brimful of push and energy, and royally endowed with every attribute that goes to make up a peerless and magnificent manhood." Later on, the novelist Owen Wister, a longtime friend of Roosevelt's, found similar qualities among the men and women he met. Wister spent several summers in the West, making his first trip to Wyoming Territory in 1885, and became fascinated with its culture, lore, and terrain.[5]

Wister launched his literary career in 1891 with *The Virginian*, which he dedicated to Roosevelt. It was the first real cowboy novel, the precursor of

Zane Grey's stories like *Riders of the Purple Sage*, and of many other western novelists' since. The story is set in Wyoming, where the narrator, an easterner, encounters "the Virginian," whose name we are never told. This model westerner is described as a tall, dark, slim, young giant with a deep personality. Naturally, as the hero in the story, he shoots the villain, a fellow named Trampas, and wins the girl, a pretty schoolteacher named Molly Stark Wood, whom he marries. The book's message is that although there are bad people in the West, there are also quintessential good guys, men of unusually heroic character forged in this uniquely American environment.[6]

Another strong influence came from the art world—the massive body of drawings, paintings, sculptures, and stories of the multitalented Frederic Remington, along with Charles Russell, Thomas Moran, Albert Bierstadt, and other artists, who captured in the popular imagination the people and places of the late-nineteenth-century West. By Remington's time, in truth, the golden age of cowboys in the cattle industry had ended, but the romanticizing of the cowboy West was just beginning. Remington's fascination with this world brought him into the same orbit with Roosevelt and generated a lasting friendship between the two. In the late 1880s, the young artist accepted a commission to create eighty-three illustrations for TR's *Ranch Life and the Hunting Trail*, which *Century Magazine* serialized before publication as a book.[7]

At least four main factors accounted for the appeal of Remington's paintings to the general public. First, they comforted higher-class whites in the East who saw themselves and their culture, extended to the West, as superior to all others. Second, the "Old West" was disappearing, and easterners grew more and more curious about this mysterious, romantic world that most of them had never seen. Third, the intrinsically masculine appeal of Remington's subjects fit with the popular literature of writers like Owen Wister and, later, rhymed with Roosevelt's political style. Finally, Remington's work captured the widely believed notion that the West held a kind of regenerative power, restoring the best of what easterners liked to imagine themselves once to have been.

Remington packed his studio in New Rochelle, New York, with bric-a-brac of the fast-disappearing frontier. He reveled in his collection of old rifles and revolvers, prized an 1840s cavalry saber among his diverse military artifacts, fastened a gigantic moose head prominently over the fireplace mantel, covered the floor with Indian rugs, and adorned the walls with drums and tomahawks and moccasins and beaded tunics. He also wrote stories of the old

West, including one entitled *Pony Tracks*, that celebrated the core virtues that he, like Roosevelt and Wister, identified in the rough-hewn ranchers he had encountered.[8]

His interest focused on such things because modern times dismayed him. Like so many Americans whose families had lived in America for generations, Remington especially lamented the impact of the "new immigration"—the influx from Eastern and Southern Europe and Asia—"foreign trash," he said, lumping them together as the "Jews—injuns—Chinamen—Italians, Huns, the rubbish of the earth I hate." America, he declared, no longer resembled the place of "our traditions." The best remedy for this overall cultural malaise would be "a real blood letting," a purifying war, and by 1898 it looked to Remington as if a fight for Cuban freedom against the decrepit power of Spain might do nicely.[9]

"This Country Needs a War"

Roosevelt, too, believed that modernity and cultural malaise had weakened young men's bodies and softened their values. By 1886, not long after taking up cattle ranching in Dakota Territory, he had come to regard the cowboy sorts he employed there—"hardworking, laboring men" and "Americans through and through"—as superior in caliber to the polyglot Knights of Labor men who had gone on strike in Chicago that year, leading to the Haymarket Riot. Reading in the eastern newspapers about the "dynamite business" going on there, he admired all the more those intrepid ranch hands "who shoot well and fear very little" and became "more furiously angry and excited than I do."[10]

If he, like Remington, saw America's laboring men as becoming undisciplined, self-serving, and lacking in what he called "the manlier virtues," Roosevelt did make an exception for the types who worked in the railroad industry—"a profession which beyond any other necessitates the exercise of hardihood, daring, self-reliance, and physical strength and endurance," as he told Charles Henry Pearson in 1894. Pearson, a British educator and historian, had just published a book entitled *National Life and Character: A Forecast*, in which he anticipated some of Brooks Adams's pessimistic conclusions on the destiny of "civilized" peoples. TR, admiring the work but disagreeing with the forecast, reviewed Pearson's book for the May 1894 number of the *Sewanee Review*. No population that had advanced beyond the "pastoral stage,"

Roosevelt instructed, "ever so tended to develop the hardier, manlier, more soldier-like virtues in the way that our railroad business has tended."[11]

Regarding the gilded youth of the privileged classes, as well as some of their vaunted professors in the colleges and universities, Roosevelt expressed the same deeper anxieties that others had voiced. He attributed the loss of influence of the "highly educated classes" to the "queer lack of Americanism" that now appeared among them. "Unquestionably the evil development of Harvard is the snob, exactly as the evil development of Yale is the cad," he judged, the latter being the "least unhealthy, though perhaps the most objectionable person." College sports, integrated within a collegiate curriculum, held promise as a preventative of such decay, but at Harvard, President Charles Eliot's "opposition to athletics" worked real harm, TR thought. "The main product we want to turn out of our colleges is men," he went on, and if Harvard could be taken as an index, America's intellectual elite stood on the verge of moral "degradation." This, as well as the pusillanimous clamoring of the "peace at any price men," he vented to Lodge in December 1895, had convinced him: "this country needs a war."[12]

Just as Roosevelt wrote those words, the United States was brushing dangerously close to a war with Great Britain—ill-advised, against the wrong enemy, and luckily averted. The crisis began as a border dispute between Venezuela and British Guiana involving some mineral-rich lands. With the British preparing to intervene and stationing warships off the South American coast, President Grover Cleveland, citing the Monroe Doctrine, warned them away from the Western Hemisphere. Suddenly, American newspapers filled with saber-rattling, and war fever quickly spread, despite that in 1895 Britain held the naval advantage over the United States by a ratio of fifty battleships to three. "I smell war in the air," Remington excitedly told Wister, as Cleveland and British officials swapped ultimatums. Support for Cleveland in Congress suddenly skyrocketed, and the jingoes started licking their chops. "Let the fight come if it must," Roosevelt scribbled maniacally, as if channeling the War Hawks of 1812, "I don't care whether our sea coast cities are bombarded or not; we could take Canada."[13]

Meanwhile, in the Senate, Lodge had delineated the case for a jingoistic foreign policy in a speech later circulated in Walter Hines Page's *Forum*, one of the three most respected highbrow magazines in 1890s America, along with *Harper's* and *Atlantic Monthly*. As partisan a Republican as Roosevelt, Lodge nevertheless represented the views of younger politicians in both parties who saw the nation's future in overseas expansion. He scorned the Democrat Cleveland for dithering on Hawaiian annexation in 1893–1894, urged wider commercial involvement in the Pacific, and echoed Mahan on the acquisition of far-flung naval bases and on America's becoming a major imperialist power. "In the interests of our commerce and of our fullest development we should build the Nicaragua canal, and for the protection of that canal and for the sake of our commercial supremacy in the Pacific we should control the Hawaiian Islands and maintain our influence in Samoa." All of that would call for a strong enough navy to protect Americans "in every quarter of the globe" and place the coasts beyond danger of successful attack. The new assistant secretary of the navy, following a Republican presidential victory in 1896, would agree completely.[14]

"Large Policy"

"What a Witches Sabbath they did hold at Chicago!" TR declared to Lodge, brimming with contempt for the Democratic Party's nominee for president, William Jennings Bryan. Perhaps no one campaigned more furiously for the Republican William McKinley in the fall of 1896 than Theodore Roosevelt, who saw this as no ordinary presidential election but one of the most pivotal of the century, more class-divided over the issues than any other in living memory. McKinley's campaign, spearheaded by his close friend, Sen. Mark Hanna of Ohio, aligned rhetorically with the interests of big businessmen, white-collar professionals, skilled workingmen, and prospering farmers. Bryan's pulled in regular Democrats but also the Populist types, including less fortunate farmers and workers who saw themselves as victims of a capitalistic system that seemed rigged against them. McKinley's regional strength lay in the Northeast and northern Midwest, Bryan's in less prosperous rural areas of the West and in the South. A loyal party man, TR traveled the country and spoke wherever the Republican National Committee deployed him. He implored audiences not to envy the wealthy but to face their depression-inflicted hardships manfully, with the same fortitude, the same heroic qualities of character, that he associated with brave soldiers.

Foreign policy featured little in the battle between the two parties or in the platform of either. That would change four years later, in the aftermath of the Spanish-American War. Instead, the presidential contest of 1896 focused on fundamental domestic issues: tariffs and monopolies and railroads, hard money versus free silver, the side effects of America's new industrial economy in general—all made painful by hard times. Voter turnout would prove unusually heavy in 1896 because of the candidates themselves and the views that made them so different from each other. Some 80 percent of the electorate showed up to vote on election day in November, and McKinley triumphed by one of the slimmest of margins in history, a mere 600,000 votes.[15]

A personal reason for TR's eagerness for Republican victory, of course, was the chance to obtain an appointment in the new Republican administration. And now McKinley owed it to him. Roosevelt wanted to be secretary of the navy, a top position, and Senator Lodge, TR's closest friend and the leader of the eastern Republicans, pushed hard for his appointment. But when the time came to stock his administration, the new president balked at such a "hotheaded and harum scarum" jingo as Roosevelt. Instead, McKinley offered him the second-highest navy department job, assistant secretary, and TR accepted.[16]

Like Mahan's, Roosevelt's credentials as a naval imperialist stood well established; he would spend most of his time lobbying Congress for increased defense spending. His very first book, *The Naval War of 1812*, which he had begun writing as a Harvard student, had marked him as a budding expert on sea power while also launching him, at age 23, on his lifelong part-time career as a historian. Published in 1882, the book sold successfully and received such glowing reviews that navy regulations as of 1886 required a copy in the ship's library of every US vessel. Thanks to the small but capable navy that Federalist leaders constructed in the 1790s, he argued, American forces had fought their best at sea during the early republic war with Britain. Their successes against enemy frigates contrasted with the mostly pathetic ground operations that had brought the nation, under the "criminal folly" of Jeffersonian governance, to the point of near disaster. As for modern policy, however, Roosevelt thought the current naval forces better equipped to meet the challenge of 1812 than the needs of the 1880s: "the necessity for an efficient navy is so evident that only our most incredible short-sightedness prevents our at once preparing one," he wrote in 1883.[17]

Starting work in April 1897, TR right away expounded the jingoism that had made the president reluctant to appoint him in the first place. In naval terms, the "Large Policy" that he shared with Mahan and Lodge meant assembling a network of bases and coaling stations, as well as increasing the number of ships, especially battleships, the kinds of modern steel combat vessels that Great Britain possessed. "I can not begin to describe the wonderful power and beauty of these giant warships, with their white hulls and towering superstructures," he gushed to Edith after reviewing the existing fleet off Hampton Roads in September 1897. Roosevelt envisioned an American navy powerful enough to rival those of the European powers and Japan, the other "new" expansionist nations that also coveted key ports and island possessions in the Caribbean and the Pacific. He argued the case in public, mostly before sympathetic audiences, reasserting the Monroe Doctrine to preempt European incursions in the Western Hemisphere. His timing seemed right, with revolutionary unrest starting to boil in Spanish-controlled Cuba and the Philippines, opening the possibility of a US takeover of the remaining bits of Spain's once-extensive empire. Just as important, Large Policy advocates agreed that such a goal, and war to achieve it, would revive the old fashioned vigor and virtue of the republic and restore an ethic of service and sacrifice.[18]

TR's reputation brought him many invitations to speak at the Naval War College in Newport, Rhode Island. Within just a few years after its founding in 1884, the school had become the major center for naval strategic planning in the country. After becoming president of the institution, Mahan brought TR to speak in 1888, and other engagements followed.[19]

The address he gave there on June 2, 1897, was titled "Washington's Forgotten Maxim"—that is, "To be prepared for war is the most effectual means to promote peace." Apart from its military implications, the speech outlined much of the social philosophy of Roosevelt's jingoism, echoing Oliver Wendell Holmes Jr.'s "Soldiers' Faith" and Mahan's strategic program more than it did any beliefs of the nation's first president. It also set forth a more aggressive view on military policy in general than President McKinley wanted at the time. "No triumph of peace is quite so great as the supreme triumphs of war," Roosevelt declared, at a time when the administration sought a resolution of the brewing trouble in Cuba *without* US military intervention. TR commented on the decaying values of urban Americans: "If we forget that in the last resort we can only secure peace by being ready and willing to fight for it, we may some day have bitter cause to realize that a rich nation which is slothful, timid, or unwieldy is an easy prey for any people which still retains those most valuable of all qualities, the soldierly virtues."

At the same time, Roosevelt was growing frustrated with his superiors and with Congress. A few days after his speech, he vented privately that he felt "hot with indignation at the seeming utter decadence of national spirit among us, and the craven policy which actuates the peace dilettante and the man to whom making money is all that there is in life."[20]

Defensive Perimeter

Apart from the reluctance of Congress to beef up naval appropriations during a time of economic depression, it irritated Roosevelt that lawmakers had balked over the annexation of Hawaii. Sailors had regarded this independent chain of sugar-producing tropical atolls 2,390 miles west of California, once known as the Sandwich Islands, as the rarest gem of the Pacific. American expansionists, like the missionaries and sugar planters before them, wanted the territory—desperately. Commercially, Hawaii's central location was vital: the islands sat midway between Alaska and the Society Islands of the South Pacific, between San Francisco and the Caroline Islands north of New Guinea. They provided a halfway point between Nicaragua and Hong Kong and fell directly on the route from South American ports to Japan.[21]

Even greater was the strategic value of Hawaii to the United States. As Mahan wrote in 1893, "Too much stress cannot be laid upon the immense disadvantage to us of any maritime enemy having a coaling station well within 2,500 miles of every point of our coast-line from Puget Sound to Mexico." Shut out from Hawaii, an enemy power would have to travel 3,500 or 4,000 miles for fuel, a prohibitive distance for maritime operations of that time. "It is rarely that so important a factor in the attack or defense of a coast-line—of a sea-frontier—is concentrated in a single position," Mahan said, "and the circumstance renders it doubly imperative upon us to secure it, if we righteously can."[22]

In the years before, the few overseas possessions under US control had served primarily as naval bases, coaling and repair stations, or sources of bird guano, prized as fertilizer for its high content of nitrogen, phosphate, and potassium. For these purposes, and not as part of a defense perimeter in the Pacific, Congress in 1867 had annexed the remote Pacific isle of Midway and, in 1878, secured rights to the harbor of Pago Pago in Samoa.[23]

In the 1870s, President Ulysses S. Grant's secretary of state, Hamilton Fish of New York, whose son would join the Rough Riders, called Hawaii a gateway to "the vast domains of Asia," then coming open to "commerce and Christian civilization." But he also knew that American ownership might "curb" the ominous rise of the Asian powers Russia and Japan. Preliminary steps toward annexation unfolded accordingly: Fish established a reciprocal trade treaty with the islands in 1875, and Congress authorized a naval coaling and repair station at Pearl Harbor in 1887. But the McKinley tariff of 1890 raised American duties on imports to record highs, causing islanders to suffer. Sugar fell into the duty-free category, but a compensatory provision for domestic sugar beet producers still disadvantaged Hawaiian growers in the lucrative American sugar-buying market. The economic distress caused by the resulting drop in Hawaiian crop prices triggered a convoluted sequence of events that, as it turned out, *should* have heightened the chances of American annexation.[24]

Recognizing that possibility in 1893, the group of white plantation gentry in the islands, many of them descendants of New England Christian missionaries, launched a coup d'état against the native queen Liliuokalani. For them, annexation meant, among other things, restored access to US consumers that the McKinley tariff had denied them.[25]

Yet Congress still held back, despite the pleading of the American minister to Hawaii, John L. Stevens, who had helped to spearhead the coup. Mainland sugar growers feared competition, and nativists doubted that the polyglot Hawaiian population—largely of Japanese extract and only 2 percent American—could fit within their preferred white Anglo-Saxon scheme of things. For Roosevelt, the international power implications of the islands mattered foremost, and he feared that the United States already was losing ground because too many Americans had grown too soft to recognize the national interest at stake. "If we take Hawaii now," TR wrote to Mahan a week after the Naval War College speech in 1897, "we shall avoid trouble with Japan, but I get very despondent at times over the blindness of our people, especially the best-educated classes." His obsession simmered further in the months that followed. "We must take Hawaii just as we must continue to build a navy equal to the needs of America's greatness," Roosevelt insisted in a January 1898 article for *Gunton's Magazine*. "If Hawaii does not become American then we may as well make up our minds to see it become European or Asiatic."[26]

In the Caribbean, Cuba constituted as prized a location as Hawaii did in the Pacific but for obviously different reasons. American expansionists had eyed Cuba, the "pearl of the Antilles," since the early decades of the nineteenth century. Increasingly, the island tied to significant commercial and strategic interests of the United States. About 700 miles across and only 100 miles south of the Florida Keys, it lay "almost in sight of our shores," as Secretary of State John Quincy Adams had longingly exaggerated in 1823. Once disjoined from the Spanish empire, he reasoned, it would have to gravitate toward the United States. Thomas Jefferson that same year wrote to President James Monroe that adding Cuba to "our confederacy is exactly what is wanted to round out our power as a nation." In 1848, President James K. Polk, acting for pro-slavery expansionists, tried to purchase Cuba for $100 million, but the proud Spanish government refused to sell, and abolitionists in the Senate opposed the idea in any case. The Ostend Manifesto in 1854, suggesting as a last resort the use of force to seize Cuba, linked the issue even more with slaveholders' territorial ambitions. In that year, President Franklin Pierce, offering $130 million, also failed to acquire the island.[27]

Some investors in the United States, especially those in the sugar market, saw a war in Cuba as a threat to recovery from the depression at home. President McKinley, for that reason and others, also hoped to avoid American military action that might appear to be an act of territorial aggression. Nevertheless, support for the Cuban revolutionaries had mushroomed in the United States right from the beginning of the renewed Cuba libre movement in February 1895. Many, though not all, Cubans hated their repressive Spanish rulers. Sympathizing Americans, drawing on their culturally engrained contempt for repressive monarchical regimes and recalling their own history of colonial subjection, equated the Spaniards with the tyrants of old. Their inhumane governance of the island registered as powerfully antithetical to the spreading of republican principles—the "contagion of liberty"—in Latin America. For jingoes, this humanitarian cause intertwined not only with national pride, profitable trading interests, and some $50 million worth of property investments on the island but also with the anxieties they expressed on the strength of their own nation at home.[28]

Part of the trouble in Cuba, as in Hawaii, resulted from US trade policy: the Wilson-Gorman tariff of 1894, which restored a duty on imported sugar, reduced the market in America for the main product that Cuba produced and threw the predominantly agricultural economy of the island into depression. But the roots of radicalism in Cuba ran much deeper than that, stretching back some three decades. Cuban rebellions against fading Spanish authority had broken out every few years, and were suppressed with similar regularity: in 1868, 1879, 1883, 1885, 1892, and 1893. To the Spanish minister in Washington, these revolutionary tumults amounted to little; he dismissed them as fictitious. But Americans increasingly did not think so, and the inflammatory presence in New York City of Cuban insurrectionist José Martí, sent there to raise funds and promote the cause, helped to convince them. That cause of the Cuban people, blacks and whites alike, he said, was the same as for all oppressed peoples everywhere. US military authorities started anticipating an intervention to free the island once and for all. Yet growing American sympathy for the Cubans was never the same thing as knowing what kind of society or government could exist there after the Spanish had departed.[29]

Cuba Libre

In 1895, a coalition of native fighters ranging sociologically from peasants to patricians joined political organizers José Martí, Máximo Gómez, and Antonio Maceo in an independence movement that reminded American newspaper readers of their own revolutionary struggle against the British long before. This time, the violence, spearheaded by revolutionary guerilla fighters, escalated more quickly than ever. Rebel radicals conspired to destroy the sugar plantations of the ruling elite, alarming Spanish investors far more than actually affecting the $50 million of American interests in the Cuban staple. The Spanish government, meanwhile, focused steadfastly on a single aim: suppression of the insurgency and preservation of Madrid's control. In the end, they would commit several hundred thousand troops, some fifty thousand of whom would eventually die in a futile struggle to keep the possession. The Spanish minister in Washington, Enrique Dupuy de Lôme, saw no possible benefit to Cuba except through the agency of Spain, and his superiors considered even war with the United States as preferable to the humiliation of giving in to Cuban radicals.[30]

To quash the rebellion, Spain called on Gen. Arsenio Martínez Campos, a relatively generous-hearted soldier who had ended a similar episode twenty years earlier. But when Campos's efforts fell short, the government in Madrid replaced him with Gen. Valeriano Weyler, thereafter dubbed "the butcher"—and for good reason. Only his egotism surpassed his cruelty. "I know I am merciless, but mercy has no place in war," the tyrannical Spaniard told visiting journalists. "I care not what is said about me. I am not a politician. I am Weyler." He promptly instituted a program of *reconcentrado*, forced "reconcentration" of the Cuban rural population into Spanish controlled towns and villages to prevent them from supplying the countryside. Then he ordered his troops to roam the interior rural areas, destroying food crops and other provisions of value to rebel guerillas. As a result, thousands of ordinary Cubans perished from the pestilence and starvation that swept the island.[31]

Weyler's brutality swelled the number of uncommitted Cubans who now joined the revolutionary cause and garnered sympathy from American editors, politicians, and ordinary statesiders, some of them eager to furnish weapons to the freedom fighters. He personified Spanish tyranny, its savagery, inhumanity, and fiendish despotism. His draconian measures inspired the Cuban-sponsored pro-rebel propaganda apparatus in New York City. They also fueled the American "yellow press"—the heavily biased newspaper network controlled by William Randolph Hearst and Joseph Pulitzer. Yellow journalists lapped up every sensational, salacious detail in hopes of whipping sympathy to fever pitch. One of the most dynamic journalists of that era, Richard Harding Davis, reporting on the ground from Cuba, sent Hearst a series of lurid stories meant to highlight the human impact of Spanish misrule. But in truth, events on the ground in Cuba unfolded more slowly. A disappointed Frederic Remington, also sent by Hearst to Cuba to prepare on-the-spot written impressions and illustrations for the *Journal*, glumly cabled in January 1897: "EVERYTHING IS QUIET. THERE IS NO TROUBLE HERE. THERE WILL BE NO WAR. I WISH TO RETURN." Hearst immediately shot back: "PLEASE REMAIN. YOU FURNISH THE PICTURES. I'LL FURNISH THE WAR."[32]

Anyone today who would lay the explanation for American intervention at the doorstep of American capitalists must contend with the sharp reality that US businessmen stood to be injured even more by war against Spain than by insurrection in Cuba. Although the violence in Cuba, the social disorder, and the escalating threat to property interests remained a major concern for American investors, some historians have exaggerated the extent that McKinley's foreign policy reflected the influence of big business. True, the desire to expand overseas markets must feature among the overarching causes of American imperialism in this period, but launching a Spanish-American war in the mid-1890s most likely would have dampened the uncertain economic recovery at home, barely underway, following the devastating Panic of 1893. American corporate power brokers, especially those with a direct pecuniary stake, favored restoration of Spanish order in the island, and pro-business Senate Republican leaders Orville H. Platt, Nelson W. Aldrich, and Mark Hanna, more restrained than the jingoes in their party, consistently urged caution in US Caribbean policy.[33]

Officially, the United States had assumed a bipartisan neutral stance, geared toward persuading Spain to end the hostilities in Cuba and lessen the chances of an American intervention. Democratic president Cleveland in 1896, to the dismay of the pro-war media and the interventionists in his party, declined to endorse a joint resolution, approved by large majorities in Congress, that declared US support for the Cuban rebellion. His view was that continuing Spanish rule in Cuba, while detestable, would still prove better than an independent but politically unstable Cuban government that might prompt intervention by other European powers. Thus, while not openly pro-Spanish, the thrust of Cleveland's policy was to perpetuate the rule of Madrid for the time being, with the hope that Spanish reforms down the road might lead to eventual Cuban autonomy. As it turned out, the policy did not work, only affording the Spanish more time to execute a brutal military solution.[34]

With pro-Cuba factions in both parties loath to see the other side receive credit for opposing Spain and liberating the island, both hammered Cuba libre planks into their 1896 election platforms. Neither could afford to be perceived among voters as in any way pro-Spanish, nor could any presidential administration. The Republican McKinley, after assuming the presidency in 1897, outwardly continued the neutral policy, favoring compromise to end the crisis and hoping to avert a US military response. Still, many accounts of the origins of the Spanish-American War have fallen short of explaining the full complexity of the diplomatic problems between the United States and Spain over Cuba between 1895 and 1898, and few have properly credited McKinley's efforts to negotiate a way around the impasse short of sending American troops. His approach did contrast with Cleveland's in a significant way, however: by increments, it ramped up diplomatic pressure on Spain to finally give up Cuba.[35]

Roosevelt, meanwhile, thought Cleveland should have recognized Cuban independence and sent the US naval fleet to Havana. Advocates for a stronger American navy and merchant marine, like Roosevelt and Mahan, saw the Cuban crisis not only as strengthening their argument but also as an opportunity to make the United States a real actor in world affairs. As for Spanish resistance, said Roosevelt, "there would not . . . be very serious fighting," and American losses would be "thrice over repaid" by the long-term results of intervention. "I am a quietly rampant 'Cuba Libre' man," he confided to his sister Anna in January 1897. "I doubt whether the Cubans would do very well in the line of self-government; but anything would be better than continuance of Spanish rule."[36]

Early on, the McKinley administration, too, explored the possibility of Spain's selling the island to the United States, but the answer came back unequivocally negative, as it had before. Then, in late June 1897, the president asserted that the United States had a right to insist that Spanish suppression of the Cuban rebellion be carried out more humanely, refraining from "fire and famine to accomplish by uncertain indirection what the military arm seems powerless to directly accomplish." Again, Madrid refused to bend, replying two months later that its actions in Cuba registered as no more ruthless than those of the Union in carrying out "total war" against the Confederate states during the US Civil War.[37]

A few tentative glimmers of hope for a peaceful solution appeared in the latter half of 1897, as the ruling Conservative Party in Spain faced mounting public criticism for its failure to end the Cuban crisis. The Conservatives' political opponents, who fashioned themselves the Liberals, advocated a political settlement that would grant Cuban autonomy. After an Italian anarchist assassinated the hard-line Spanish premier Antonio Cánovas de Castillo in August 1897, the new government in Madrid under Cánovas's replacement, Práxedes Mateo Sagasta, recalled Weyler from Cuba. Sagasta, acting for the queen regent, had no desire for a war with the United States and believed that a negotiated peace with the rebels, thus appeasing the Americans, might turn out as the best strategy for resolving the internal turmoil in Spain over the seemingly endless rebellion. In late October and into November, the Sagasta government halted the reconcentration policy and gave amnesty to political prisoners, including some Americans, being held in Cuban jails. Then, on November 25, it announced an autonomy plan that would have provided Cubans a greater degree of self-government than ever but without repudiating Spanish sovereignty, meaning that its military control and conduct of foreign relations for the island would remain intact. Still, in all, the new prime minister would not countenance US intervention on the island, announcing that "no Spanish party, certainly not the Liberals, could assent to foreign interference in our domestic affairs or with our colonies."[38]

McKinley's annual message on December 6, 1897, indicated a willingness to hold back and allow these Spanish reforms time to work. If they did not, he added, then the United States stood prepared to take action on its own. This patient stance, ostensibly sympathetic toward Sagasta and stopping short of recognizing Cuban belligerency, elicited cries of protest from the most ardent rebel supporters in both parties, Democrat and Republican,

President William McKinley, about 1898. The Republican McKinley, TR's predecessor in the White House, presided over the sudden transformation of the United States from a continental empire into a transoceanic one. Library of Congress, LC-USZ62-13025

but public opinion by the imprecise indications of that day still seemed to back the president. Meanwhile, however, McKinley ordered the navy's North Atlantic squadron to embark on winter maneuvers off Key West, where the battleship USS *Maine* had already been stationed, and asked Secretary of the Navy John Davis Long to instruct the commander of the European squadron to suspend the expiration of sailors' enlistments. The message for Spain: the United States was preparing for war.[39]

By this time, too, other international events heightened the urgency of resolving the Cuban crisis as soon as possible, by American force if necessary. In Asia, European powers potentially hostile to US interests pushed for trade advantage in the Far East, China in particular, as evidenced by the Germans' occupation of Kiaochow (Jiaozhou) Bay in November 1897. Apart from just Cuba, the ongoing instability of other Caribbean islands, again resulting from the growing uncertainty of Spanish rule there, might invite other nations, including imperial Germany, to challenge the Monroe Doctrine. Rear Adm. Arent S. Crowninshield, sent to the Dominican Republic to assess the threat of German influence, wrote ominously to Secretary Long, "I do not hesitate to predict that before many years have passed, Germany will succeed in acquiring one or more territorial possessions in the Western Hemisphere."[40]

"Remember the *Maine*"

McKinley was only edging toward war, but Roosevelt could barely wait. "We ought to go to war with Spain, unless she gets out peaceably, within the next month," he said privately on November 4, 1897. "Bluster which does not result in fight," he told the US ambassador to Britain, John Hay, "is both weak and undignified." But at that point he still credited McKinley with deft handling of the "Spanish question so as to avoid the necessity of war, and yet uphold the honor of our country and to procure for the insurgent Cubans infinitely more than Cleveland was able to procure." By Christmas, however, with Madrid possibly buying time by promising reforms and autonomy for Cuba, TR's frustration once again exceeded his limited ability to contain it. Congress had dithered on the annexation of Hawaii, and the steady breakdown of order in Cuba made British or German intervention more and more likely. "I wish we had a perfectly consistent foreign policy," he confidentially told family friend William Astor Chanler on December 23, one premised on every European power being "driven out of America, and every foot of American soil, including the nearest islands in both the Pacific and the Atlantic, should be in the hands of independent American states." Taking Hawaii still seemed to him the more pressing matter, but failing also to take Cuba, which he thought no grant of autonomy rather than independence could ever pacify, meant that "it will remain in the hands of a weak and decadent nation [Spain], and the chance [for some other power] to take [it] will be just as good as ever."[41]

Spain's reform program went into effect on January 1, 1898, but in Cuba the ideological damage had been done; the rebels refused to entertain any outcome other than independence. Meanwhile, pro-Spanish groups there refused to cooperate with the plan for Cuban autonomy. As the revolution grew more and more likely to result in rebel success, loyalist (pro-Spain) islanders, who feared being abandoned to the insurrectionists, erupted in a spate of anti-American riots that January in Havana, advocating continued Spanish control of the beleaguered island. These events strengthened the position of hardliners in Madrid. In response, the Spanish government now prepared troop reinforcements to be sent to Cuba, purchased additional weapons and ammunition from Germany, and, in a move that looked like preparing to confront the American navy, pursued negotiations with Great Britain and others for the acquisition of additional ships while speeding repairs on vessels they already had.⁴²

Increasingly doubtful that Spain could make its colonial adjustments work, and reviled, especially by Democrats in Congress, for being "pro-Spanish," McKinley faced a shrinking range of options. He worried, now, for the safety of US nationals living in Cuba and for the security of American property there. So, for protection, he dispatched the *Maine* to Havana in mid-January. One of the most advanced and supposedly invulnerable battleships in the navy, the *Maine* stayed moored in the harbor for a month with its crew of 290 sailors, 39 marines, and 26 officers.⁴³

As relations with Spain continued to spiral downward, William Randolph Hearst on February 9, 1898, received an interesting letter that insurrectionist agents had stolen from the mail in Havana and delivered to the New York newspapers. It was a private communication from the Spanish minister Dupuy de Lôme to a friend in Cuba, penned back in mid-December, describing President McKinley as "weak and a bidder for the admiration of the crowd, besides being a would-be politician who tries to leave a door open behind himself while keeping on good terms with the jingoes of his party." Hearst, without checking for authenticity, published the letter immediately in the *New York Journal*. The McKinley administration insisted on a formal apology, accompanied by the minister's removal. Shamed personally and compromised officially, De Lôme cabled his resignation to Madrid but not before the public outcry in America further intensified the indignation toward Spain. "THE WORST INSULT TO THE UNITED STATES IN ITS HISTORY," screamed the yellow press headlines. With Congress demanding that the administration's consular correspondence on Cuba now be released to the press, McKinley gave in on February 14, knowing that the reports would only give fodder to the jingoes and conceding that the chances of averting war now appeared slight.⁴⁴

Then came the fateful evening of February 15, 1898. In Havana, it was the second night of the Carnival, a traditional pre-Lenten celebration much like the Mardi Gras in New Orleans. As usual on that occasion, the streets teemed with revelers donning festive masks and costumes; happy sounds of music, dancing, and laughter filled the tropical air; and popular cafés crowded with customers, many of them European and some American. On board the *Maine*, however, all was quiet on deck. A Marine corporal softly bugled taps at about

9:10 p.m., though most of the crew had already retired to their hammocks. Capt. Charles B. Sigsbee sat in his cabin writing a letter to his wife. The officer of the watch, Lt. John Hood, relaxed on the port side, his feet propped up on an outer rail as he gazed at the city lights and listened to the faint Carnival noises drifting pleasantly across the harbor.[45]

Suddenly, at 9:40 p.m., there came a powerful shuddering from beneath the bow, Hood later recalled. As he instantly turned his head in that direction, a massive blast, like a volcano erupting, sent everything flying. It was as if a huge front section of the battleship had suddenly disintegrated. "I saw the whole starboard side of the deck and everything above it as far as the aft end of the superstructure spring up into the air with all kinds of objects in it—a regular craterlike performance with flames and everything else coming up," said Hood. Another witness reported a huge column of dark smoke soaring 150 feet skyward. Gigantic pieces of the vessel—everything from chunks of wood and ship's equipment to cement boulders and jagged lengths of steel, along with human body parts—shot in every direction. Some of the debris rained down as far as half a mile away. In only a moment, dozens of mutilated sailors, their limbs severed, found themselves thrashing in the water, shouting desperate cries for help.[46]

On shore, Walter Scott Meriwether, a former naval officer and now a correspondent for the *New York Herald*, had just walked into one of the busy nightclubs when the horrific blast jarred his ears, shattered the windows, and drove customers under the tables. "The city shook to a terrific explosion. Amid a shower of falling plaster every light in the place went out, as did every other electric light in the city," he said later. At first, no one in Havana could imagine what had occurred; one man, groping around with Meriwether in the darkness, guessed that the arsenal across the bay somehow must have ignited. But shortly after, as a squadron of Spanish cavalry galloped by and bits of information circulated in from witnesses, the astonishing reality started to dawn on everyone: the *Maine* had blown up.[47]

The reported toll of losses staggered readers' imaginations, many of them now too young to remember the sickening casualty lists that newspapers printed during the Civil War. At final official count, 260 sailors, marines, and officers perished—some 75 percent of those on board—and of the number of men rescued, only sixteen came through uninjured. Thirty-six of the victims, as later reported, were African American cooks and stewards. Except for the men obliterated in the blast, most burned alive or drowned. A majority of the officers lived, including Captain Sigsbee, their quarters located safely under the stern of the ship, the opposite end from the crew. Sigsbee, the last man to leave the doomed ship as it sank in 30 feet of water, made his way in a small boat to the *City of Washington*, an American steamer anchored close by. "Public opinion should be suspended until further report," he cabled futilely to Secretary Long.[48]

The dreadful news from Havana generated almost instantaneous media reaction in the United States. A major crisis loomed, with "Spanish treachery" to blame. "NOW TO AVENGE THE MAINE," trumpeted Hearst's *New York Journal* in headlines four inches high. The flamboyant Hearst made the most of it, quickly offering a $50,000 reward for "the detection of the Perpetrator of the *Maine* Outrage." Lusting for power, journalistic or otherwise, he had purchased the newspaper in 1895 and became obsessed with the unfolding Cuba story. Further, like the jingoes in general, he regarded war as a necessary tonic for cultural malaise at home.[49]

Hearst and Pulitzer actually represented only a small part of the journalistic community. The media frenzy, in truth, involved thousands of independent newspapers throughout the nation, blaring similar headlines to 15 million readers. The number of daily newspapers in America had multiplied by a factor of four between 1870 and 1900, while ten-cent, illustrated magazines like the *Saturday Evening Post* and *Muncy's* had proliferated from roughly 600 in 1865 to some 4,400 by 1890. If the Spanish-American War of 1898 was media-generated, then editors and publishers all over the country, not just in New York, scrambled to foment it. Proof of Spanish responsibility for the *Maine* incident never surfaced and probably did not exist, but most of the American press and public opinion in general fixed blame resoundingly on the "treacherous Dons," as if they had fired on the Stars and Stripes. The groundswell of patriotism that immediately followed resembled that of the Union states to the news of Fort Sumter in 1861, complete with a made-for-order battle cry inscribed on everything from lapel badges to toothpick holders: "Remember the *Maine*, to Hell with Spain."[50]

This far-flung media explosion stoked the clamor for war already rising around the country. The pressure soon concentrated more heavily than ever on the White House. Receiving the news at about one-thirty in the morning, Secretary Long asked Commander D. W. Dickens to go and tell McKinley. "The President came out in his dressing gown," Dickens remembered. "I handed him the dispatch which he read with great gravity." As administration officials scrambled to insulate McKinley from the din of reporters' demands for retaliation against the Spanish, McKinley turned to George Cortelyou, his chief of staff who would later fill the same role for President Roosevelt. Cortelyou, with utmost restraint, tailored press statements during the tense months preceding the outbreak of war. Despite his efforts, daily coverage of the White House became regular fare for newspapers all around the country—and has remained so ever since.[51]

Never one to act precipitously, McKinley moved with extreme caution. Evoking the memory of the first president on Washington's birthday a week later in Philadelphia, it was that leader's "exercise of a sober and dispassionate public judgment" that the one *now* in Washington's shoes chose to emphasize. Behind the scenes, however, McKinley would step up military preparations, asking Congress in early March to pass a $50 million appropriation for national defense, which it did by a unanimous vote in both houses.[52]

At length, the McKinley administration's methodically appointed board of inquiry would seize on the explanation that most Americans suspected from the start: external explosion, caused by a deliberately placed Spanish mine. Assistant Secretary Roosevelt fretted, meanwhile, that the longer the president delayed war, the more time the Spanish would have to marshal their navy or, alternatively, gain support from sympathetic European powers. "The coincidence of her destruction with her being anchored off Havana by an accident such as has never before happened, is unpleasant enough to seriously increase the many existing difficulties between ourselves and Spain," Roosevelt wrote Secretary Long on February 16, while urging preparedness to strike "a paralyzing blow at the outset" if war were now to come. To others, privately, he loosened his full outrage—and also, by now, his complete loss of faith in the administration. "I would give anything if President McKinley would order the fleet to Havana tomorrow," he wrote the same day to Benjamin Harrison Dibblee, the young All-American captain of Harvard's football team. "This Cuban business ought to stop. The *Maine* was sunk by an act of dirty treachery on the part of the Spaniards *I* believe; though we shall never find out definitely, and officially it will go down as an accident."[53]

New Rochelle

Early on the morning of February 16, 1898, James Waterbury, a Western Union agent, telephoned Frederic Remington at home. The *Maine* had been blown up in Havana harbor, Waterbury reported, expecting a colorful response. After a brief, shocked silence, Remington barked "RING OFF," abruptly ending the call so that he could contact his publishing friends in New York City right away, especially Hearst. To Remington, the news meant that the war he, like Roosevelt, desperately hoped for had already begun.[54]

There was no time to waste; the 37-year-old Remington would sail back to Cuba to witness the war in person. Too fat, out-of-shape, and devoted to liquor and cigars to even dream of enlisting, he could still contribute in other ways. All things military obsessed him as much as they did TR, and besides, Remington needed a new venue to revive his creative passion for the fast-fading old West. Now he would have the chance to sketch, and later paint, Americans who knew the sting of battle, just as an earlier generation of artists, including Winslow Homer, had during the Civil War. "The creation of things by men in time of peace are of every consequence," Remington later wrote, "but it does not bring forth the tumultuous energy which accompanies the destruction of things by men in war. He who has not seen war only half comprehends the possibilities of his race."[55]

This fascination with soldiers and fighting must have started from his boyhood in Canton, New York, where just two months after Frederic's birth on October 1, 1861, his father, Seth Pierre Remington, received a commission as a major in the Eleventh New York Cavalry. The elder Remington finally returned home four and a half years later, promoted to colonel, a hardened battle veteran, and a true war hero in the eyes of an adoring young son. Frederic would embark on schooling at Yale University's School of Fine Arts in 1878 but only stay for a year and a half. While there, his interests gravitated more to the "manly" pursuits of football and boxing than to academics. He went west for the first time in 1881, only dabbling in cattle and sheep ranching before heading back east in 1886, to New York City, where he studied under J. Alden Weir at the Art Students League.[56]

Even though Remington had never come close to being either a cowboy or a soldier, he did little to discourage eastern art buyers from the impression that he *had* been. The cowboy mythology he had helped to construct buoyed not only his own market but also that of his close friend Owen Wister and, for that matter, Roosevelt. By the mid-1880s, his sketches, illustrations, and other artwork on western themes filled the pages of *Collier's*, *Harper's*, and *Century*, all catering primarily to male readers at a time when popular fascination with the dying old West was cresting.[57]

His work took him to venues other than the far West. In 1894, when President Cleveland sent two thousand federal troops into the Chicago area to quell the Pullman Strike, Remington was there, too, covering the scene for *Harper's Weekly*. That experience brought out the ugliness in him, as would his coverage of Cuba. He mingled among the army men bivouacked on the lakefront, especially admiring the officers whose role as custodians of public order impressed him far more than did the plight of the "malodorous" palace car workers. The potential altercation between "mob and soldiers" had been "hot stuff," he wrote to English journalist Poultney Bigelow just after returning home. "Got to have a big killing in this country," Remington enthused, hoping to dispose of "the lice from Central Europe." But by April 1896, a war to depose the Spanish in Cuba intrigued him more, though he thought as poorly of the native Cubans as of the unhappy railway workers. A fight for Cuba libre seemed in keeping with the antislavery legacy of the Civil War. "It does seem tough that so many Americans have . . . got to be killed to free a lot of d—— niggers who are better off under the yoke. There is something fateful in our destiny that way," he confided to Wister. He later added, "Say old man, there is bound to be a lovely scrap around Havana—a big murdering—sure."[58]

Apart from their common interest in western subjects, it was Remington's jingoism considerably more than his raging bigotry that accounted for Roosevelt's friendship with him. After the artist had accompanied TR on an inspection tour of the Atlantic squadron, the assistant secretary was glad to have such an "ally" in making "the American people see the beauty and the majesty of our ships, and the heroic quality which lurks somewhere in all those who man and handle them." With the coming of war with Spain, Remington wanted to be in Cuba for one of the same reasons that Roosevelt did: "to see men do the greatest thing which men are called upon to do," only in his case, to capture it with both his pen and his brush. For both, there was a sense of personal urgency in the endeavor. "We are getting old," Remington told Wister in 1897, "and one cannot get old without having seen a war."[59]

War!

Accident or not, the destruction of the *Maine* worsened the diplomatic impasse between the United States and Spain. Most members of Congress held the Spanish fully responsible. Even those who grudgingly reserved judgment on the cause of the explosion still said that the Spanish could have done more to assure the safety of a US ship in Cuban waters. The greatest pressure, however, came from public opinion, galvanized by the yellow press—but only in part. In fact, jingoism had spread across the nation like prairie fire, fanned by media headlines and editorial commentary everywhere. Newspapers across the country called for intervening in Cuba, reflecting values and beliefs about America's position in the world already established in readers' minds.[60]

Thanks to the well-publicized brutal acts of Weyler, the Spaniards had been dehumanized by American media in general. Their leaders both in Cuba and in Spain represented the utter antithesis of republican values as embraced in the United States. Roosevelt wanted to "throttle the sons of Spain," citing their inhuman treatment of the native Cubans. Beyond that, he regarded the Spanish as lacking the principles he associated with Anglo-Saxons, as well as being deficient in ambition and moral fiber. He had written in 1895 that *character* in a nation, "entirely independent of any religious considerations," determined its capability of social progress just as much as it affected the reputation of an individual man or woman. "The best type of soldier or citizen," he insisted, "feels infinitely more shame and misery from neglect of duty, from cowardice or dishonesty, from selfish abandonment of the interests of the organism of which he is a part, than can be offset by the gratification of any of his [selfish] desires." When he read Edmond Demolins's 1897 *Supériorité des Anglo-Saxons*, TR became even further convinced that Spanish culture fell short of Britain's and his own. Later, in Cuba, noting that his troopers had started referring to Spaniards as "dagoes" or "greasers," he felt tempted to tolerate it.[61]

Ideological forces by themselves cannot explain Americans carrying themselves off to war. "Words are not things," as one prominent scholar once cautioned. Historians smitten by rhetoric sometimes forget the determinative power of contingent events. Even so, while ideas alone do not turn the wheels of history, they do lubricate the turning and influence the direction. When the "wolf rises in the heart," as Roosevelt put it, leaders can then more easily mobilize belief into a course of action.[62]

Amid the growing popular uproar against Spain, members of both parties demanded that McKinley respond militarily. But the president, tormented by the horrible memory of his own war—the blood-soaked corpses stacked at Antietam—still hesitated. He clutched the dimming hope of a diplomatic settlement to end the Cuban issue and avert the loss of American lives. Yet he desired strategic and territorial concessions from Spain that perhaps only war could achieve: US control of the Caribbean and a further extension of

American influence in the Pacific. Roosevelt, meanwhile, polished the plan already drawn up at the Naval War College in case of war: a blockade of Cuban ports, a dispatching of four cruisers to the Spanish coast, and orders to the Asiatic squadron to capture the city of Manila in the Spanish Philippines. He regarded as unmanly McKinley's indecision in the months after the *Maine* disaster. The commander-in-chief had "no more backbone than a chocolate éclair," he vented privately.[63]

By the third week of March, the pressure on McKinley from Congress as well as the general public had become too much. Some of the president's advisers reported him looking more and more haggard, the nervous strain registering on his face. On March 17, Sen. Redfield Proctor of Vermont delivered his conclusions based on a recent trip to Cuba. He had found the native population desperate for "freedom and deliverance" and desolated by the "worst misgovernment" he had ever seen or imagined. The response to Proctor's words, both in the Senate chamber and in the press, said Sen. Francis E. Warren of Wyoming, evinced "a raising of the blood and temper as well as of shame that we, a civilized people, an enlightened nation, a great republic, born in a revolt against tyranny, should permit such a state of things within less than a hundred miles of our shore as that which exists in Cuba." Increasingly, business leaders, too, spoke in favor of war—another shift. Then, on March 19 came the almost inevitable conclusion of the four-member *Maine* inquiry board.[64]

In one more last-ditch attempt at peace, the administration offered to mediate between Spain and the Cuban insurgents. From this, McKinley omitted the threat of an ultimatum or an outright demand for Cuban independence, either of which the Sagasta government would have rejected outright for fear of triggering a revolution at home. When Spain gave its final reply—another unflinching "NO"—on March 31, McKinley, now frustrated and exhausted, resigned himself to fight.[65]

On April 11, the president sent his message to Congress recommending US military action as the only solution to the Cuban crisis. The document was as revealing for what it did *not* say as for what it did. An end to the conflict between Spain and Cuba was its goal, *not* Cuban independence, and it contained no promise that Americans would fight for the latter. For the insurrectionists in Cuba, who regarded themselves on the cusp of ousting the Spanish on their own, McKinley's position must have seemed more exasperating than welcome. On the other hand, when on April 20 Congress enacted the Teller amendment, a public disclaimer of any US intentions to annex Cuba after the war, both McKinley and the jingoistic "Large Policy" advocates also felt betrayed. As for what the message *did* say, US troops would protect American commercial and business interests on the island, safeguard American lives and property there, and stop the ongoing "menace" to peace for the US government. Further, "the cause of humanity" required an end to the "barbarities, bloodshed, starvation, and horrible miseries" in Cuba. It was no answer, he added, "to say this is all in another country, belonging to another nation, and is therefore none of our business." On the contrary, "it is specially our duty, for it is right at our door."[66]

McKinley had tried to avoid war. Now his patience had run out, as had almost everyone else's. Two weeks later, on April 25, Congress declared war against Spain. The "jingo doctrines" had prevailed, but partly because there remained little alternative.

Manila Bay

Land operations would take time to organize, but the fighting at sea commenced almost immediately, in the far South Pacific, and American naval power would make the difference. Roosevelt, back on February 25, acting in place of Secretary Long, had issued secret orders to Commodore George Dewey, instructing him to prepare his small, unarmored Asiatic squadron of cruisers for action in the event of war. It would face Spain's similarly small, also unarmored, flotilla in the Philippines. TR did *not* act out of turn—or behind Long's back—in issuing the order; in fact, he was only carrying out a naval plan in place since 1896, and Long did nothing to countermand it. The strategy guaranteed America's west coast security against potential Spanish attack by sea and prevented that part of the enemy navy from ever reaching the Caribbean. Jingoist officials in Washington also figured that American occupation of the Philippines would increase pressure on Spain to abandon Cuba, while leaving the United States the option later to establish a naval base in the Philippine Islands—and perhaps more.[67]

Spain had ruled the Philippines since the early 1500s, the beginnings of its world empire. The islands featured key harbors and commanded water routes between China and Southeast Asia. For generations, Spanish merchants had shipped sugar, hemp, and tobacco through Manila to markets in China. But in the Philippines, too, Spain's grasp had loosened in the latter part of the nineteenth century. Indeed, a story similar to the one in Cuba was unfolding there: a revolutionary uprising of the native people, led by Gen. Emilio Aguinaldo, in the radical spirit of liberty, equality, and fraternity.[68]

In the early morning hours of May 1, Dewey, aboard the USS *Olympia*, steamed into Manila Bay and, at 5:41 a.m., turned to his captain and said: "You may fire when ready, Gridley." Fire they did, one withering barrage after another in the hours that followed, until the Spanish struck their colors at 12:40 that afternoon, having lost some 381 sailors and all of their ships. By contrast, Dewey suffered no lost vessels at all and only a few men dead or wounded. For the remainder of the war, the American squadron would maintain a blockade of Manila Bay while US land forces commanded by Gen. Wesley Merritt, and Filipino insurgents under Aguialdo, held the islands.[69]

Just like that, without much of a far-Pacific *imperial*—as opposed to *naval*—strategy ahead of time, the United States had acquired the Philippines. It had happened even though the plight of its oppressed local population had never registered on the humanitarian radar of the American public as that of the Cubans had. It remained to be seen later what Congress would do with the islands—whether the United States would keep them as part of a new, farther-flung empire and, if so, whether the insurgent population would stand still for a new imperial power merely replacing the old instead of the independence that they, like the Cubans, longed for.

As would prove to be the case again and again in American wars to come, US war makers had embarked on a foreign struggle without as much preparation—or deliberation—as they should have. The unforeseen price, in both lives and treasure, would prove greater than expected. The benefits would not altogether justify the sacrifices, and soon enough many at home would start saying so. This "new test" of America's institutions, of national policy, and of its people themselves would, editor Walter Hines Page wrote in the June 1898 *Atlantic Monthly*, "change our very character, and we are now playing with the great forces that may shape the future of the world—almost before we know it."

But it was not so much the *fact* of American empire as it was the nature and direction of it that now was changing, with startling rapidity. A generation of young leaders who had taken no part in any great military adventure had now grown to manhood, and Theodore Roosevelt wanted to be the leading voice of that new generation. The news from Manila had arrived without anyone knowing the full meaning of it. "The very swiftness of these events and the ease with which they have come to pass," Page concluded, "are matters for more serious thought than the unjust rule of Spain in Cuba, or than any tasks that have engaged us since we rose to commanding physical power."[70]

The Spanish-American War had indeed come about as a war of *choice* for the United States, not of *necessity*, and anti-imperialists would later say that fact in itself made it wrong. And yet was it an "unjust" conflict? The answer to that question, for the most part, is no. By the moral standards of that day— and perhaps still—the American decision for war in 1898 was justified, the aims at the start of the fighting more honorable than not, though hardly selfless.

If a "just" war can only be waged as a last resort, then President McKinley did so. Had the United States acted against Spain on the basis of legitimate authority? Yes, assuming that the long-standing American assertion of international rights and privileges under the Monroe Doctrine could be taken as legitimate. If war is "just" only when fought to redress a wrong suffered by an innocent party, then also yes, because the long-exploited and oppressed Cuban native population deserved a liberator, even if "liberation" did not rank among the highest motivations on the American side. If war is to be "just," it must be launched with a reasonable chance of success, as loss of life in a hopeless cause is unjustifiable. For the United States, this one was. Finally, the ultimate goal of a "just" war must be to reestablish peace. That question would become more and more complicated as events unfolded. To answer it, one must judge whether the situation of people once governed badly by the Spanish tyrants turned out better or worse in years to come as a result of American intervention, influence, and rule.[71]

3

Teddy's Terrors

WHEN HE HEARD OF ROOSEVELT'S INTENTION TO VOLUNTEER, John D. Long, President McKinley's 59-year-old secretary of the navy, thought the idea was preposterous. "His heart is right and he means well," Long wrote of his impetuous assistant secretary, but did Roosevelt have any idea of what he was getting into? The odds were far greater that he would perish from tropical fever in Cuba than that he would return as a war hero. Had he considered the possibility of being disfigured or maimed or killed in battle? Secretary Long chalked up the behavior to the younger man's "vainglory," his having "lost his head to this unutterable folly of deserting the post where he is of most service and running off to ride a horse."[1]

Even McKinley, twice, implored Roosevelt to reconsider. Beyond that, most of his closest friends simply could not understand the compulsion. "I really think he is going mad," one of them, Winthrop Chanler, remarked. "Theodore is wild to fight and hack and hew. It is really sad. Of course, this ends his political career for good." Henry Cabot Lodge, TR's best friend and a US senator from Massachusetts, feared the same. Lodge urged him to stay in the Navy Department, not only for the sake of Mrs. Roosevelt and their six young children but also for the promising future in Washington that might unfold for him.²

"My friends have been making me very miserable with their appeals during the last few weeks," TR told another friend, John Proctor of the Civil Service Commission.

"I suppose I have been the worst of all," Proctor answered.

"Yes," Roosevelt replied, and then he stopped right in the pathway, put both hands on Proctor's shoulders, and looked at him in a way that Proctor never forgot. "Proctor," he said, "I am going to Cuba. I will take all the chances of meeting death by yellow fever, smallpox, or by a Spanish bullet just to see the Spanish flag once on a battlefield."³

Historians who have tried to deconstruct TR's psyche have explained his determination to volunteer as, among other things, his being embarrassed by his father's decision not to fight in the Civil War. Some people close to him thought this to be so, yet in all of his massive private correspondence Roosevelt never stated such a motivation directly. The quality that he worshipped most about his father was the elder Roosevelt's self-sacrificing civic-mindedness, as evidenced throughout his life and practiced consistently during that war. The explanation that TR *did* give for his choice to volunteer made better sense: "a man's usefulness depends upon his living up to his ideals in so far as he can," he told his friend, the Harvard-trained physician William Sturgis Bigelow, in late March 1898. "I have consistently preached what our [political] opponents . . . call 'jingo doctrines' for a good many years. One of the commonest taunts directed at men like myself is that we are armchair and parlor jingoes who wish to see others do what we only advocate doing." His credibility would be lost, he went on to say, if he did not try to "live up" to those "doctrines." Further, to have stayed home after urging others to fight would have left a stain on his character as damaging as anything else to any political future he might have.⁴

This is not to deny that his reasons for fighting were self-interested, complicated, and perhaps mysterious even to himself. Significantly, his own statements at the time, including the one to Bigelow, *did* imply consideration of his political image, thus his prospects for career advancement. One historian has attributed TR's actions to "social and psychological needs" arising from "deep personal sources of frustration, anxiety, and fear." That may be so, but intriguing as they are, psycho-historical diagnoses can be difficult to prove. Another interpretation finds Roosevelt to have been driven by homicidal "bloodlust" for the sake of fulfilling a warped notion of manhood. This conclusion risks being more present-minded than historical, possibly obscuring more than illuminating the cultural context of TR's decision. Besides, many thousands of other Americans of that time also expressed an eagerness for battle.[5]

In the end, Roosevelt's own account for his actions remains as persuasive as any. His deeply rooted sense of personal honor and commitment to traditional civic values—mixed with his political ambition—compelled him to practice what he preached and justified his encouraging others to follow.

Joining the Fight

Since his days in the Dakota Territory, Roosevelt had dreamed of organizing a western cavalry outfit. In August 1886, while at his ranch in Medora, Roosevelt learned that an American army captain had been killed by Mexican troops in a border incident. He immediately wrote to Secretary of War William Endicott, offering to raise some companies of "horse riflemen" in case of war with Mexico. "I think there is some good fighting stuff among these harum-scarum roughriders out here," he told Lodge, then a US congressman. It would be "as utterly reckless a set of desperados as ever sat in the saddle." In 1895, while serving as police commissioner in New York City, he had contacted New York governor Levi P. Morton regarding his chances of being offered a captaincy in a volunteer regiment in the event of war with Spain. And as war loomed in early 1898, he had entreated Col. Francis V. Greene of the Seventy-First New York Regiment, Secretary of War Russell A. Alger, and army general-in-chief Nelson A. Miles about commanding a cavalry unit. Finally, on April 25, the day that war was declared, he received the go-ahead for his Rough Riders regiment. Roosevelt always figured his own best role to be *army* service, near the spray of bullets. The navy would not do. "I shall be useless on a ship," he confessed.[6]

Those who knew him most closely sensed, however, that his decision to fight came after more soul-searching than outsiders could have realized—and was less impulsive than some historians have thought. TR later wrote that he "would have turned from his wife's deathbed to have answered the call"; there might never arise another "chance to cut my little notch on the stick that stands as a measuring-rod in every family." Roosevelt was given to hyperbolic, self-aggrandizing statements. That declaration, made in retrospect, was one of them. In fact, his wife, Edith, revealed privately that he had spent many sleepless nights pondering what to do. No one knew better than she the vulnerabilities and fears lurking behind his public bluster and manly pronouncements. He always depended on the women in his life—now, mainly, his wife and sisters Anna (Bamie) and Corinne. They cared for him, chased away his self-doubts, and lifted his spirits in moments of melancholy. Edith referred to him as her "sensitive plant."[7]

Part of the reason for that insomnia and the moments of uncertainty about going to war was Edith's health. She actually *had* come unnervingly close to death during the weeks just prior to his departure. Unlike Theodore, Edith had viewed the country's gradual slide into war against Spain with mounting dread. Meanwhile, on November 9, 1897, she had given birth to her fifth child, a son, Quentin, but her recovery had been agonizingly slow. Not until Christmas, her husband wrote, was she "beginning to look and feel herself." But then, in the first week of January, she came down with a mysterious affliction accompanied by an unremitting high fever. At first, the family feared that she had typhoid, the disease that had taken Theodore's mother on that terrible day in February 1884, when his first wife, Alice, also had died. At the same time, their oldest son, eleven-year-old Ted, was suffering from severe headaches, attributed to nervous exhaustion because of his father's overly intense expectations of him, said the boy's doctor.[8]

Increasingly alarmed about Edith's decline, Theodore canceled a series of business engagements in New York in order to stay at her bedside. Far more fragile psychologically than he ever revealed in public, it would have devastated him to lose her. And if she had died, would he have gone on with the Rough Riders anyway, as he later declared, or retreated within himself, as he had done before in the wilds of Dakota?

No improvement followed over the next four weeks, her temperature never falling below 101 degrees. On February 22, she noted a strange swelling just above the pelvis. Distracted also by the news of the *Maine*'s sinking the week earlier, Theodore called in an expert on abdominal tumors, Sir William Osler of the Johns Hopkins University, who diagnosed her as "critically ill," with a dangerous abscess in the psoas muscle, requiring risky surgery. The antibiotics that would be employed for such internal infections today did not exist then. Undergoing the operation on March 6, Edith remained incapaci-

Theodore Roosevelt and family, about 1894. Roosevelt holds Archie (*left*); Theodore III is standing next to Alice (*center*), with Kermit and Ethel in front of Edith (*right*). Library of Congress, LC-DIG-pmsca-39691

tated for another two weeks. Not until March 21 could Theodore say with any certainty, writing to Brooks Adams, that "she is crawling back to life." Even so, Edith remained weak and "terribly wasted" until early April.[9]

Finally, only days before McKinley's war message to Congress, she felt well enough for a spring-morning carriage ride with her husband. Relieved at last, Theodore proceeded with plans to accompany the cavalry regiment he envisioned. Mostly concealing the worry she now felt for *his* safety, Edith gave her reluctant blessing for him to go and join the fight. "I can never say what a help and comfort Edith has been to me," he told his sister Corinne on May 5, a week before he left for Rough Rider training in San Antonio.[10]

Citizen Soldiers

Biographer Kathleen Dalton has noted that charismatic leadership such as TR's involves an interaction between the leader and those being led; followers are not a passive, unthinking part of that relationship. TR had appealing qualities—his charm, energy, electric presence, and sense of humor, along with his moral leadership rooted in traditional American ideals—that drew people to him. It would become so, as well, with the men who volunteered as Rough Riders.[11]

Historians who have written full-length studies of the Rough Riders have focused much more on what they *did* than on what they *meant*, both to themselves and to other Americans. Few, moreover, have analyzed their composition as a group. Although billed as an "all-American" fighting force, the Rough Riders would pass no multicultural muster of today. The regiment reflected its time, along with all the prevailing social biases. It included no women, of course, and no African Americans in those days of a strictly segregated military. Nor did it contain many names reflecting the "new immigration" from Eastern and Southern Europe or Asia. Few Hispanic surnames appeared. The roster featured only a smattering of Catholics and Jews. And one report found twenty-six "full-blooded Indians" in the regiment.

Yet many commentators thought the regiment to have been strange in design for that time. "In its ranks, serving as privates, are men of all social conditions and racial differences," exaggerated the *Springfield Republican*. "On this account alone we are proud of 'Teddy's Terrors.'" All volunteers, they constituted a band of citizen soldiers but hardly the most conventional citizens. As critics initially judged them, the Rough Riders' faults of composition seemed certain to outweigh their military potential. Some noted that about half the regiment consisted of the people *least* likely to sacrifice for *any* cause: a bunch of rowdy, law-flouting, ungovernable far westerners on the one hand; on the other, a contingent of spoiled, soft, overprivileged sons of the wealthy eastern elite.[12]

This amalgamation, though criticized by many at the time, represents one of the most significant aspects of the regiment. The Rough Riders' two commanders, Roosevelt and fellow Harvard graduate Leonard Wood, believed the unusual mix of troopers held great symbolic as well as military potential. They wanted the experiment to show that Americans all around, whatever their political, social, and sectional differences, still had greatness in them. According to the regimental roster stored in the National Archives, the troopers covered 145 different occupations, professions, and trades. Only 160 of the final total of 1,252 enlistees described themselves as "cowboys," along with another 58 who identified as "ranchers" or "cattlemen." Apart from those, the combination included 87 miners, 53 farmers, 44 clerks, 34 laborers, 32 attorneys or lawyers, 31 railroad men, 26 students, 23 printers or reporters, 17 blacksmiths, 15 teachers, 15 polo players, 14 musicians, and 13 carpenters.

In addition, 29 regular army men joined the regiment as volunteers. For occupational range, the regiment featured a confectioner, two florists, a pair of nurserymen, three insurance agents, two singers, a hotel keeper, a pharmacist, four watchmakers, and a sculptor. The vast majority of the men were, of course, young—in their 20s—and unmarried. Given their wide variety of backgrounds, the Rough Riders never actually constituted the wild bunch of "cowboy" soldiers that the newspapers—and later historians—found to make such engaging copy. As the regiment's story evolved, however, some of the scribes around the country started to find more interesting their real identities in contrast with their popular image. As one would say shortly after the Battle of San Juan Heights, it had been "childish" ever to imagine that every man was a "cowboy."[13]

Further, unlike volunteer regiments of the Civil War era, the Rough Riders belonged to no single state; the recruits hailed from forty-two states, North and South, West and East, as well as three territories and thirteen foreign countries. In that sense, they mirrored the whole nation, which contradicted their media image as "cow-punchers" plus an incongruous smattering of eastern "dudes." As the *New York Advertiser* observed just after the war, "Texas feels as much local pride in them as does New York." The *St. Louis Republic* added that "the blue and the gray march shoulder to shoulder, and the rich and the poor meet on a common level." Among the troopers could be found "the sons of federal and confederate soldiers, and the sons of millionaires of the east ride side by side with the cowboy of the western plains." It is true that the majority of the Rough Riders came from western states and territories, including 127 from Texas, 120 from New Mexico, and 103 from Indian Territory. Apart from those, however, well over a third came from places other than the far West: from the old Northwest, 195 volunteers; the old South, 142; the middle-Atlantic states, including Roosevelt's New York, 148; New England, 43; and 63 showed up from outside the United States.[14]

A motley bunch of volunteers such as these, once proven in battle, TR maintained, could represent the best of American manhood—"cowboys," "dudes," and all others in between made useful to the state. "The contrast between the citizen one day and the soldier the next, in the United States, has been the marvel of the old world," bragged an editorial in the *Denver Rocky Mountain News*. Together, the recruits were to feature qualities of character still needed to preserve a now-democratized republic, build the nation, and expand an empire.[15]

If Roosevelt considered himself and his recruits prepared for a war against Spain, the US military in general was not. The navy, thanks in part to Roosevelt, stood ready, with its 196 ships, 73 of them fighting vessels, including 5 battleships, 4 of those top of the line—in all, far superior to the Spanish fleet. But the army's condition that spring and for several months afterward proved to be one of "transition accompanied by confusion," in historian Graham Cosmas's phrase. The disarray, especially the haste and ineptitude lasting at least through August, reflected the social and political contexts of the decision for war. "The United States was groping . . . into the complicated game of international power and diplomacy, aware of her strength and desirous of using it, but unsure for what purposes," writes Cosmas. In April 1898, US regulars numbered only 28,000, mostly scattered among various posts in the far West. That number amounted to roughly a twentieth the size of Germany's army, a thirteenth of Great Britain's, and less than a third of Spain's. In addition, state governors could mobilize militia and national guard companies, adding about 100,000 undertrained ground troops carrying obsolete weapons. The War Department had no prearranged contingency plan for Cuba; little knowledge of Spanish forces there, which numbered somewhere around eighty thousand regulars; no particular faith in getting help from the local insurgents; an encumbering lack of detailed geographical information about the island; and no logistical experience in managing an amphibious invasion since Gen. Winfield Scott's assault on Veracruz in 1847, during the Mexican-American War.[16]

These deficiencies notwithstanding, the last thing that many regular army commanders wanted was a sudden influx of war-crazy volunteers, and there existed no shortage of those. Beyond sympathy for the oppressed Cubans, the *Maine* disaster in mid-February had stirred a warlike spirit throughout the nation, spreading among all classes and sections. State and federal authorities soon found themselves deluged with applications to join the armed forces. Pennsylvania coal miners, some of whom had once served in Central European armies, contributed to a multitude of willing recruits, as did labor unions, Republican political clubs, Civil War veterans groups, national guard units, college fraternities, civic organizations, and various millionaires willing to arm and equip men at their private expense.[17]

After the news began to circulate that the War Department had approved Roosevelt's regiment of cavalry volunteers, some regular army officers immediately started venting their doubts to the press. Those doubts included suspicion of volunteer forces generally. "The hardest work to perform with such troops would be keeping them in order," an unnamed military source told the *Springfield Republican*. A raw amateur like Roosevelt, for example, "would have to prove himself a great military genius" to keep them all from being killed. If "a band of American cowboys set out to show Spaniards how to make war[,] there's simply no knowing what may happen." Furthermore, changes in military tactics since the Civil War and technological advancements in weaponry arguably called for reliance on a standing force of trained professionals. So said the West Point–educated infantry lieutenant George B. Duncan in an article for the *North American Review*. The old idea that "a uniform makes a soldier" must be abandoned, he explained. Success in future wars would depend on skill in the use of weapons and in "fire discipline, combined with implicit obedience to and trust in commanders." These requirements could not be met in volunteer training camps held for just the days or weeks—not months—that might now remain prior to an attack on the United States by the more militarily experienced Spanish.[18]

In this argument for a professionalized military, however, the army ran up against a philosophical issue much older than the Union itself. It was the fear that a large regular force, especially if under control of ambitious, power-hungry men, would threaten *internal* security, thus endangering the republic even more than any foreign foe could. The historical example of Gen. George Washington's keenness to surrender command of the Continental Army at the end of the Revolutionary War, rather than using that force to seize political power as a less virtuous leader might have done, still resonated ideologically. In Congress, one speech after another emphasized the social importance of recruiting volunteers as opposed to relying completely on the regular army. That would include men from all classes and every ordinary occupation, lovers of country rather than seekers of pay, citizen soldiers and not "hirelings" and "mercenaries." As one congressman put it in early 1898, the tradition of citizen soldiers had proven sufficient in fighting American wars of the past and, more important, promised never to "menace our liberties." Even if this fear was just an "old bugbear," said Duncan, applying no longer since the Civil War, the belief in non-professional armies still dominated in American political culture.[19]

Aside from the supposed dangers of a professionalized military, both of the great revolutions of the eighteenth century—the American and the French—had emphasized a fundamental connection between soldiering and citizenship. That meant tying the privileges of liberty together with the responsibilities of membership in a body politic. A willingness to face danger for the sake of protecting freedom or defending a common cause had become a test of a man's maturity and of his fitness to meet the challenges of adulthood in a free society. Further, the general public, by every indication, still celebrated citizen soldiering over the professional variety, especially later when the fighting in Cuba had mostly ended and the volunteers had once again proven themselves. "The American is not a born soldier, but he is a born patriot," trumpeted the *Philadelphia Enquirer*. "He knows by instinct and education how to fight for his country." The *Buffalo Commercial* proudly echoed that sentiment: "Our fighting men, regulars and volunteers, are in the army of their own free will. There is not a conscript under the American flag. Their hearts are in the cause."[20]

Following the old-fashioned American military and political formula, McKinley at first asked for 125,000 volunteers (soon increased to 267,000). Congress also had authorized him to "call into the actual service of the United States the militia of the several states." Meanwhile, it passed the War Revenue Act authorizing $200 million for the expansion of the regular army to 61,000 men.[21]

Skilled in building political coalitions, the president used army commissions not only to consolidate support for his administration but also to advance reconciliation between North and South. He called for civilian volunteers from every state in the Union. The last time a president had asked southerners to defend the country—Abraham Lincoln in April 1861—four southern states, including Virginia, seceded from the United States, joining the seven that had already formed the Confederate States of America. Over the years since the Civil War, the Republican Party had garnered only very limited support in the South. In the presidential election of 1896, the electoral votes of *all* the former Confederate states had gone to McKinley's Democratic rival, William Jennings Bryan. McKinley, of course, could not be sure that his strategy might not backfire. Would asking southerners to fight on the federal side now produce a renewal of old sectional animosity?

Happily, as it turned out, the answer was no. Volunteers of every description appeared from all over the country, their eagerness reflecting not only the lingering economic effects of the Panic of 1893 but also ardent expressions of restored patriotism in all sections. By mid-May, every gray state had promptly filled its quota, reported the *New York Tribune*, and "in many cases double the number called for" now awaited acceptance. Of these thirty thousand men, the *Tribune* estimated 90 percent of them to be former rebels or sons of ex-Confederates. Even Roosevelt, the New Yorker of prominent Dutch lineage, advanced McKinley's credibility in the South in his being, a Charleston newspaper later would note, "half a Southerner, at least, by reason of his maternal ancestry" from Georgia. And his Rough Riders regiment was "largely composed of volunteers from Texas" and other former Confederate states, wrote the columnist.[22]

Early on, it had helped that McKinley appointed ex-Confederate leaders Fitzhugh Lee, who had been governor of Virginia, and Joseph Wheeler of Alabama to be major generals in command of volunteer forces. Lee prided himself as the grandson of "Light Horse Harry" Lee and a nephew of the most revered Confederate in the South, Robert E. Lee. He had served as an officer throughout the Civil War, riding with the romanticized Confederate cavalry commander, Gen. J. E. B. Stuart, and earning promotion to major general in August 1863.[23]

The 62-year-old Wheeler, a former cavalry officer who had been wounded three times while fighting under Gen. Joseph E. Johnston, claimed the dubious honor of having sixteen horses shot from under him during the Civil War, at battles including Shiloh, Murfreesboro, Chickamauga, and Atlanta. Before all that, Wheeler had graduated from West Point and fought for two years in the Mexican-American War. In 1898, he was serving his last of eight terms in Congress, where, though a Democrat, he had bolted against Cleveland's anti-inflationary support for the gold standard and had become a leading proponent of populist free silver in the House of Representatives.

Representing Alabama, he had promoted economic reconciliation between North and South, but fellow congressmen knew him best for his eccentricity, his inexhaustible nervous energy and zeal. They dubbed him "Jack-in-the-box" because of his penchant for suddenly jumping up from behind his desk on all occasions. As war approached, Wheeler became an almost daily visitor at either the White House or the War Department, obsessed with receiving a commission to fight the Spanish. "God forbid that the growing generation should prefer to be money changers rather than brave soldiers, fighting and if need be, dying, in the front rank of battle," he announced, sharing Roosevelt's attitude. Aging, slight in stature, and weighing just 110 pounds at the most, "Fightin' Joe" no longer looked much like a soldier. Even so, McKinley handed him command of a brigade of volunteer cavalry, the one that would include the Rough Riders.[24]

"Cowboys"

In keeping with Wild West legend, some of the most colorful volunteers for cavalry service did come from the western states and territories. But the wildest of these did not make it into Roosevelt's regiment or, for that matter, get into the war at all.

They varied even further across the social spectrum, from frontier celebrities to suspected murderers. Counting on his fame as a showman, "Buffalo Bill" Cody extravagantly promised a force of thirty thousand, mostly western roughnecks and Indian fighters, along with their own motley assortment of guns and horses. Frank James of Missouri, the former Confederate bushwhacker and sketchy brother of deceased gang leader, train robber, and killer Jesse James, scratched up an outfit of men that he knew. In Chadron, Nebraska, "Doc" Middleton, "famous on the border," said one western editor, "as an Indian fighter, highwayman, bad man, frontier marshal and all-round tough citizen," was busy organizing a regiment of "rough riders" and ended up with a hundred men "fully equipped for field service," or so he claimed. As for the local observation that many of his recruits were "old outlaws, road agents and dangerous frontier criminals," Middleton replied, "I've got nothing to do with that.... In this Western country, you see, it is not considered good manners to inquire too closely into a man's past." LaCrosse, Wisconsin, reported Dr. D. Frank Powell to be composing another group to be called "Wisconsin Rough Riders," which included a large number of Winnebago Indians. From Wyoming came an offer from George R. Shanton, "a well known Laramie cowboy," to raise within ten days a company of fifty "rough riders and expert shots." In St. Louis, 49-year-old "Captain" Frank M. Walters, a Civil War veteran, Populist politician, and operative for the Missouri Labor Bureau, managed to collect twenty-five unemployed former "Texas rangers and daredevils" from the western plains, all judged "equal to those of [Confederate raider William] Quantrill in bravery and devil-may-care fighting capacity."[25]

Roosevelt's plan differed from all of these in that he envisioned making the frontier less alien from establishment values. He wanted its people and the best of their character to be mainstreamed more into American life. More likely useful by that standard, Wyoming judge Jay L. Torrey raised an outfit of "Rocky Mountain Riders," and in Sioux Falls, the attorney general of South Dakota, Melvin Grigsby, who boasted four-and-a-half years of Union cavalry experience in the Civil War, gathered another contingent of "cowboy" types. Several western newspapers credited Torrey as the "originator" of the idea of enlisting frontiersmen in the Cuban campaign. Quietly preceding Roosevelt's efforts by two months, he had already assembled a regiment of "hardy riders" from Wyoming, the western parts of the Dakotas, northern Colorado, Montana, and Idaho. Both his troop-raising and Grigsby's would receive the official green light from Washington shortly after Roosevelt's did, but it remained to be seen which group, if any, would be sent first to Cuba.[26]

Meanwhile, in Yavapai and Maricopa counties of the Arizona Territory, a citizens' group started planning right after the *Maine* disaster to gather an entire regiment of Arizona volunteers—enough, they imagined, to fill the army's entire need for mounted forces. Two leaders of the Cuban rebels, traveling around the West to promote the Cuba libre movement, had conducted a meeting at the Yavapai Courthouse, pleading their cause as comparable to the American war for independence and inspiring the eager crowd to pledge considerable funding as well as men. Territorial governor Myron H. McCord barraged President McKinley's mail with entreaties on behalf of the grassroots organizers: James McClintock, a Phoenix newspaper publisher; Alexander O. Brodie, an 1870 West Point graduate, Indian fighter, cattleman, and mineral prospector; and William Owen "Buckey" O'Neill, mayor and former sheriff in the town of Prescott. "No better material for cavalry purposes can be found anywhere in the world, than among the cowboys of Arizona," McCord boasted. With the mining and cattle industries still in the doldrums from the Panic of 1893, the Arizonans figured they could easily round up three squadrons, an estimated 1,056 southwestern men, already well-versed in horsemanship and use of firearms. Brodie, the old soldier, would command them. All of it might advance the cause of Arizona statehood, they believed. Their disappointment registered deeply when they learned that Roosevelt and Wood would receive regimental command and that only 170 of their total (and later 200) would be accepted into the Rough Riders. Brodie, McClintock, and O'Neill, however, would go along as officers.[27]

Apart from economic motivation, patriotic impulses, or just evading the sheriffs, much of the groundswell of volunteers around the country responded to the cachet of being a "rough rider," as in the popular entertainment craze of the day. The attraction drew on the romantic imagery of the "old West," a place then palpably disappearing. What many Americans had come to *believe* about the West, however much distorted, influenced their behavior. High among those beliefs rested the notion that the frontier could regenerate manly virtue, shore up character, steel a man's soul, and make him a better citizen as well as a hardier person. "There will be some historic fighting done by these [western] rangers," boasted the *Idaho Falls Times*, "and the scenes that were part of the life of Custer, Jack Crawford and Buffalo Bill will be again enacted, but with better weapons and with some of the comforts and conveniences of civilization." True, the golden age of the cowboy in the West actually did not last long. Many of the real cowboys had been, in fact, African Americans looking for a livelihood somewhere different from the post–Civil War South. Western investors found profits by employing people to round up Texas longhorns and push them north to railheads in Kansas and Missouri. Herding steers reached a high point in the 1880s, but by 1895 that kind of cattle industry had mostly ended. But the romanticizing—meaning largely, the fictionalizing—of cowboy life was only beginning, and it did not take long for the myths to crowd out the reality.[28]

Beyond pursuing the cowboy myth, however, many Americans in the 1890s had plenty of financial reasons to worry about their future and to try new opportunities when they could. If the Chicago World's Fair signified that America stood on the "threshold of a great awakening" of both technology and spirit, as President Cleveland declared on its opening day in May 1893, then the onset of the Panic of 1893 quickly dampened the general mood. It would register as the worst economic depression in American history up to that time. In fact, calamity had struck even before Cleveland took office that March. A month later, the news hit that the Philadelphia and Reading Railroad had filed for bankruptcy, and the stock market reacted with the largest single-day losses to date. That spring, stocks would plummet, thousands of businesses would go bankrupt, and millions of Americans would lose their jobs. Then, on May 5, just days after the Chicago fair started, came news that the National Cordage Company had collapsed, followed by another market slide that ignited a financial chain reaction. Banks everywhere called in loans and suspended further ones. The shock forced additional railroad failures, including the bellwether Northern Pacific and Union Pacific lines. By the end of the year, some five hundred banks and sixteen thousand other businesses nationwide had gone under.[29]

As unemployment increased to almost 20 percent of the workforce, many companies slashed the wages of laborers who remained, and labor protests followed. In addition to the 1894 Pullman crisis, a succession of miners' strikes broke out farther west, including one in the gold-producing region around Cripple Creek, Colorado, and another by the bituminous coal workers of the United Mine Workers Union. The growing numbers of roving jobless people—"vagrants" in the unsympathetic vernacular of the day—rose alarmingly. That signaled what many took to be a serious public danger to the rest of the population.[30]

Patriotic motivations aside, there is little question that the lingering depression of the mid-1890s made the flood of volunteers in 1898 greater than it might have been otherwise. Although the crisis had begun to lift by mid-1897, estimated unemployment rates still ran around 12 percent of the workforce at the start of the Spanish-American War. The second and third largest categories of the Rough Riders' rank and file were "miners" and "farmers," occupational groups hit so hard by the depression that many gravitated to the new People's Party in the early-to-mid 1890s. And now, thousands of new employment opportunities had suddenly opened in the field of soldiering. Military service "in defense of the flag" could appeal for many different reasons.[31]

Gathering Men

Of all the volunteer cavalry options before McKinley, Roosevelt's proposal held the greatest organizational advantages. Few others could match TR's combination of being well connected in Washington while offering personal experience and contacts in the West as well. Besides, unlike some of the other would-be regiment commanders, TR sensed that he lacked the military knowhow to command such an outfit all by himself. When McKinley's secretary of war, Russell A. Alger, offered him the colonelcy of the First Volunteer Cavalry, he refused, proposing instead regular army captain Leonard Wood, with himself as lieutenant-colonel—the second-in-command. Alger promptly approved, with the formal announcement coming on April 25.[32]

The 37-year-old Wood, a New Hampshire native, was a Harvard Medical School graduate and career army officer. He had received the Congressional Medal of Honor in 1885, as a captain in the Eighth Infantry, for heroics that included hand-to-hand combat against renegade Apache Indians in Arizona and their elusive leader Geronimo, the "wily savage," as newspapers dubbed him. He and Roosevelt became fast friends in Washington while TR was in the Navy Department and Wood served as President McKinley's personal physician. A man of rare athletic ability, Wood sometimes joined the

"Sunday scrambles" in Washington—on foot, over treacherous terrain—that Roosevelt liked to organize for himself, his children, and whoever else might be talked into going along. On those occasions, the obsessive Theodore usually outwalked everybody—except Wood. Roosevelt admired Wood almost beyond limit and later wrote that he "combined, in a very high degree, the qualities of entire manliness with entire uprightness and cleanliness of character." Every inch the professional soldier, it would not bother Wood so much when the press paid scant attention to him in favor of his more colorful—and *much* more voluble—subordinate. Accepting the appointment and its rapid promotion to colonel, Wood immediately coordinated with the territorial governors of Oklahoma, Arizona, New Mexico, and the Indian Territory to find the toughest and best men available in those places.[33]

Roosevelt, meanwhile, delayed only briefly his resignation from the Navy Department after the formal April 25 war declaration against Spain. With Edith finally recovering, he finished remaining duties while attending to arrangements for uniforms, supplies, weapons, and ammunition for the Rough Riders. For himself, he ordered from Brooks Brothers an "ordinary cavalry lieutenant colonel's uniform in blue Cravenette" and contacted an animal dealer for "a couple of good, stout, quiet horses," specifying that they "not be gunshy." He also made a point of fortifying his investments and insurance policies, making certain that his death, should it come in Cuba, "would not very materially affect" his family's income.[34]

With Wood scouring for recruits in the West, where the feeling for war brimmed over, TR selected men from other parts of the country, including the Northeast. Within just a few weeks, he found himself swamped with twenty-seven sacks of mail, all bulging with applications. As word spread, the total number of volunteers reached some 23,000 for a regiment that the War Department originally limited to just 780 troopers but soon after raised to 1,000; the final number listed on the National Archives roster was 1,252. All those accepted as recruits had to be able to ride, shoot, endure pain, and put up with hardship. All had to embrace the Spartan attitude of public need over private comfort. Almost all could qualify to the standard of being law-abiding, respectable citizens.[35]

Although the western component would provide the regiment with its unique tone and lasting reputation, Roosevelt worked frenetically in these early weeks to include as many from east of the Mississippi as he could. He wanted to prove that they, too, especially young men of the privileged classes, had lost neither patriotism nor a sense of obligation to serve cause and country. No matter where they came from, he later wrote, they had to be men "in whose veins the blood stirred with the same impulse which once sent the Vikings over sea." To New York City reporter and Kentucky native John William Fox on April 25, he wrote, "We are to try to raise the regiment in the Rocky Mountain States; but it may be that I have a chance to put in some eastern men, though this as yet I cannot promise. Could you get a hundred men, either where you are or at your home in Kentucky[?] . . . They must be sound in body and heart, able to fight, and willing to obey." On the same day, he also wrote his friend William Austin Wadsworth of Geneseo, New York: "It may be that I can get them to include a company from New York. Set about at once finding out how many men you could get. Do you think you could raise 100? Do you think you could raise 50? . . . [Y]ou must have everything ready so I can slash you in if there is a failure of recruits in the West."[36]

Roosevelt also recognized the symbolism of including some Ivy League athletes. He telegrammed Harvard football coach Guy Murchie, who had recruited a group of young men at Harvard: "Bring on your men so that we can enlist them at eighteen fourteen G Street, Washington, D.C., at ten Thursday morning, May fifth without fail." Another he sent to journalist and social reformer Lincoln Steffens on May 4: "There are a number of Knickerbocker and Somerset Club as well as Harvard and Yale men going as troopers, to be exactly on a level with the cowboys." The following day, he announced proudly to his sister Corinne, "I have about twenty five 'gentlemen rankers' going with me—[including] five from the Knickerbocker Club, and a dozen clean-cut, stalwart young fellows from Harvard; such fine boys." And to former Virginia governor Fitzhugh Lee on May 6, he cabled: "Young Simpson is with me, and he is a gallant young fellow. If he earns his commission I will do my best to get it for him."[37]

San Antonio

The assembled Rough Riders had just begun their military training in Texas when an anonymous reporter for the *Chicago Record* encountered Roosevelt in San Antonio's Alamo plaza. There he was, wandering contemplatively among the blossoming magnolias, dressed in his officer's khaki uniform, hands behind his back, head bent downward. Rigorous exercise since childhood had given him a stout build, though he was only 5 feet 8 inches in height. His increasingly famous cowboy-style mustache, drooping at the corners, complemented his short-cropped hair and a florid complexion. "His nose is thick, his chin square and aggressive, eyes blue gray and so penetrating in their look that the thick glasses, flashing with every quick movement of the head, seemed superfluous," the writer observed. The corners of his eyes wrinkled up in mirth, and when he smiled or talked, "a set of beautifully white and strong teeth" captured one's attention. "His manner is animated, his speech rapid, yet curiously distinct and emphatic." Altogether, "he impressed me as energy personified," with an irrepressible combativeness standing out as his most "prominent characteristic." Asked to remark on his military philosophy, the pugnacious lieutenant colonel replied: "Hit 'em, hit 'em, hit 'em," fiercely pounding his left palm with his right fist.[38]

Colonel Wood struck the reporters as markedly different from the impetuous, more "picturesque" Roosevelt. In fact, many at the time spoke of the regiment more as Roosevelt's than as Wood's. The same Chicago columnist described Wood almost as the opposite of TR: "quiet and undemonstrative." Yet he cut a far more imposing figure. "His chest is deep as that of one of Du Chaillu's gorillas[,] and his shoulders remind one of the Farnese Hercules." Fellow officers stood in awe of Wood's strength. He was known as the best boxer in the army and the only white man who could tire out an Apache on the trail. He commanded almost automatic respect from the volunteer recruits in camp. If Wood "had a reproof to administer he did it quietly, almost gently, but every rough rider in the regiment seemed to know intuitively that he was the last man in the world to be trifled with."[39]

Whatever the personal appeal of their commanders, the question remained: could they transform this kind of regiment into an effective fighting force? More specifically, given cultural norms of the Gilded Age, could the Ivy League "dudes" among them, including scions of the eastern elite, get used to the principle of merit instead of money or social status? One Washington, DC, writer, in early May 1898, marveled—and probably doubted—that privileged "Eastern athletes and Western veterans are all to serve side by side in Roosevelt's regiment without regard for birth, education, wealth, or previous condition. It is to be a regiment in which the best men will get to the top by fighting." Another Washington pundit, noticing that some recruits from the eastern clubs passed through the capital with their "high-priced cooks and valets" in tow, quipped that "Roosevelt's rough riders are a feature of this war that makes the whole business approach comic opera." Alfred R. Rowley, in the African American *Indianapolis Freeman*, cynically added, "No one ever suspected that the American millionaire possessed any such democratic sentiment as patriotism." The editor of a Fresno, California, paper jibed, "A lot of people may laugh at the 'dudes,' but some of them can put up a pretty good fight, judging from the newspaper accounts of their prowess with decanters, champagne bottles and other movables. Many a bloody battle has been fought by the dudes in the Hoffman house and other Gotham resorts."[40]

It little aided their credibility that some of the New York clubmen—the "Gilded Gang," as another Chicago reporter styled them—showed up at training camp wearing tailored suits and spent their first night not with the other recruits but at a nearby luxury hotel. A Dallas newspaperman gloated that the next day they would be exchanging multiple-course dinners and hot baths for "the coarse blankets and fried bacon of the fierce men from the west." If it seemed inconceivable that men so pampered from birth could ever hold their own in battle, the idea that they could ever blend effectively with hardened western members of the regiment registered as even more unlikely. But as one dubious observer put it, "Possibly, . . . if they get into a fight the difference in social status may not count for much."[41]

This ridicule from the press reflected the extent that ordinary Americans viewed with contempt the quintessential upper-class "clubman." In the common impression, such types contradicted everything democratic: overly rich, exclusivist, condescending, unproductive, and self-interested. Many of the urban "club" types did fit the mold as idle young bachelors practicing the institutional amenities of extreme affluence: fancy bars and restaurants, cigars, reading and gaming rooms, pools and gymnasiums, and regular sleeping quarters away from home. A number of such patrician organizations had popped up during the mid- to late-nineteenth century: in Boston, the Somerset Club; in Philadelphia, the Rittenhouse Club; in San Francisco, the Bohemian Club; and in New York City, the Union League, the Century Club, the Metropolitan Club, the Harvard Club, and the Knickerbocker Club, just to mention a few. In the mid-1890s, the *New York World* somehow produced a final tally of 37,737 male members of the city's generally resented privileged clubs. Roosevelt himself belonged to more than one.[42]

In addition, many college graduates of that day little more resembled citizen-soldier material than did the effete "clubmen" of the big cities. At a time when only a handful of every five thousand Americans ever attended any college, the most prestigious eastern private ones, especially the Ivy League, tailored themselves to serve the white, Anglo-Saxon elite. The Harvard of Theodore Roosevelt's day was a place of only about eight hundred undergraduate students, some two-thirds hailing from places within a hundred miles of Cambridge, Massachusetts, and more than half groomed at such esteemed preparatory institutions as Exeter, Andover, and St. Paul's. Roosevelt's class of 1880 included only three Roman Catholics and no Jews. "Judged by the color of their skin, the churches they attended, the number of syllables in their names," wrote historian David McCullough, "they were as homogenous an assembly of young men [and, of course, only males] . . . as one could imagine"—the antithesis of the increasingly conflicted, multicultural society that post–Civil War America was becoming.[43]

Roosevelt himself, as a young man before going to live in Dakota Territory, also had suffered the kind of taunting that his privileged-class cavalry volunteers now encountered. It bothered him. Never one to take personal insults lightly, he lashed back at his assailants. In 1881, while launching his political career as a 22-year-old New York state assemblyman, Roosevelt dressed for work as he understood a proper, high-society gentleman should, which often included his favorite purple satin waistcoat. When he spoke from the floor, he did so as was usual for him then, in cultivated terms and with a high-pitched, pretentious-sounding "Harvard accent." These quirks of style scarcely fit in the company of typical New York state politicians of the time, a rough-hewn company of "saloon-keepers, horse-car conductors, and the like," as TR later described them. They immediately classified him as a "chief of the dudes," called him "Jane Dandy" and "Punkin-Lily," compared him to Oscar Wilde, and in various other fashions impugned his heterosexuality.

One day, when he heard that ex-prizefighter "Big John" McManus and a little bunch of Tammany Hall jokers were conspiring to capture him in a blanket and then fling him up and down in the air, he vowed that enough was enough. "By God," Theodore exclaimed, charging up to McManus, "if you try anything like that, I'll kick you. I'll bite you. I'll kick you in the balls. I'll do anything to you unless you leave me alone." On another occasion, several years later in a bar somewhere near Medora, a drunken lout came up to Roosevelt and proceeded to make fun of his nearsightedness and his corrective pince-nez lenses. Tough guys in the West were not supposed to be seen in public wearing spectacles. "Four eyes," the man called Roosevelt scornfully, as he sneered at the New Yorker's unimposing stature. Rising to the challenge, Theodore recalled his amateur boxing skills, honed at Harvard, and left his tormentor lying unconscious. If there was one thing he could not stand, it was bullies.[44]

It did, however, come as a relief to Wood and Roosevelt that their eastern volunteers, especially the Ivy Leaguers, not only ignored the mockery heaped on them but also refrained from demanding commissions, often accepting the rank of private instead. This ethos of troopers living on equal terms, expecting no reward but the satisfaction of having served, remained crucial to being a Rough Rider. Roosevelt made this clear from the beginning. In Washington, before allowing any to be inducted, he gathered together his eastern recruits and told them that they would not only be expected to fight but also to "perform the weary, monotonous labor incident to the ordinary routine of a soldier's life." They might face deadly fever as well as bullets, should expect to "do their duty as readily if called upon to garrison a fort as if sent to the front," might be asked to undertake "irksome and disagreeable" chores as well as dangerous ones. They would have to "obey unquestioningly," make "no complaint of any kind," and vow not to back out once they had signed on. That policy interested the press precisely because it contrasted so radically with the experience of the eastern club crowd, just as did their unprecedented social mixing with unmannerly western men. Nor were the officers, Roosevelt and Wood included, to expect privileged treatment. In his letters at the time and in his retrospective 1899 account, *The Rough Riders*, TR would emphasize repeatedly that once in Cuba, even he and the other officers in the regiment ate, drank, washed, and sheltered on equal terms and under the same squalid combat conditions as the lowest-ranking troopers.[45]

As for the western recruits, whose rough style the two commanders counted on to give the regiment its "peculiar character," Roosevelt identified in them—or perhaps only imagined—the heroic frontiersmen's qualities of character that he glorified in *The Winning of the West*. Their stout-hearted, regenerative example, he believed, would not only inspire their fellow troopers but also provide models of strong manhood for Americans across the country, perhaps for generations to come—*if*, that is, they gained distinction in battle, an all-important part of the formula.

Meanwhile, TR did everything he could, via his talents with the media, to draw coverage of his men and of himself, boasting that the Rough Riders could "whip Caesar's legions" and calling them "children of the dragon's blood." Many, he stressed, had come from "the lands that have been most recently won over to white civilization," the places where "the conditions of life are nearest those that obtained on the frontier when there still was a frontier." His western men obviously reminded him of the types he had known earlier in Dakota—"splendid" examples, he later wrote, "tall and sinewy, with resolute, weather-beaten faces, and eyes that looked a man straight in the face without flinching. . . . hardened to life in the open, and to shifting for themselves under adverse circumstances." Even though most had never been "cowboys" at all, TR, like the press, promoted that image for popular consumption. They and their leaders, he said, "had shown their energy by settling in the new communities and growing up to be men of mark."[46]

But serious questions lingered as to whether such fiercely independent, sometimes ungovernable western men could be turned into soldiers any more than the self-indulging "dudes" might be. Could they be instructed to work together as a unit or take orders from others very different from themselves? One thing for sure: The ones charged with drilling such a group into military shape would face an arduous task. As one southwestern editor quipped, "The temerity required in telling a Texan how to handle a horse or gun almost baffles the imagination." But if the "experiment" of Roosevelt's "theatrical" regiment finally collapsed, noted other doubting correspondents, the *real* rough riding outfits, like Grigsby's or Torrey's, could easily replace them without any further "grand-standing."[47]

At times, even Roosevelt and Wood questioned the practicality of their task, though not openly. Near the end of May, less than a week before boarding rail cars for Tampa, where they would embark for Cuba, a *Boston Journal* correspondent reported the officers' disappointment with some of the men, especially those from the Indian and Oklahoma Territories. But the two colonels remained "determined to make the best of the situation" by applying "strict discipline to all the rowdies in the regiment." TR tried to win men over by eating the same chow and sleeping in the dirt and rain with them, but the "untamed spirit" of some still asserted itself. One bunch of Oklahoma men refused at first to serve under any officers from New York, claiming they could "win no glory under the command of 'blasted dudes.'" For gamblers and drinkers among the men, the saloons of San Antonio beckoned irresistibly, one newsman revealed. Another noted some of the Rough Riders "raising Cain" one night, eight being thrown into jail for "running amuck and fighting with everyone who would fight with them." In addition, a trooper from the Indian Territory, Levi Jones, had to be dismissed upon discovery of his involvement in a train-robbing episode for which he had spent time in a penitentiary.

Staff of the First US Volunteer Regiment, the "Rough Riders," in Tampa, Florida, 1898. *Front row, left to right*, Maj. Gen. Joseph Wheeler, Col. Leonard Wood; Lt. Col. Theodore Roosevelt; *back row, left to right*, Maj. George Dunn, Maj. Alexander O. Brodie, and Chaplain Henry A. Brown. Library of Congress, LC-DIG-ppmsca-37597

Worse still, another of the western recruits, James Redmond, who joined the Rough Riders under a false name, was wanted for murder in Kansas City.[48]

By contrast, the sizeable Rough Rider contingent from Arizona showed considerable promise, perhaps because they showed up with their own local leaders already in control. Of the two hundred or so of them, the story of

Capt. Buckey O'Neill seemed best to encapsulate much of the legend—and some of the salient truths—of the "Wild West."

O'Neill had been mayor of the town of Prescott before volunteering, and in years before, had tried many occupations, including public service jobs as Yavapai County probate judge, sheriff, tax assessor, and ex-officio school superintendent. Roosevelt described him in paradoxical terms: "iron-nerved, iron-willed fighter," a "gambler who with unmoved face would stake and lose every dollar he had in the world," yet "he, alone among his comrades, was a visionary, an articulate emotionalist." His Irish-born father, John O'Neill, who most likely had immigrated during the potato famine of the 1840s, served as a captain in the 116th Pennsylvania Volunteers, part of the "Irish Brigade." Shot repeatedly at the Battle of Fredericksburg, one bullet tearing through a lung, the elder O'Neill emerged from the Civil War so heavily scarred that he walked with crutches the rest of his life.[49]

Born and schooled in Washington, DC, the son inherited the audacious spirit of his war-hero father. Drawn by the great silver discovery of 1877, Buckey first arrived in the Arizona Territory two years later, at age 19, and stayed briefly in Tombstone when Wyatt Earp and his brothers kept order there. He knew the Earps personally and worked at the pro-Earp newspaper, the *Tombstone Epitaph*, before moving on to the mining-rich town of Prescott in 1882. He earned the nickname "Buckey" not for his personality or his newspaper-reporting style but for his gambling habit, "bucking the tiger" being synonymous for the saloon game of faro. He came to favor bourbon whiskey and got addicted to the Bull Durham cigarettes that he skillfully rolled for himself. In Prescott, he established his own newspaper, *Hoof and Horn*, aimed at cattlemen and touting the economic prospects of the territory.

Taming his vices a little, Buckey married a Prussian-born, 21-year-old Prescott schoolteacher, Pauline Marie Schindler, in 1886. She, too, had grown up amid military tradition, her father being a purchasing agent for the army at Fort Whipple in Arizona Territory. Together, they became moderately wealthy by a variety of investments, including onyx mines around Mayer, Arizona, copper mining near the Grand Canyon, and early railroad development in the region. Meanwhile, Buckey continued his modest literary career as a writer of short fiction on sensational western themes, most of the stories appearing either in the *San Francisco Examiner* or the *Argonaut* magazine during the 1890s. He also dabbled in Populist politics, following the radical political economy of Henry George.[50]

While serving as a Yavapai County judge, Buckey had won election as county sheriff, the job that provided his real bona fides before joining the Rough Riders. As one story went, four disguised men robbed the Atlantic and Pacific express train in the railroad town of Canyon Diablo on March 20, 1889. In classic wild western style, close to a similar experience that Roosevelt had earlier with thieves in Dakota Territory, O'Neill organized a small posse and gave chase. After a few weeks and 600 miles of riding, they finally caught up with the culprits near the Mexican border. A short rifle battle ensued without serious casualties except for O'Neill's horse, killed under him. On a different occasion, a friend encountered Buckey on the street in Prescott and noticed his arm in a sling. It turned out that while pursuing a "Mexican desperado," he had been shot but had captured the man anyway. "Buck, you are a handsome, educated and refined gentleman, so why not leave that kind of business to others and get into civilization?" the friend asked. O'Neill's answer reflected his devotion to public service: "Well, life is short, and death is long; whenever you are called you have to go, so what is the difference?" In all, he reportedly had killed five men "who defied him and the law."[51]

The point is that O'Neill modeled the character traits that TR and Wood expected from the best "cowboy" recruits. Roosevelt knew the overall quality of the western men because, as the *Portland Oregonian* explained, "he has lived among them" and could appreciate their "value in war," knowing that "the Western cowboy offers . . . manly virtues, and, in a military point of view, even his failings partake of merit." In this tougher strain of American manhood, "the vices that enfeeble and emasculate men of the towns are to him unknown," the columnist continued. However "blunt and picturesque" his language might be compared to that of finely cultivated men, his speech lent itself "not to flattery or lying." And safe to say "he never donned his chaps or buckled on his deadly 'gun' in a more welcome cause than the honor of the nation which he feeds in time of peace." Referring more specifically to the Arizona recruits, especially the groups of thirty-eight and thirty from Phoenix and Prescott, respectively, the *Dallas Morning News* reported such men to be "fitted to endure hardships that would speedily prostrate a city bred man."[52]

In the end, of course, the fighting would be the proof of their worth. Maybe they reflected "democracy as Washington, Jefferson and other fathers of the republic dreamed," an Omaha columnist reminded readers, but "crowns must be won before they can be worn." And nothing that happened in San Antonio could have dispelled the journalistic cynicism that still surrounded them.

"Teddy's Terrors . . . are no more soldiers than these war correspondents around here are," grumbled the crusty, English-born Alfred O. Andersson, covering the scene in San Antonio for the Scripps-McRae league of newspapers. These volunteers, having "pronounced notions" and "not accustomed to obeying implicitly," had been so "puffed up" in the press that "they now think they are the whole thing," when, in fact, the McKinley administration would have taken no "particular stock" in them had not the regiment's officers exerted "big pull at Washington," at the expense of the army's regular horse soldiers.[53]

TR did not like the expression "Teddy's Terrors," but he at first avoided the phrase "Rough Riders," too, fearing that it might become a term of reproach. Because of the popular association of "rough rider" with entertainment programs on the one hand and with westerners who disregarded order and discipline on the other, Roosevelt preferred calling them the regiment's official name—First United States Volunteer Cavalry—because it sounded properly military. "Don't call them rough riders," he told writers in San Antonio, "and don't call them cowboys." It would be alright to dub them "mounted riflemen," he added, but "if any man believes this regiment will go on the hippodrome order he has made a bleeding mistake—particularly when we get in the midst of the fight." Still, newspapermen could not resist the alliterative nicknames for the regiment. And one western scribe, ominously, said those appellations made him think of another: "Custer's Cavalry."[54]

4

Crowded Hour

THEY LANDED ON JUNE 22, 1898, at Daiquirí, a forlorn village on the southern coast of the island, 20 miles east of their strategic objective, the ancient city of Santiago. No Spanish forces showed up to oppose them.

A vital seaport of some thirty thousand inhabitants, Santiago de Cuba had been established nearly four centuries earlier by Spanish conquistador Diego Velázquez de Cuéllar. From there, in the earliest days of the Spanish empire, Hernán Cortés launched his 1518 expedition to the coast of Mexico, and Hernando de Soto his to Florida in 1538. Now, by taking that city and later, if still necessary, Havana, American forces would destroy the last remnants of Spanish rule in the New World—a historic moment. The US land invasion numbered some seventeen thousand men, volunteers and regulars. It included two cavalry regiments of black "buffalo" soldiers, the Ninth and Tenth, assumed to be immune from tropical diseases because of their African bloodlines. In all, it was a massive force, yet the American invaders would face serious trouble if things did not go as planned.[1]

In Washington just a week before, the Newlands resolution authorizing the annexation of Hawaii had passed the House of Representatives by a vote of 209 to 91. The measure now went to a still-reluctant Senate, where anti-imperialist opposition from both parties had been enough to deny the two-thirds majority needed. But in the White House, President McKinley now threw his full weight behind Pacific expansion. "We need Hawaii just as much and a good deal more than we did California," he had told Cortelyou on May 4.[2]

In New York City, popular frivolities mirrored the public image of TR's "cowboy" regiment. A sombrero-style headgear of the western plains had become all the fashion for chic young people. "It is the favorite outing hat of the Fifth avenue girl. And also of her brother. Whether he has gone off to the war with Colonel Theodore Roosevelt's band of rough riders or whether he plans to be among the chosen few at the summer resorts," reported one major newspaper. Available in cream, gray, black, and a dun shade, the hat gave the impression of being "big and flashing and Western-like," and, when given an "indefinable touch" of the wearer, it became "the most picturesque thing in town." The more that it suggested "the genuine cowboy," the more appealing it was. "Such are fashion's eccentricities."[3]

On Long Island Sound, as the early summer days melted one into another, Edith Roosevelt waited for news of her husband. Anxiously, she scanned the newspapers for dispatches from Cuba. Her heart pounded whenever she spied the postman approaching Sagamore Hill, possibly with a letter from Theodore or, more frightening, a telegram that would devastate her. She wrote him that their eldest son, Ted, hoped there would be at least one big battle and that his father could be in it but come out safe. Otherwise, her missives concentrated on lighthearted subjects, concealing her deepest feelings, lest they sadden him too. Despite this intention, she said: "Always I have the longing and missing in my heart, but I shall not write about it for it makes me cry."[4]

In Boston, Harvard professor William James would attend a protest meeting at Faneuil Hall. In doing so, he would join scores of others who worried about the moral consequences of American foreign conquests. Jingoes viewed the matter with frightening naïveté, James thought. But most Americans, rightly or not, believed otherwise. "The hauling down of the Spanish flag and the hoisting of that of the United States means more than on its face it indicates to the popular mind," warned the *Springfield Republican*. Those who identified as anti-imperialists would never constitute a majority of public opinion and varied widely in their individual perspectives, but they could agree on at least one thing: the overextension of US influence beyond its own shores would be hard to reconcile with the deeply engrained early republic creed of governance by the consent of the governed. "Human nature is everywhere the same," James fretted, "and at the least temptation all the old military passions arise and sweep everything before them." America's new empire, soon to unfold, appeared to him a mixed blessing at best—and at worst a historic disaster.[5]

First Days

The landing had to be coordinated with naval events: first, the locating of Admiral Pascual de Cervera's Spanish squadron in the Caribbean; then, the US navy's containing of the enemy vessels so as to guarantee safe passage of the vulnerable transport ships, packed with soldiers, leaving Tampa for the southern coast of Cuba. The North Atlantic squadron, under Rear Adm. William T. Sampson, had located Cervera near Martinique on May 13, only to have the Spanish commander elude them long enough to take shelter in Santiago harbor six days later. On that same day, however, a friendly agent in the Havana telegraph office learned of the enemy's arrival in Santiago and promptly alerted the Americans. Sampson thereupon steamed toward the Cuban city, arriving on June 1, confirmed Cervera's presence there, and blockaded the extensive narrow-necked harbor. That action trapped the Spanish force inside but, given the enemy's mines and fortifications, Sampson could not penetrate far enough to destroy the anchored ships. Thereafter, the Spaniard troops would be fighting not just to defend Santiago but also to save Cervera, on whose naval force depended almost entirely Spain's slim chance of winning the war.[6]

The Rough Riders, along with the whole Fifth Corps, under command of Maj. Gen. William R. Shafter, had departed Florida in such disarray that many of the troops, including at least a third of the First Volunteer Cavalry, and all but a few of the horses, had to be left behind. The remainder of the regiment, following Wood, now headed westward on foot, through the overgrowth and toward the hills that guarded the city. Those 20 miles from Daiquirí would prove merciless, exhausting, anxiety-ridden, and bloody. The men would have to slog through forbidding terrain, lugging cumbersome supplies on their backs—"Wood's Weary Walkers" the now-dismounted cavalrymen now mordantly called themselves. And they would also have to move quickly, as they knew that Spanish defenders were mobilizing as fast as possible to stop them.

In Shafter's Cuban strategy, speed mattered most. If successful, he would pin the roughly twelve thousand Spanish defenders against Santiago Bay, lay siege, rout them piecemeal, and pressure Cervera's ships out of their safe haven and right into Sampson's awaiting guns. The sooner American forces captured Santiago, the faster they could be evacuated from the island, avoiding the rainy-season diseases that might decimate them by thousands, as they had the British in late 1741, during the War of Jenkins' Ear. The Spanish controlled the hills to the east of the city and were filling the jungle with snipers and experienced jungle-fighters prepared to delay the American advance as long as possible. The Fifth Corps would have to slug their way from the coast to the outskirts of Santiago and drive the Spanish troops from the San Juan Heights.[7]

For their principal weapon, the Rough Riders relied on the Springfield 1896 model Krag-Jørgensen bolt-action carbine, of Norwegian design, as opposed to the older Springfield 1873 model single-shot rifles issued to other volunteer regiments. The regular army had adopted the Krag, with an effective range of 1,000 yards, as its standard long rifle in 1892. The carbine version resembled the rifle except for its 22-inch, as opposed to 30-inch, barrel. Before leaving Washington, Wood and Roosevelt had used their influence with the War Department to ensure that their troopers would carry the same, up-to-date firearms that the regulars employed.

The Krag featured several key advantages over the 1873 Springfield make. Light in weight, the carbine provided easy maneuverability, lending itself conveniently for operation on horseback. It took a five-shot 30-caliber magazine clip of ammunition, which, upon reloading, provided the capability of firing about fourteen rounds per minute, as opposed to the earlier one-bullet, 45-caliber breechloader, requiring about a minute for just a few well-aimed shots. Further, even though the older Springfield's deadly, flesh-ripping 45-caliber shells promised greater knock-down power, the lighter, smaller-caliber bullet of the Krag enabled each trooper to pack and carry a third more ammunition.[8]

Most importantly, the Krag fired smokeless powder cartridges, as opposed to the black powder rounds of the 1873 model rifles. Nitrocellulose-based smokeless powder, first developed in 1884 by French chemist Paul Marie Eugène Vieille, furnished not only three times the explosive force as the same amount of black powder but also the distinct benefit of concealing from the enemy the exact position of an unexposed shooter. By contrast, the cloud of white smoke from black powder rounds immediately made attacking soldiers, regardless of cover, a discernible target for returning fire, thus elevating the number of casualties.[9]

Everyone knew that the quality of a soldier's weapon and ammunition might be all that stood between life and death in combat. In answer to angry protests on the home front, several factors explained why the other volunteer regiments received the obsolete 1873 models instead of the Krags. At the start of the war, the older rifles were the only type that the government held in any considerable stock, as well as the only weapon with which the volunteers, largely drawn from National Guard units, had already become familiar using. Some military authorities regarded the Krag as too complicated for hastily trained, nonprofessional troops to operate, as well as too difficult to repair if it jammed during battle. Also, with pressure mounting on the War Department to bring an army together quickly, it would have taken months to provide all of the volunteer forces with new-production Krags. Finally, as a *New York Tribune* columnist grumbled, "Congress, in its parsimonious wisdom," had "time and again, refused to furnish the War Department with money either to acquire or to manufacture . . . any considerable amount of smokeless powder," as it cost three times as much as ordinary black powder. In the fighting to come, G. P. Nuttall, a London correspondent with the 33rd Michigan Volunteers, noticed the men discarding their old-fashioned Springfields and snatching up the Krag-Jørgensen rifles whenever regular army troops fell, also "taking the cartridge belts, so as to have the proper kind of ammunition."[10]

On the opposing side, the enemy's Mauser rifles posed a more formidable threat than either Springfield product, especially for attacking forces fighting in the open. Its smokeless powder ammunition gave hidden Spanish snipers a terrifying advantage over invaders probing their way through unfamiliar Cuban terrain. The German-manufactured model 1893 bolt-action Mauser held five smokeless rounds of slightly smaller caliber than the Krag bullet, but it could be reloaded fast by inserting a stripper clip of rounds from the top of the open bolt. The Mauser bullet also traveled at higher muzzle velocity, and therefore flatter trajectory, extending the effective range of Spanish fire to about 2,160 yards, more than twice that of the Krag-Jørgensens. Overall, the Spanish infantry, concealed in lowland chaparral and well fortified on the high ground, would be defending Cuba not only from every key geographical position but also with a superior weapon.[11]

A Mauser slug made a small, deeply penetrating wound, likely fatal if involving vital organs or the spine but otherwise often survivable. One war correspondent, after talking with wounded American soldiers, concluded that the Spanish ammunition was the "most civilized . . . ever used in warfare, as it makes a clean, neat wound, and while disabling a man temporarily, does not cause nearly so much suffering as various others." That fact, together with the advent of antisepsis (minimizing infection) and the soldiers' careful application of their bandage packets, would save many who would have died from similar wounds thirty years earlier. "The surgical axioms which relate to gunshot injuries will have to be revised," an army physician told the *New York Journal* during the war. Another surgeon, estimating the Civil War death rate for perforating wounds of the abdominal cavity at nearly 90 percent, guessed the figure at about 3 percent in Cuba. And further, "the amputation percentage is practically non-existent. . . . There will be no 'piles of mangled limbs' in this war."[12]

Beyond the standard Mauser shells, however, Spanish snipers also employed a brass-coated, exploding type of projectile that inflicted ghastly damage upon impact. "The brass rips on touching, and tears the flesh horribly, while the small brass splinters cause blood poisoning," as one reporter informed readers back home. In addition, the Spanish riflemen sometimes cut a small cross through the tip of the Mauser bullet, causing it to mushroom horribly on striking.[13]

Yet a far more hideous threat than Spanish bullets haunted every American sent to Cuba that summer: a terrifying disease that killed half its victims. It went by various names—"yellow jack," "the yellow plague," "bronze John," and "the black vomit." Its symptoms frightened no less than Ebola or Marburg, but unlike those other hemorrhagic diseases, the yellow fever virus spread in a way difficult to avoid: the bite of an infected female of the *Aedes aegypti* species of mosquito. No preventative vaccine existed in 1898—and no cure, even today. The soldiers called it "black vomit" because victims with advanced cases, one historian explains, "vomited up something that looked roughly like coffee grounds but was actually stomach lining and intestine." Difficult to diagnose in early stages, the disease easily passed for malaria, dengue fever, and various other tropical diseases, as well as several forms of poisoning. The "yellow," or bronzing, appearance referred to the jaundice that frequently accompanied other symptoms. No one knew how to treat yellow fever, except caring for the high body temperature, dehydration, respiratory difficulty, and tissue damage it caused.

After initial infection, the virus incubated in the body for several days. Then, two levels of sickness followed: first an "acute" phase, with symptoms of fever, muscle pain, backache, headache, shivers, loss of appetite, vomiting, and then, after all that, either recovery or just a brief period of remission. In the second, more toxic phase, high fever returned along with abdominal agony and melting of soft tissue, resulting in bleeding from the mouth, nose, eyes, and stomach. Toward the end, blood filled the vomit and stools of the victim, kidney function deteriorated and, after several more days, death came as almost welcome relief.[14]

On June 23, in the muggy discomfort of midday made worse by a torrential downpour, the Rough Riders began their march along the muddy road to Siboney, another squalid town about 7 miles west from Daiquirí. Wheeler's orders were to follow in support of Gen. H. W. Lawton's Second Infantry. After a sparse dinner of hardtack, bacon, and coffee, the men slept miserably on the soaked ground, tormented by the pernicious flies and sheets of mosquitoes. They had no insect repellent, only mosquito netting that helped a little but not enough. Hordes of ants invaded their camps, some hundred varieties of them, including an aggressive stinging type, along with an invasive kind of land crab that somehow presented itself everywhere.[15]

Roosevelt seemed almost to enjoy the physical hardship. Up to a point, it added to the challenge he sought and constituted further proof of his fortitude and that of his men. Late that night, he admired "the splendid bodily vigor" of Allyn Capron and Hamilton Fish, the captain and the sergeant, as they stood talking in the flickering light of the campfires. "Their frames seemed of steel, to withstand all fatigue; they were flushed with health; in their eyes shone high resolve and fiery desire." These words, and other remarks like them, might strike some modern interpreters as denoting a kind of homoerotic attraction on TR's part. They more likely reflected the male fitness craze of that time, widely promulgated as an antidote to neurasthenia, as well as Roosevelt's obsession, since the asthma-induced weakness of his youth, with building up his body and his physical stamina in comparison with other men.[16]

The 26-year-old Capron had married his teenage sweetheart, Lillian, in 1890 and then enlisted in the army as a cavalry private, moving up the ranks with unusual rapidity before leaving Oklahoma Territory to join the Rough Riders. His father, Allyn Sr., also a captain, a West Point graduate, and decorated veteran of the Lakota Wars, commanded an artillery battery near El Caney in Cuba, not far from his son. The 25-year-old Fish, the wealthy New Yorker and son of Grant's secretary of state, had turned himself into "one of the best non-commissioned officers we had," said Roosevelt. "He never complained and never shirked any duty of any kind, while his power over his men was great."[17]

To Roosevelt at that moment, the two young men, so radically different in background, symbolized the very best of American manhood, and "two better representatives of the American soldier, there were not in the whole army." Both, like Roosevelt himself, longed to "show their mettle" and brimmed with confidence that, if they lived, they "would win honorable renown" and "rise high in their chosen profession."[18]

Las Guásimas

On the following morning, June 24, the blazing sun rose from behind the mountain peaks, lifting a curtain of early mist to reveal a panorama of narrow jungle valley that traced irregular paths between Siboney and the San Juan Heights, looming to the northwest. The hills provided the people of Santiago, and the Spanish garrison there, a natural barrier against aggressors approaching the city. The defenders had fortified those hills to their deadly advantage. They also had spread mobile bands of snipers and guerrillas all through the jungle and chaparral lying east of those hills, the route that the Americans had to traverse. The American force that day included an advance column of General Lawton's US regulars taking the main road toward Santiago. About a half hour behind them came a detachment of Rough Riders, spearheaded by Capron's L Troop, moving parallel to the regulars along a dense ridgeline 500 feet above.

The two American lines of attackers planned to converge at what Cuban scouts had reported to be the edge of Spanish defenses, about 4 miles up from the coast, near a location called Las Guásimas. The name referred to a type of tropical flowering tree that proliferated at the spot where the road and the trail converged. Dozens of field glasses trained on almost every foot of ground as the blue-uniformed troopers penetrated the thickets, seeking the enemy. Abandoned Spanish blockhouses here and there seemed to indicate that the Spanish, strangely reluctant to engage, might have retreated toward their entrenchments in the heights. Officers and men puzzled over the disappearance of the foe, even wondering whether the Spaniards would ever make a stand. Could it be that their commander, Gen. Arsenio Linares y Pombo (known as Linares), had sensed the odds against him and would surrender without giving them the fight they had anticipated?[19]

By about 9:00 a.m., not enough air stirred even to flutter the leaves of the coconut trees along the line of march. As the remaining part of the regiment progressed, single file, along the main hillside trail, Rough Rider officers had to call several halts, allowing the men to rest. To soldiers trained for mounted service, this kind of arduous travel on foot—climbing with loaded packs in the heat of the day—proved quickly exhausting. Wood marched them hard, for fear of missing the first strike against the Spanish. They started casting aside their blankets and other articles too burdensome to carry. A few troopers fell out of the ranks, finding refuge in the shade of the trailside brush. Dr. Henry La Motte's ambulance corps busily attended to cases of heat prostration. A dozen mules carrying reserve ammunition and hospital supplies also had to stop frequently, the sun enervating pack animals as well.

Yet there was still no contact with the elusive Spanish. As the Rough Riders sweated through the tunnels of foliage, they violated one of the cardinal tenets of a combat mission: keep quiet while approaching a hidden enemy. Overconfident and, from their inexperience, underestimating the foe that lurked somewhere ahead, a few of the troopers started talking, laughing, arguing, and cussing the heat. Some lamented Wood's unrelenting pace; others mused on how nice a cold beer would taste. The novelist Stephen Crane, covering the Rough Riders as a freelance journalist, said they made "more noise than a train going through a tunnel." The "clatter of tongues" continued, Crane noted with escalating discomfort, even after the officers ordered "Silence in the ranks!" Edward Marshall, correspondent for the *New York Journal*, later recalled one of the regiment's physicians rattling through on a mule. Roosevelt's agitated effort to keep him quiet made an even louder racket.[20]

As the troopers wound their way along the narrow path, some of the journalists wondered about the unusual bird sounds emanating from the surrounding thicket. As Crane noted, his anxiety mounting, "those of us who knew [the calls of bird species] heard going from hillock to hillock the beautiful coo of the Cuban wood dove—ah, the wood dove, the Spanish guerrilla wood dove which had presaged the death of gallant marines" (who had landed a few days earlier at Guantánamo). Roosevelt, who knew his birds better than anyone, also noticed the incongruous wildlife sounds but failed to react at first. "It was very beautiful and very peaceful," he later wrote, "and it seemed more as if we were off on some hunting excursion than as if we were about to go into a sharp and bloody little fight." Mentioning the cooing to some of the troopers along the line, Crane recalled, they "said decisively that the Spaniards did not use this signal."[21]

Little did the troopers know. The suspicious sound they were hearing, that innocent-sounding wood dove, was an omen of death.

Eyewitness accounts vary as to what happened next. It began at the vanguard of the column. Suddenly, Mauser rounds started popping, cutting through the dense underbrush on both sides of the trail, peppering tree trunks, and thudding into human flesh. It looked as if the regiment had blundered right into a sucker's trap, although debate about that would follow. In any case, they had found just what they expected: the front-edge Spanish line.

For those immersed in the fog of battle, there is no "big picture." Time speeds up. Consciousness quickens. Fear intensifies. Decisions erupt from impulse. "Don't think . . . that there is a wild kind of joy about the music of whistling bullets; there isn't," Rough Rider Private Carl Lovelace of Waco, Texas, later told a friend back home. Almost immediately, a Mauser slug found young Hamilton Fish's chest. He would be the first of the regiment to die, his sacrifice quickly symbolizing courage regardless of social class for readers back home. Urging his men toward the sudden gunfire, Capron also fell, the bullet hitting between the left shoulder and neck, passing through his lungs and exiting out the right side of his waist. The young captain lay in agony as troopers around him returned fire. He lived just over an hour, the first of the Fifth Corps officers to perish in the war.[22]

A little farther back, Colonel Wood barked urgent instructions: "Deploy!" "Lie down!" Panicked men scattered right and left, searching frantically for attackers nowhere to be seen. "This is what made it so hard for us in the fight," Roosevelt wrote afterward. "It was very trying to stand, or advance slowly, while the men fell dead or wounded, shot down from we knew not whence; for smokeless powder renders it almost impossible to place a hidden foe." Edward Marshall took a bullet that lodged painfully within an inch of his spine. He managed to crawl up against a tree and continued to scrawl on blood-stained pages what he witnessed in the hours that followed. Correspondent Richard Harding Davis meanwhile discarded his notepad and grabbed a carbine. It was he, Roosevelt said, who spotted their Spanish adversaries in the jungle cover before them. Peering through his field glasses, Davis shouted, "There they are Colonel; look over there; I can see their hats near that glade."[23]

As the shooting intensified, Wood, the experienced commander, kept calm. By instinct, he stayed on his feet, exposing himself to enemy volleys, and assessed the predicament rationally. "Don't swear, shoot!" he shouted at the troopers. The example of leadership under pressure powerfully affected Roosevelt; he would try to replicate it in the days ahead. After some two hours of intense firing along an expanding front—roughly a thousand US troops against fifteen hundred Spanish—sixteen Americans lay dead, half of them Rough Riders. Another thirty-four of Wood's men had been wounded among the American total of fifty-two. Spanish losses totaled many more, perhaps as many as 250 killed and wounded. "My gun got so hot I could not hold it," 21-year-old Private Will Freeman told his mother back in Ypsilanti, Michigan.[24]

By Civil War standards, as Wheeler told everyone, Las Guásimas barely amounted to a skirmish. Even so, it was the first American military engagement involving volunteer forces since 1865, the first on foreign soil since 1848, and the first against a European foe since the War of 1812. Primarily because of the Rough Riders' high-profile image, the newspapers treated the minor contest as a major story. Impatient to find meaning in the events, they asked what this first performance under fire at Las Guásimas revealed. Much of the commentary addressed an overarching question that Roosevelt's regiment had raised from the beginning: Could citizen soldiers answer the needs of an advanced, expanding nation, its interests now involving overseas action? Or would those needs now require professional armies and an end to long-standing tradition?[25]

As they do today, the media moguls of 1898 quickly buttonholed military "experts," veteran commanders of previous wars, for commentary and analysis. What first impressed Gen. Nathan Dudley, he told the *Boston Journal*, was that the Rough Riders had stood their ground in this first fight, resisting the urge to retreat. Dudley knew both sides of the army, having served in the Civil War as a colonel of Massachusetts volunteers and, afterward, as a regular officer, taking part in various Native American wars and in Mexican border conflicts. "Not having the close training of the regular cavalry," he said, "the Rough Riders could not be expected to take advantage of natural defences, as the regulars do." Their "splendid courage" had yet to be tempered "by the prudence which always characterizes brave and disciplined soldiers." They had "learned a lesson which only can be learned under fire." Gen. Charles H. Grosvenor of Ohio, who had fought as a colonel with the 18th Ohio Infantry at Chickamauga and at the Battle of Nashville, also praised the "great bravery" and "splendid spirit" of Roosevelt's men but, like Dudley, faulted them for exposing their positions so much to enemy fire. The Rough Riders had been overly eager to prove themselves, whereas the object of fighting, he instructed, "is not to display reckless courage so much as it is to win battles."[26]

Had the ill-trained Rough Riders blundered into an "ambush" at Las Guásimas, giving credence to those who had doubted them all along? The *Philadelphia Inquirer* called the encounter "one of those dearly paid-for experiences by which fresh troops, bubbling over with ambition, learn how to make war," while the regulars, simultaneously attacking the Spaniards, "did just as much service with considerably less sacrifice of life." Armies are threatened with disaster and nations imperiled, the writer added, by "soldiers whose chief object upon the battlefield is the winning of personal glory"—an implied reproach of Roosevelt. Several correspondents on the scene also supported the "ambush" view. Even Richard Harding Davis, always quick to defend the Rough Riders, conceded that they had been "surprised."[27]

It surprised no one, however, that Roosevelt hotly disputed this version later, and so did other Rough Riders. The impression of an "ambush," he contended, had come from two or three writers located safely in the rear of the column, far from harm's way. There, they witnessed how the appearance of stragglers and the wounded produced "a good deal of panic and confusion," so their first reports described with "minute *in*accuracy" what had happened at the front. Further, Roosevelt held little regard for the "realistic modern novelists" (like Crane) who had never ventured close to a fight themselves. As for Marshall and Davis, who *had* put their own lives at risk, they "showed as much gallantry as any soldier in the field."[28]

Capt. John R. Thomas, who took charge of L Troop right after Capron fell, also tried to correct the newspaper accounts after he was sent home, crippled by a Mauser bullet to his right leg. Troopers near the front of the column, he explained, had already learned from some men of another regiment that Spanish forces were close, as they had been heard working during the night. Capron and six other Rough Riders had gone ahead of the others and come across the body of a dead Cuban. Ten or fifteen minutes later, Capt. Thomas Isbell had spotted a Spaniard in the brush and fired at him. That was the first shot of the fight, according to Isbell, and the enemy retaliated with the volleys that hit Capron and Fish. Isbell himself took seven bullet wounds during the fray but still walked back to the American field hospital, 4 miles to the rear. "It has been said we were ambushed, but that is not so," Isbell insisted. Twenty-seven-year-old Rough Rider corporal Harry C. White, an electrician from Somerville, Massachusetts, blamed the forbidding Cuban environment for what had befallen them. "It is the wildest country I ever saw or imagined," he wrote back home, "and a splendid country for just such ambushes as we ran into yesterday." Probably the most common Rough Rider perspective came, however, from Private Charles C. Bull, a 21-year old Californian, who found the whole argument pointless: "The odds were three to one against us," he estimated, incorrectly, "but we drove the Spaniards out of a strong hold in two hours, which the Cubans have been trying for three years to take. They nearly had us ambuscaded but we would have whipped them anyway." Sgt. Walter S. Cash of Colorado Springs, agreed: "We knew that the Spaniards were in ambush, and we were trying to beat them out."[29]

The estimations of Bull and Cash probably came closest to being the dominant view, both among the troopers and on the home front. They echoed what Roosevelt had promulgated to the press. It was the idea that Americans, with a heritage such as theirs, would always prevail, no matter the odds. "It is very easy for civilians who have kept out of the war to sit . . . and explain just how this fight should have been fought," chided a columnist in Boston, but still, for a comparatively small price in casualties, American troops had in just "one blow . . . cleared the way . . . straight through to the gates of Santiago." To another, in Minneapolis, Las Guásimas had recalled the best traditions of citizen soldiery: the "pioneer days of New England when men fought single handed in defense of families, when women took the old muskets and for hours held the redskins at bay until relief came." A commentator in Springfield, Massachusetts, thought Colonel Wood's injunction "Don't swear; fight!" would be just as fitting as advice for society generally.[30]

In any case, people concluded what they wanted to—or perhaps needed to. Many later impressions originated in sympathetic reporting from Cuba, as in one of Davis's dispatches for the *New York Herald*. Gushing over the bravery that "soft" Ivy Leaguers had displayed, he wrote: "The grit of the cowpunchers has never been doubted, but whenever we have wished to illustrate the fact that the swell [privileged-classes] will fight, we have had to refer to the English Guardsmen and Dandies of Alman Balaklava. Now we can refer instead to the courage of the young men of the universities and of the Knickerbocker

Club. . . . It is a more up-to-date example, and the men are Americans." In other words, a Phoenix pundit quipped, the "dudes" had "quit sucking cane handles" and learned to "chaw terbaker."[31]

Buckey

After the clash at Las Guásimas, it took six days in the mud, daily downpours, and punishing heat for Shafter's Fifth Corps to assemble the troops and supplies needed for the Santiago offensive, beginning with the series of ridges known as the San Juan Heights. Shafter's calculation called for General Lawton's five to six thousand men, less than half of the American troops, to capture the heavily garrisoned village of El Caney first, preempting Spanish reinforcement of Santiago and cutting off its water supply. The remaining forces would then launch a perilous frontal assault on the fortified hills directly to the west—about 8,400 of the soldiers who remained able-bodied, including the dismounted cavalry units under Wheeler and three batteries of artillery.[32]

In the late afternoon of June 30, the Rough Riders gathered up three days' rations from their supply of tainted bacon, greasy beans, soaked hardtack, and foul canned beef. Then they proceeded to their assigned position along the Las Guamas Creek, putting them less than half a mile from Kettle Hill, so named because of the ruins of an old sugar mill visible on top. San Juan Hill, with its formidable blockhouse, loomed in the near distance. Meanwhile, a tropical fever had felled General Wheeler, leaving him incapacitated and requiring Wood's being promoted to brigadier general and put in charge as Second Brigade leader while his exuberant backup, Roosevelt, became a full colonel, in command of the First Volunteer Cavalry by himself.[33]

Shafter's overall plan was to drive the Spaniards off the heights and westward toward Santiago, following with a siege that, he hoped, would last only briefly until the enemy surrendered the city. Meanwhile, Linares had played right into Shafter's hands, deploying his army of ten thousand all around the eastern perimeter of Santiago instead of concentrating his forces at the most likely points of attack. As a result, fewer than a thousand Spanish infantry actually defended the hilltops, hoping that their possession of the high ground, the positioning of snipers and skirmishers below, and the unbearable heat of summer would undercut the American strategy.[34]

By the time the morning fog had burned away on July 1, Roosevelt had moved his men far enough to be within view of the Spanish entrenchments on the hill before them, careful to guard against a surprise attack on their right flank. To reach their designated place in the line, facing Kettle Hill, the Rough Riders had proceeded along a narrow path shrouded by thick undergrowth, crossed two streams, and hurried through an open field. Frederic Remington, having returned to Cuba for Hearst's *New York Journal*, described the scene: "As the troops came pouring across the ford" of the San Juan River, "they stooped as low as they anatomically could, and their faces were wild with excitement." Remington noted how the "older officers stood up as straight as on parade," a display of fearlessness for their men to see. "They may have done it through pride or they may have known that it is better to be 'drilled clean' than to have a long ranging wound. It was probably both ideas which stiffened them up so."[35]

By 11:00 a.m., as Capt. George Grimes started firing his howitzers toward Santiago, American forces had received a return volley from the Spanish lines, igniting over the Rough Riders' location. The Spanish cannon shells "sounded like a hurricane coming through the air," young George Reubelt of Key West, Florida, wrote to his parents afterward from his hospital bed. "They burst in about 200 pieces[,] and if they explode above a regiment of soldiers very few would be uninjured." The Americans answered ineffectively with Krag-Jørgensen fire from ground level, accompanied by their long-range artillery. As Remington later said, "It was thoroughly evident that the Spaniards had the range of everything in the country. . . . Some as gallant soldiers and some as daring correspondents as it is my pleasure to know did their legs proud there." Some of the men dropped flat, hugging the ground like starfish, he reported. "BANG!" Over and over again, the shells exploded right over them.[36]

As the troopers waited behind cover, they also heard the thunder of American cannons from El Caney, to the north. From nearer to them came the clatter of the Hotchkiss batteries that supposedly would soften Spanish defenses before the order to "charge" that everyone knew was coming. But when? The signal to advance had to be issued by the generals stationed in the rear. While the ensconced troopers sat more and more anxiously, Spanish defensive fire began pounding down upon them, every unnerving explosion sending barrages of shrapnel screaming over their heads. Enemy snipers started to zero in as well, their Mauser bullets making a "nasty, malicious little noise," like the spirit of a "very petty and mean person turned into sound," said correspondent Edward Marshall, who somehow managed to survive the one that nearly pierced his spine.³⁷

As at Las Guásimas, appearing fearless under fire—even to the point of being targets for Spanish sharpshooters—had become almost a mantra for Wood and Roosevelt. By western custom, such behavior supposedly denoted the height of male courage, proof of one's fitness for command, and was intended as an inspirational example for the troopers. Historian James McPherson has written that during the Civil War, as well, the only thing many soldiers dreaded more than being wounded or killed in battle was to be perceived as cowardly in the eyes of their peers. So as not to "shame" themselves in front of their men, the lower-ranking Rough Rider officers followed their commanders' example. Having seen Colonel Wood leading his horse up and down in range of Spanish fire, 21-year-old trooper Harry Van Treese wrote his parents, "Don't you think if such men as that can face the enemy[,] I can afford to fall[?]" Gauging the opinion of other Rough Riders, "our officers are brave men," said Private Mason Mitchell of New York City after returning home, wounded on July 1. "They always led in person, and we think, though we say it in their praise, that often they exposed themselves unnecessarily." In private letters to Henry Cabot Lodge, TR would later disparage the grossly overweight Shafter for never coming within 3 miles of the actual fighting: "Our General is poor; he is too unwieldy to get to the front."³⁸

For Arizonan Buckey O'Neill, who viewed the Spanish as contemptible and inept from the start, the braggadocio of daring enemy marksmen to target him came all too naturally. As his troopers crouched nervously at the base of Kettle Hill, gazing up toward the heavily fortified entrenchments, Captain O'Neill paced before them in open view, stopping only now and then to extract his tobacco pouch and roll another Bull Durham. Seeing this, Lt. Woodbury Kane, whose K Troop waited cautiously nearby, tried urging Buckey to find cover. Indeed, as Private Jesse Langdon later recalled, *everyone* was telling him to "lay down," but he would not do it. Another witness, Private William A. Larned of Summit, New Jersey, reported to his father a week later that O'Neill then remarked, as it was his habit of saying, "There is no bullet made that can kill me."³⁹

At about ten o'clock, O'Neill went over to the left of the line to confer with Capt. Robert D. Howze, an aide to Gen. Samuel S. Sumner. No news yet from command; the Rough Riders were to continue standing ready.

Then, only a moment later, a Mauser round fired from above suddenly struck O'Neill right through the mouth, exploding out the back of his head. The sight horrified every man there, as they all ran to his aid but to no avail. Like many a brave Union soldier who once fought beside O'Neill's father at Fredericksburg, Buckey met death instantaneously. "Even before he fell," Roosevelt wrote afterward, "his wild and gallant soul had gone out into the darkness."[40]

Oyster Bay

Edith had spent the early morning hours of Friday, July 1, 1898, resting on the west porch of the Roosevelts' comfortable Victorian manse, which they called "Sagamore Hill." Two of her younger sons, Kermit and Archie, lounged at her side. As a boy, Theodore had enjoyed many summers vacationing on Long Island, his parents intent on having a family escape from the city heat. In 1880, prior to his marriage to Alice, his first wife, he had purchased for $30,000 a tract of 155 acres on Cove Neck, a peninsula close to the village of Oyster Bay. Then, six years later, he hired the New York architectural firm of Lamb and Rich, for a cost of $16,975 (more than $500,000 in today's dollars), to build a twenty-two-room, Queen Anne shingle-style house to accommodate the brood that he and his new wife hoped to raise there.

Accustomed, like Theodore, to financial ease since childhood, Edith had wanted for nothing; her father, Charles Carow, was a wealthy shipping entrepreneur in New York City. Their well-appointed family home stood at Livingston Place, near Union Square. Upon marriage to Theodore in 1886, she had come to love "Sagamore Hill" as much as he, and so did their six children.[41]

But now all she wanted was to see Theodore return home alive and in one piece.

The only letter she had received from him since the Rough Riders' departure for Cuba recounted the Las Guásimas fight. It spared few details. Theodore had come out unharmed, but Edith hardly could have found comfort in his vivid description of the experience. "One man was killed as he stood beside a tree with me," he told her. "Another bullet went through a tree behind which I stood, and filled my eyes with bark. . . . The fire was very hot at one or two points where the men around me went down like ninepins." In still more graphic detail, he went on to tell of the health-threatening living conditions:

sleeping on the ground and being so drenched in sweat that he and the men had not "been dry for a minute[,] day or night."

Beyond all that, much of the Rough Riders' baggage had disappeared, quickly stolen, the troopers lamented, by the impoverished Cubans they encountered on shore. "I have nothing with me," Theodore informed Edith, "no soap, toothbrush, razor, brandy, medicine chest, socks or underclothes." By the time they finally had a chance to bury those killed at Las Guásimas, "the vultures were wheeling overhead by hundreds. They plucked out the eyes and tore the faces and the wounds of the dead Spaniards before we got to them and even one of our own men who lay in the open." As if to insult the fallen soldiers, "the woods are full of giant land crabs," which slowly "gathered in gruesome rings" around the corpses, he reported, scarcely imagining how it all might affect her.[42]

San Juan Heights

The looming terrain consisted of a series of low-lying hills running north-and-south, less than 2 miles to the east of Santiago. An arc of US forces, about half of the whole Fifth Corps, now faced the two most prominent, and militarily crucial, of these hills, San Juan and Kettle. The latter rose closest to the Rough Riders' position in the American line. The shot that killed Buckey O'Neill most likely had come from a sniper hidden somewhere up the slope, and once they began their onslaught, *all* of the advancing forces would lie under full view of the fierce Spanish defenders on the hilltops, making the Americans fully vulnerable to murderous rifle and artillery fire from above.

Awaiting instructions from the generals, Roosevelt's impatience grew, as did that of his troopers. By his later account, he sent "messenger after messenger" imploring General Sumner for permission to advance, but there was no response. The brutal midday heat now added to their misery. As one o'clock neared, TR considered sending the men forward anyway, never mind the lack of explicit orders or the possibility of being court-martialed later for doing so—if the attack were to fail.

Just then, at last, Lt. Col. Joseph H. Dorst came galloping "through the storm of bullets" with the official command from Shafter to advance, supporting the regulars in their assault of the hills. At that instant, as TR later wrote, "I sprang on my horse and then my 'crowded hour' began." Starting from his spot in the rear, where the colonel normally stayed, Roosevelt moved up through the lines, instructing troopers of his First Volunteers, along with elements of four other cavalry regiments, to rise from their "safe" positions and follow him over the deadly open ground, "toward the guns." All the different units would soon be "more or less intermingled" in a combined American attack—a direct frontal charge up Kettle Hill.[43]

Several units of regulars, including the African American buffalo soldiers of the Ninth Cavalry, were to spearhead the charge, but TR later said that he found those men still lying in the tall grass instead of advancing. "I got my men moving forward, and when the 9th regiment of regulars halted too long firing, I took my men clean through it, and their men and younger officers joined me. At the head of the two commands I rode forward," much aided, he reported, from being the only one on horseback. Roosevelt, of course, was determined to prove the mettle of his volunteers, even if that meant denigrating the regular US forces. Other Rough Riders on the scene would later credit the African American troopers with far more initiative—and greater courage—than TR did at that moment, or would afterward.[44]

Acting half from bravado and half from conviction, Roosevelt consciously made himself a prominent target for the Spanish riflemen. Clad in his ordinary cavalry uniform, a blue flannel shirt with white suspenders and khaki trousers, he tied to his brown felt officer's hat a blue-and-white polka dot bandana, "floating and flapping out" behind him, said regiment chaplain Henry A. Brown of Prescott, Arizona. It was the defiant emblem of a warrior, as TR's men did not fail to notice. "He's a perfect devil in action," reported one of the Rough Rider troopers afterward. "He's always ahead, waving on the men with his sword in one hand and a big revolver in the other, and yelling all the while like a garret full of cats let loose." Another, when asked later, said, "He led us mounted. His marvelous courage was inspiring." Twenty-three-year-old Private Fred Chilcoot, from Nebraska, put it most succinctly: "He never said 'Go on, boys.' He was in front and called 'Come on, boys.' "[45]

Reflecting Civil War experience, regular military tactics of the time advised against frontal assaults over open ground against entrenched enemy positions. Combat manuals also instructed that a regimental colonel should command from the rear, better to see what his men were doing ahead. But in Rough Riders' style, one threw caution to the wind. Roosevelt had decided that if he were to fall, it would be as Col. Robert Gould Shaw had at Fort Wagner in July 1863: at the front of his regiment. "No one who saw Roosevelt take that ride expected he would finish it alive," said Richard Harding Davis, who was there.⁴⁶

TR's fearlessness that day would stand beyond serious question. Other Rough Riders, however, would later register somewhat different accounts of those first moments of the attack. According to 34-year-old Private Thomas J. Laird, another from Prescott, Arizona, the famous "charge" began more-or-less spontaneously, contrary to Roosevelt's version. Born in Wisconsin, Laird had migrated west and become a miner, but the mining slump in central Arizona probably helped to explain his volunteering for the army. Tired of the Spanish shells that exploded over the grass and bushes where they lay waiting, Laird recounted, many of the troopers started moving forward on their own. "They were pouring so much lead into us and killing us like dogs that I guess the boys thought like me—that we might as well die in trying to capture the hill ahead as to lay down and be shot to pieces." So "with a yell," they started, "without any command from our officers." Soon after Laird and his group started forward, he remembered, the Ninth and Tenth African American cavalry regiments, positioned to the right and left of the Rough Riders in line, "also broke away from their officers to help us out, as we were in a bad fix." Those African American troopers, Laird said, "came on like a pack of blood hounds[,] and in one hour we took the hill and drove the Spaniards out."⁴⁷

Forty-year-old 1st Sgt. (later 2nd Lt.) William E. Dame of Cerrillos, New Mexico, also reported his impressions soon after the event. A New Englander who, like Laird, had moved west to seek fortune as a miner, Dame later wrote of being under rifle and artillery barrages for two hours before the Rough Riders began their advance on Kettle Hill. "We swept forward under a heavy fire, being compelled to lie down *frequently* until we reached the line of the 10th [African American Cavalry]," who wanted to know who they were and where they were going. By his account, Dame replied, "Rough Riders going to take that hill. Get out of the way or fall in with us." One of the veteran Buffalo Soldiers then exclaimed: "I will be damned if those Rough Riders will get ahead of me," whereupon the entire line, whites and blacks together, "started to run for the hill, stopping only when the top was reached," then turning, after about an hour of continued firing, toward San Juan Hill and joining the fight for that one as well. "The Spanish . . . have a large amount of ammunition and their rifles are superior to ours," said Dame, "but their marksmanship is very poor." Still, they could "keep up a hot and steady fire which is decidedly uncomfortable."⁴⁸

Many rank-and-file Rough Riders spoke gratefully of the black soldiers who fought beside them. One was Sgt. Garfield Hughes of Albuquerque, New Mexico, just 18 years old when he joined the Rough Riders on May 2. He remembered the Spanish entrenched in rifle pits 4 feet deep, "but the Tenth, Ninth, and First regiments of regulars and the Rough Riders, all cavalry, run them for half a mile," he wrote to his father, who was editor of the *Albuquerque Citizen*. "Colonel Roosevelt is as brave as they make them," he testified, but also "the colored troops, the Ninth and Tenth, are the best fighters in the army." Private Kenneth Robinson, of New York City, shot in battle on July 1, agreed: "There is not a man in the rough riders but takes off his hat to the negroes. They not only fought like devils, but they were the readiest to come to our help when we were wounded." West Point graduate Tom Roberts, a white lieutenant in the Tenth Cavalry, heard nothing but praise for his "colored soldiers" and remembered one of the Rough Riders telling him he would never forget those men: "They saved our regiment." Billy Larned, who shortly before had seen Buckey O'Neill die, credited the African Americans for his own survival: "If it had not been for the colored Regular cavalry, who were on our flank, we would have lost three times as many." The *Cleveland Plain Dealer*, though with racial condescension, went even further: "Scarce used to freedom themselves, they are dying that Cuba may be free. . . . They bore themselves like veterans [which they were], and gave proof positive that out of nature's . . . peaceful, dareless and playful[,] military discipline and an inspiring cause can make soldiers worthy to rank with Caesar's legions or Cromwells's army."[49]

In all, the famous "Charge of the Rough Riders" actually consisted of soldiers of different regiments, whites and blacks combined, creeping forward in small groups, sometimes running, often stumbling down, fighting for cover, then moving ahead again. "Our men staggered and threw themselves on the ground," said one reporter within watching distance. "Again they started, and again they prostrated themselves, but on, on, on, up, up, up, they went until, with a cheer, they sprang over the trenches dividing the sides of the hill." As the troopers advanced, Roosevelt bravely rode back and forth along the front line, urging his own men to keep going. Other commanders, including the later-famous 1st Lt. John J. "Black Jack" Pershing of the "Buffalo Soldier" Tenth Cavalry, did the same, shepherding the blue-uniformed mass of men now rushing in a jagged lane that extended more than half a mile. At one point, TR reported having found a Rough Rider cringing behind a bush and ordered him to get up and fight. "Are you afraid to stand when I am on horseback?" The man gathered himself, rose to his feet, and then immediately fell dead, drilled by a Mauser bullet probably meant for the colonel. Many of the troopers, however, went forward eagerly and without inordinate fear. One of them, William J. Pollock, a Pawnee Indian, let loose with a shrill war cry that everyone later remembered. But to the press corps watching from a safe distance, including Stephen Crane, and to a host of foreign military observers, the situation appeared hopeless: a "very gallant, but very foolish" maneuver, said one, almost certain to be an "absolute slaughter" of the American attackers.[50]

The very concept of "charging," of carrying the fight straight into the enemy, without flinching, carried special significance for the Rough Riders. Aboard the transport en route to Cuba, as one correspondent reported, the young Captain Capron had impressed on the other officers his theory that "the only way to get out of an unpleasant predicament ... was to charge through it and do it quickly." Apart from training, however, Roosevelt's men assumed a responsibility to prove the character of Americans: their commitment to principle, their courage, their iron will. "The Spaniards say we are American devils: that we violate the rules of warfare." said Capt. William Llewellyn in a letter sent back from Cuba. "When they fire volley after volley at us, instead of retreating as we ought, our trumpeters sound the charge." As Private Dudley Dean of Boston, a railroad worker in civilian life, told his father: "It is this advancing in the face of fire by the Americans that the Spanish do not understand." Spanish prisoners often confirmed this. As one of them said, "They did not fight us as other soldiers. When we fired a volley, they advanced instead of going back.... We are not used to fighting with men who act so." Foreign military observers noted the same, as Corporal J. D. Honeyman of San Antonio observed to his sister: "This is the record [with the reporters] we have been trying to make for ourselves." The Rough Riders "did not flinch," said one of newsmen covering the July 1 attack. "Fighting like demons, they held their ground tenaciously, now pressing forward a few feet, then falling back under the enemy's fire." But still, "the western cowboys and eastern 'dandies' hammered the enemy from their path." As Private Allen M. Coville, of Topeka, later told a small Kansas paper, "some Spaniards that we have captured say we do not fight fair, that we shoot and advance and shoot and keep on advancing."[51]

As they moved up the gradual slope, Roosevelt's troopers could see clearly the massive iron sugar-boiling kettle and the frantic Spanish marksmen in trenches firing down at them. The colonel now galloped ahead, one bullet grazing his elbow and another scraping "Little Texas." At a wire fence 40 yards from the summit, he dismounted and, with the men around him, ran toward the enemy trenches, shooting at Spanish soldiers willy-nilly as they fled for their lives. TR later bragged that he personally killed one of the Spaniards with the Navy Colt revolver he carried, a pistol that had been salvaged from the battleship *Maine*. As Third Cavalry sergeant J. E. Andrews said later, "I'll never forget the way our boys walked up that hill, from the top of which came a storm of bullets. . . . They were yelling all the way up." At one point, claimed Andrews, who had been hit in the abdomen, he told Roosevelt and another Rough Rider officer "to lie down or they would be shot, but they wouldn't." In the brief melee that followed, Americans from various regiments, including the African American Ninth and Tenth, succeeded in claiming the hilltop, planting yellow silk guidons to mark their conquest. "The fighting from the first engagement to the last I was in was desperate," Rough Rider 1st lieutenant Joseph A. Carr of D Troop told reporters after being sent home to Washington, DC, seriously wounded. "We were not supported by artillery, and it was a test of what American nerve and determination could do."[52]

Soon enough, the triumphant Americans on the summit of Kettle Hill received another heavy barrage from the Spanish firing pits on another ridge about 500 yards forward, the one actually named San Juan Hill. For a moment, Roosevelt and several Rough Riders took cover behind the huge iron kettle, now theirs, and watched the second fight as it unfolded. There, an American brigade of regular forces under the command of 63-year-old Maj. Gen. Hamilton Hawkins, a career soldier who had fought at the Battle of Gettysburg, charged into a hail of Spanish bullets and artillery shells from the crest of San Juan. "The fire was terrific," said Carr, "and our men went right into the teeth of it." One of Hawkins's young first lieutenants, 31-year-old Jules Garesche Ord of the Tenth Cavalry, a white man, led the Buffalo Soldiers into the fray, urging his men onward until being fatally shot just several strides from the top.[53]

Just when it looked as if disaster lay in store for the attackers at San Juan, everyone suddenly heard over the din of carbine shots a deafening *bam-bam-bam-bam*, the sound of Capt. John H. Parker's battery of American Gatling guns. Each of the Colt-manufactured precursors of the twentieth-century machine gun poured its murderous 700 rounds-per-minute onto the Spanish positions. In all, these terrifying ten-barrel, rapid-fire weapons sent some eighteen thousand bullets toward the enemy within just eight and a half minutes. Amid the horrible carnage, dozens of panic-stricken defenders, in white-and pale-blue pinstriped garb, again fled from the fortifications, as the cavalry regulars used their Krag-Jørgensens to cut down many of them as they ran.[54]

Other Americans behind the lines, meanwhile, beheld a scenario of grievously wounded men limping or being carried back to ill-equipped field hospitals. "The sight of that road as I wound my way down it was something I cannot describe," said Remington. "The rear of a battle. All broken spirits, bloody bodies, hopeless, helpless suffering which drags its weary length to the rear, are so much more appalling than anything else in the world." Half-naked men sat down on the roadside, exhausted. Some troopers, shot in the lower extremities, hopped in on one foot, using their rifles for crutches. Others, out of their minds from sunstroke, wandered to the rear. Soldiers arrived carrying officers on makeshift litters or bearing them on their backs. "Dead men, horses and mules and millions of dollars' worth of stuff was lying on the ground," Sgt. Horace Gilbert of the Third Infantry told a friend back in Sioux City. "The smell was terrible," he added. Remington saw one man stooping over, arms drawn up, flapping his hands downward at the wrists. "That is the way with all people when they are shot through the body," the artist explained, "they want to hold the torso steady, because if they don't it hurts." Margherita Arlina Hamm, perhaps the first female journalist to cover a war from the front lines, blamed Congress and selfish businessmen for the distressing camp and medical preparations: "In many cases the scenes would make a person's blood boil at the indecent indifference and soulless greed displayed by seemingly respectable men." Aside from that, however, the work there of Clara Barton and the other Red Cross women, Hamm added, "should never be forgotten."[55]

By the end of the fighting that afternoon—the Spanish counterattacks met in turn with heavy American carbine fire and the continuing report of Parker's Gatlings—the enemy force had been driven off the hills, fleeing toward Santiago where they prepared for a drawn-out shelling, just as Shafter had anticipated. Yet the obese commanding general, tormented by gout and malaria, felt hardly like celebrating. The price of victory on that decisive day of the war had been higher than expected. In all, the Fifth Corps had suffered over 1,300 casualties, and of Roosevelt's First Volunteer Cavalry, 15 killed and 73 wounded from among the 583 fit for duty that morning. Even so, the

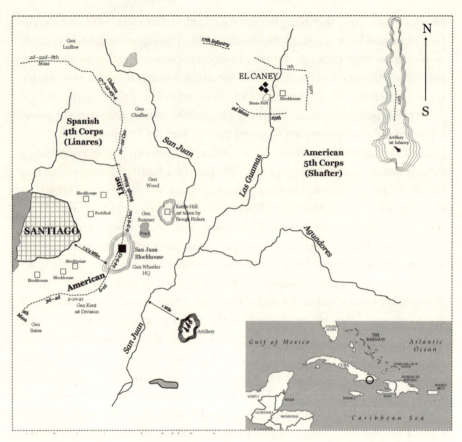

Positions of American regiments at the end of the day, July 1, 1898. Map prepared by Margot S. Gibson-Beattie

American losses paled in comparison to those of the Spanish; 30 to 50 percent of them reportedly had fallen in the fighting for the San Juan Heights. Even General Linares, leading the desperate fight in person, had sustained an arm wound so disabling that he had to step down from command, Gen. José Toral replacing him.[56]

Just two days later, on July 3, Cervera ordered his squadron commanders to take their ships, steaming at full, single file out of Santiago harbor and through the bay, headed for open water in a desperate attempt to escape. Sampson quickly closed in, taking less than four hours to reduce the Spanish vessels, four cruisers and two destroyers, to flaming hulks. With that, and with the army's triumph on land in Cuba, the United States now ruled the Caribbean.[57]

The last battle for Santiago, a minor one, came on the afternoon of July 10, consisting mainly of small arms and cannon exchanges. Finally, on July 17, Toral agreed to "capitulate," a euphemism for the sake of Spanish pride. Units of the Fifth Corps thereupon marched into the city square and raised the stars and stripes atop the municipal palace. Spain formally asked for peace on July 18, and President McKinley issued a protocol to that effect on August 12, 1898. Meanwhile, Maj. Gen. Wesley Merritt, commanding American forces in the Philippines, pushed into Manila, delivering the city, as Dewey had the bay, to American control. The fate of those islands, too, would be decided at the formal peace conference with Spain, scheduled to convene in Paris that October.[58]

Much of the blame for Spain's loss of the San Juan Heights—and therefore, of Cuba—must fall upon its leadership. As it turned out, Linares had failed to reinforce this position properly, choosing instead to hold nearly ten thousand Spanish reserves in Santiago. As a result, the Spanish entrenchments to the east, crucial to defending the city, had been poorly constructed. Rather than being concentrated on the crest of the San Juan Heights, where they could have had a clear field of fire all the way down the hills, Spanish soldiers had dug in sparsely. That spared the Americans the full force of near point-blank enemy rifle fire upon the advancing regiments below. In retrospect, given the opportunity Linares had, the "Battle of San Juan Hill" could have been a stinging US defeat and far more of a bloodbath for the Americans than it was.[59]

The dispute over who deserved primary credit for the victory commenced almost as soon as the shooting stopped. Afterward, Roosevelt would claim that the Rough Riders took Kettle Hill with the help of men of the Tenth Cavalry, along with primarily the Third Cavalry regiment of (white) volunteers. Eager to promote his regiment's image along with his own political fortunes, the Rough Riders' commander would in little time employ his literary powers to seize control of the historical narrative. So would journalists like Richard Harding Davis, who spent much of the Santiago campaign touting the merits of TR's First Cavalry volunteers. As one scribe wrote shortly afterward, the San Juan Heights action, and especially "the charge" of the First Volunteer Cavalry, now revealed "what a tremendous effect the daring of the rough riders has had on the rest of our troops." These volunteers had "set the pace for other volunteers," showing the "good solid basis for our boasts of our citizen soldiers." Further, said the *New York Times*, the Rough Riders had shown that "in extreme cases men of high individual courage, intelligence, and self-

Colonel Roosevelt and his Rough Riders after the "Battle of San Juan Hill," 1898. Cropped out of this picture, on both the right and left sides, were some of the African American troopers of the Ninth and Tenth Cavalry regiments who participated in the famous "charge" on that day. Library of Congress, LC-USZC4-7934

reliance, led by men like themselves, may be as efficient a fighting force as an equal number of men who have been drilled to respond to orders with the precision of a machine." Today, military historians—following Pershing's subsequent account and those of others who questioned a central role of the Rough Riders—tend to credit more heavily the Tenth Cavalry of regulars, along with TR's volunteers and the other regiments present.[60]

In all, some fifteen thousand men of Shafter's Fifth Army Corps—all who remained fit for action—participated in the July 1 fighting near Santiago, divided between the operations at El Caney and the San Juan Heights. About thirteen thousand of those men were white and roughly two thousand black—twenty-six regiments in all, including three volunteer ones, the others regular. In the official count, 205 US soldiers lost their lives in the action, along with another 1,180 wounded. Casualties among the officers proved especially high: twenty-two killed, ninety-four wounded.[61]

Roosevelt afterward gave his reason for the Rough Riders' heavy casualties: "we did the charging; and to carry earthworks on foot with dismounted cavalry, when these earthworks are held by unbroken infantry armed with the best modern rifles, is a serious task." Yet some of the regular army veterans held a different view. Said one, Private George Tallman of the Twentieth Infantry, the "rashness" of the Rough Riders "in running into that Spanish pocket [of fire] would have caused their complete annihilation had it not been for the Tenth colored United States cavalry[,] who so nobly came to their rescue."[62]

Faneuil Hall

Since long before the Revolution, the massive, three-story Georgian building in old Boston, near the historic harbor, had served as a meeting hall for groups of every description and purpose. William James knew it well, and so did most of the others, half of them women, who had showed up for the mass meeting on June 15, 1898, to protest the war that most other Americans supported with enthusiasm.[63]

Anti-imperialists around the country, including Massachusetts civil rights lawyer Moorfield Storey, Stanford University president David Starr Jordan, immigrant and civil service reformer Carl Schurz, and diplomat Charles Francis Adams already had registered their opposition. They feared the transformation of the United States into a militaristic power. In Boston, Gamaliel Bradford, a retired banker and active antiwar publicist, had organized the Faneuil Hall event, appealing to any others who would "stand up . . . against the insane and wicked ambition which is driving the country to moral ruin."[64]

Bradford chaired the meeting, contending in one of several major speeches that in spite of the war's just having begun, plans for the subsequent peace required immediate attention. "A faction is hard at work to commit the country to action from which it cannot afterwards recede," he warned, referring to the jingo element in both parties, especially the Republicans. Those "factions," he believed, included greedy businessmen as well as ambitious politicians—"imaginations thirsting after military and naval glory." Storey's keynote address reinforced these points. To "seize any colony of Spain and hold it as our own, without the free consent of its people is a violation of the principles upon which this government rests," he insisted, noting that when ancient Rome began its litany of conquests, the Roman Republic began to decay.[65]

Battlefield successes did little to change this oppositionist sentiment. In a Fourth of July oration in Philadelphia, Republican and former US senator from Vermont George F. Edmunds warned that imperial power would require "maintenance of great standing armies and navies, with the enormous expenses and other evils attending their existence." The "strange" thing about it all, said a columnist in Austin, Texas, on July 21, was that both political parties had been "willing to involve the nation in war with Spain without knowing anything about the condition of the country for war, . . . anything about the people for whom they were going to war, . . . anything about the strength of the people with whom they were going to war." Beyond that, if the revolution in the Philippines proved extensive, spreading throughout the islands, said the *Helena Independent*, then "the task presented to the United States military and naval authorities will be one of great magnitude."[66]

The organizational efforts in Boston would lead, in November 1898, to the formation of the American Anti-Imperialist League, with former US senator George S. Boutwell of Massachusetts as its president. Over the next few years, the movement would spread as a network of such organizations, claiming more than 700,000 supporters around the country. Many of that number had at first supported the war for humanitarian reasons—contempt for Spanish tyranny that they shared with most other Americans—but the series of military successes, beginning with Dewey's at Manila Bay, raised the question of what US policy makers would do with the former Spanish possessions that American forces now were conquering. Although losing their battle for majority support, they still argued that further imperial expansion did not fit with American traditions, that the only proper outcome of the fighting would be the full independence of the liberated provinces, especially the Philippines.[67]

The 80-year-old Boutwell, an ardent abolitionist in pre–Civil War days, had in the mid-1850s been present at the founding of the Republican Party, had pushed in the House for adoption of the Fourteenth and Fifteenth Amendments in the late 1860s, and in the Senate had sponsored passage of the Civil Rights Act of 1875. In foreign policy, he had long opposed American expansion in the Pacific, counseled against acquiring Hawaii, and lamented the gradual shift of the McKinley administration toward the jingoistic perspective of Lodge and Roosevelt.[68]

In the end, he would walk away from a Republican Party that he believed had lost its ideological soul, scorning the young imperialists and damning the party's general support for annexing the Philippines in 1899 instead of granting Filipino independence. "Is it wise and just for us, as a nation, to make war for the seizure and government of distant lands, occupied by millions of inhabitants, who are alien to us in every aspect of life, except that we are together members of the same human family?" he later queried. His answer and that of all other anti-imperialists would remain an emphatic no.[69]

More simply, Boutwell thought America had no business trying to govern faraway places, especially while it abandoned more and more the cause of equality for African Americans at home. Though not always for that reason, anti-imperialists in general would agree that solving problems at home should take precedence over the spreading of US influence abroad. Winning the war with Spain had proven much easier than would forging the peace afterward and determining the kind of nation Americans might have as a result.

Prescott

Anticipating the Fourth of July, its roughly 3,500 citizens had yet to learn of Buckey O'Neill's death. Everyday life in Prescott, and throughout Arizona Territory, had gone on pretty much as usual that early summer of 1898. The days had been hot, local temperatures averaging 96 degrees in the shade. That surprised no one, of course; folks simply accepted the heat, as modern air conditioning did not exist. Harry Shumate, owner of a general store and soda fountain on Montezuma Street, announced his "having secured the services of a first class ice cream maker," ready to crank out "sherbets and ices" of all fruit flavors. In addition to that, a carload of watermelons had just arrived from Phoenix. If they wished, patrons might stay around and listen to the store's "fine gramophone" as they ate their warm-weather treats. Meanwhile, the tavern keepers along "Whiskey Row," across from the courthouse, traded briskly in an alternative kind of refreshment. Elsewhere, the town's "baseball boys," donning brand-new uniforms made for them by Mrs. W. J. Mulvenon, prepared for a ballgame, scheduled for 11:30 the morning of the fourth. In appreciation of her generosity, the Prescott nine had promised to "fight harder than ever to see that their colors triumph on the diamond." Some of the younger townsfolk planned to attend the Fourth of July ball to be held that evening in a local dance hall, featuring the town's new string orchestra. And in countless backyards and pastures, the holiday's festivities would be punctuated by fireworks.[70]

Still, the impact of the war at home, and especially the nagging worries about relatives fighting in Cuba, had altered the lazy rhythms of summertime. News from the soldiers changed what people talked about casually and drew attention to new oddities. In one tidbit, noted in Prescott's only newspaper, the *Weekly Journal Miner*, Mrs. Ella Williams now owned "a beautifully designed souvenir spoon, portraying the battle ship *Maine*," which she had received from one of the troopers in Tampa, an assurance that all was well. The men in uniform *had* done well, but everyone waited precariously for the "vacant chair" that a few families might have to accept. "We had hoped to have you always among us—that you never would have a more serious battle than the common every day 'battle of life.' But we are all 'creatures of circumstance,'" the *Weekly Phoenix Herald* later counseled. It comforted Prescott readers to learn that "the Rough Riders captured a spy the other day and turned him over to the Cubans, who made short work of him." But the papers also published the names of the killed and wounded at Las Guásimas, including two from Captain O'Neill's company. Neither had been known well around town, but a few remembered one, Ed Liggott, as a reliable marksman and expert rider, "very enthusiastic" for the cause. The minister at the Methodist Episcopal Church planned for his traditional Independence Day sermon on the evening of Sunday, the third of July, followed by the choir's rendering of Rudyard Kipling's 1897 "Recessional":

> God of our fathers, known of old,
>   Lord of our far-flung battle-line,
> Beneath whose awful hand we hold
>   Dominion over palm and pine—
> Lord God of Hosts, be with us yet,
> Lest we forget—lest we forget![71]

The whole mood of the town quickly changed into one of shock, and then anguish, when the word arrived that O'Neill had been killed at Kettle Hill. It came clattering off the telegraph wires on Saturday, July 2. The news not only jolted Prescott but also launched a wave of grief throughout the territory.

The dreaded telegram reached Pauline O'Neill when she stepped off the train in Prescott upon returning from a business trip. "Kind hands and loving hearts led me home," she wrote. "The agony was so great that I could not weep for days." The last letter she had received from Buckey was dated June 27, the day after the Las Guásimas fight. "It was short, and only written to let me know that he was still unharmed. He had to make the letter brief, because he wanted to help bury the dead." She had hoped to visit him that coming winter in Havana, where he figured the Rough Riders might be sent by then. Being told that he "fell, killed instantly, as he was leading his men to victory" gave but cold comfort.

She remembered, now half bitterly, that meeting in the Prescott Court House on the evening of February 16, after the destruction of the *Maine* had been reported. "Mr. O'Neill felt that his country would demand his services," and he declared before everyone "that he was ready and willing to shed his heart's last drop for . . . his country." When the audience applauded, Pauline's soul plummeted, for she knew "that in case of war his honor would demand that he keep the promise so solemnly made to his fellow men." A friend later remembered his stressing the importance that Arizona men do their part to help the territory be admitted to the Union: "Who would not gamble for a new star in the flag?" On April 28, Buckey returned from Phoenix with his captaincy in his pocket and was mustered in the following day. "I went to the train on May 4th to see the gallant Rough Riders leave," recalled Pauline. "At the last good-bye he said: 'My dear, the war will not last long, and I will return in ninety days.'" Now, it had "all ended"—all but the unshakable despair of having lost him.[72]

As for others throughout the territory, the legend of Buckey O'Neill grew much faster than it took for memories of the actual man to fade. As in past wars, the fight against Spain converted citizen soldiers into cultural icons, prescriptive models of upright behavior for the moral instruction of people back home. "He left a beautiful home, a noble wife, riches, political preferment—everything that man could desire, to go to the front and fight for freedom," gushed the *Weekly Phoenix Herald* two weeks later. "No Knight Templar who did battle with the Saracen to rescue the holy sepulcher from infidel hands was actuated by more chivalrous motives." Another tribute fashioned O'Neill as an archetypal democratic hero, recalling that Buckey "had a warm place in the hearts of more people in Arizona than any other man in the Territory. He was one of the people; he was a living example of the broadest western generosity and nobleness of character." Phoenix city officials postponed the extensive Fourth of July demonstration they had planned for that Monday because of Saturday night's sad report. When their parade did take place, on the evening of July 6, one onlooker noted that while "the cheering was liberal," the "awful shadow of the sorrowful news that has been echoed back from Santiago seemed to hover like a spell over the vast concourse." Instead of laughing and bravado, "there were sober faces and firmly set lips."[73]

As the years passed, the citizens of Prescott would go on claiming, rightly or not, that they had furnished the first volunteers for the war. Yet some still must have wondered what might have been if events had turned just a little differently—if Buckey had lived, come home to Pauline, worn the laurels of a war hero, and gone on to become governor of Arizona, as some had predicted. Or what if the war had not been fought in the first place? And what if, in that hot summer of 1898, ordinary life in Prescott had just unfolded peacefully as it normally did, undisturbed?[74]

As it was, the townspeople expected a monument, "in memory of Captain William O. O'Neill and his comrades who died," to be erected on the courthouse plaza. One was: a larger-than-life bronze of a cowboy rider on horseback, created by sculptor Solon Borglum and unveiled on July 2, 1907—the sixth year of Colonel Roosevelt's presidency.[75]

It stands there still today.

5

New Empire

EARLY IN 1899, A NEW PAINTING on display in a gallery window on Broadway near Madison Square increasingly attracted the attention of New York's shopping masses. "Seventy-five percent of those who pass the window daily stop and look at it," said the art critic for the *Philadelphia Inquirer*. "This would seem to indicate that the pictorial side of the late war appeals strongly to the public taste. . . . [T]he war seems to have had a marked effect in stimulating American artists in the production of military pictures." The dealer who owned the gallery added that "the public is ripe for works of this kind." Indeed, it was. The painting employed "the language of imperial progress," says one historian. It was a dramatic scene of Col. Theodore Roosevelt and the Rough Riders at the start of their now-celebrated charge up "San Juan Hill."[1]

In the new work, Frederic Remington reflected not the war he had observed personally but the one that he thought the public wanted to imagine. While in Cuba, he did not witness the actual charge, but his picture conveyed symbolic qualities that he, too, found in the Rough Riders: courage and conviction, military fortitude and camaraderie. It shows a blue-shirted Roosevelt on horseback, pistol drawn, leading from the front, exposed to enemy fire, conducting the mass of troopers in their assault up the slope. In the foreground, Lt. Woodbury Kane, Harvard graduate and peacetime yachtsman, dressed in the khaki uniform of an officer, runs forward with his men of K Troop, some of them falling but the others still advancing, bravely. The scene reflected the way that many Americans of the time had come to view and accept war, with touches of romantic heroism but also the unsparing reality of sacrifice. It would become the most famous work of art associated with the Spanish-American War.[2]

One of its admirers was Roosevelt, who knew Remington well. "It seems to me that you in your line, and [Owen] Wister in his, are doing the best work in America today," TR had written to the artist back in November 1895. As for the painting, he confessed in 1899: "he portrays me with a decorum of attitude which was foreign to my actual conduct at the time; but it is a good picture."[3]

There is one element of truth in the picture, however, that catches the viewer almost by surprise. It takes a second look at the painting to find it—the solitary black face among the charging troopers, the second man behind the figure of Woodbury Kane and to the right of him in the picture. Is this Remington's grudging token of respect for the black soldiers who fought alongside the Rough Riders that day? Perhaps, and yet the young man remains somehow alone, segregated here and, by custom, everywhere in American society. Still, there he is, in this melee of combat, the moment that conferred upon Roosevelt the lasting fame that he so craved and many others also deserved.[4]

Afterward

Even more than Spain's defeat on land, the loss of its Pacific and Caribbean fleets had spelled a final demise for the Spanish empire. There remained no choice but surrender. Had the Spaniards continued the war without naval forces for their defense, US warships could have attacked the enemy coasts with abandon, probably triggering revolution against the decrepit monarchy at home.

The final collapse of the Spanish empire changed the balance of power throughout the world, and advocates of the "Large Policy" in the United States received by naval power one key component of their overall agenda—American domination of the Caribbean—along with another part they had not clearly planned: partial control of Pacific trade via the Philippines. The annexation of Hawaii, at last, in 1899 would add another piece, and the build-

Frederic Remington, "The Charge of the Rough Riders," 1898. The Spanish-American War stimulated the popular market for military paintings, this one becoming the most famous. It represented the event not as it actually occurred but as the public wanted to imagine it. Courtesy of the Frederic Remington Art Museum, Ogdensburg, NY

ing of the Panama Canal in the early twentieth century would complete the scenario.

After impassioned debate on the ideological propriety of including the Philippines, along with Puerto Rico, Guam, and control of Cuba among Spain's cessions to the United States, the Senate would ratify the Treaty of Paris on February 6, 1899. Anti-imperialist objections would make the issue close, the treaty barely receiving the constitutionally required two-thirds majority, 57 to 27—only one vote to spare. All but two Republicans, 72-year-old George Frisbie Hoar of Massachusetts (Boutwell's successor) and Eugene Hale of Maine, would vote in favor. The Democratic senators would divide on the question, southerners generally opposing.[5]

Still, in all, the Spanish-American War had changed—in part, by reinstating—the way that most Americans thought of themselves and saw the place of their nation in the world. The Rough Riders' sacrifices, observed the *Dallas Morning News*, "tell . . . of American bravery without regard to birth, wealth, or station, and how the country's peril is the real leveler of all her citizens." The war's outcome, however, would reaffirm a sense of pride in American expansion not seen since the 1840s era of "Manifest Destiny." As a minister speaking in Chicago said, "History has no precedent, no comparison. The theatre in which the great drama of war was enacted was vast, far transcending our original expectations and designs." The new overseas frontier, so promoted by American expansionists and so lamented by anti-imperialists, had come into being. President McKinley's willingness to support, and the Senate's decision to accept, the annexation of the new conquests would further establish the imperial mission that now loomed.[6]

Relative to the Civil War, the fighting in the Spanish-American War had taken a very small toll in American lives; fewer than five hundred soldiers had died in battle. But ten times that many would perish from disease, inadequate medical care, and appalling camp organization. The most life-threatening experience for the Rough Riders, and for most of the troops, came *after* their days of heaviest combat. Although Spanish bullets still whizzed around them as they huddled in trenches on the outskirts of Santiago, food poisoning and the lack of clean water threatened them even more, as did malaria and yellow fever.[7]

Feeling stranded in the tropical mud, Roosevelt had experienced his last weeks in Cuba as the darkest of the war. He feared that a "military disaster" impended, despite the triumphs on the battlefield. "For God's [sake]," he implored Henry Cabot Lodge, "have heavy reinforcements sent to us instantly." There was little question that army and civilian managers in Washington, including McKinley's inept secretary of war, Russell Alger, had botched transportation arrangements and provisions for the soldiers—the "embalmed" roast beef, the "disorganized" medical care, the absence of planning. Roosevelt said so in a series of outraged letters that offended the military bureaucrats responsible, costing him the Congressional Medal of Honor that he unashamedly sought. But now, luck as much as anything rescued the Rough Riders. Cuban guerillas had kept Spanish counter-attackers at bay, Rear Adm. William T. Sampson's navy had routed the Spanish fleet as it tried to escape from Santiago harbor, and the enemy garrison of some 24,000 men had surrendered soon after.[8]

Back home, meanwhile, Roosevelt's popular reputation rose to near-epic levels. His image in military uniform made the cover of *Harper's Weekly*, while drawings and photographs of his regiment in action around Santiago filled its pages. News of the Rough Riders circulated all through the country. Editorial columns everywhere showered praise on their commander. One quoted an astonished trooper from the Empire State as saying, "a couple o' years ago we people of New York didn't think Teddy knew enough to review a parade of cops!" Now, commented the *Springfield Republican*, the Rough Riders looked like "a stroke of genius, for they hit the popular fancy and created an enormous interest in the man who created them."⁹

When he began his Navy Department job in 1897, TR had no clear future in elective politics. Old Guard Republicans controlled New York, and the McKinley administration hardly imagined him on a national ticket. But now, declared the *New Haven Register*, "the American people are very sensitive to such influences as Roosevelt personifies, and if they make up their mind that the qualities of the fighter . . . ought to receive civic recognition, [then] nothing short of a cyclone can stop their planning and plotting for it." Such adulation crossed the sectional divide as well. On August 15, the southern segregationist (and Republican) minister Thomas F. Dixon told a crowd at the Grand Opera House in New York City that "every man must love and admire any American who has the courage of his convictions, and such a man is Theodore Roosevelt." As wartime service had advanced every chief executive but one since Ulysses S. Grant in 1868, the politically savvy Lodge quickly detected a president in the making. TR had hinted at political advancement as among the reasons for his volunteering. Now, his reputation for battlefield heroics placed him well ahead of all possible contenders in either party except the incumbent president himself. Even before the shooting had stopped, Lodge started pulling strings to get his friend nominated for governor of New York, a stepping-stone to higher office—and then, after McKinley, to the presidency no later than 1904.¹⁰

It may seem to modern observers that it somehow tainted TR's "hero image" that he would use it for political advancement, but he lived in a society that *expected* him to do exactly so. Americans still mostly subscribed to traditional values but no longer defined their heroes quite as they had in early republic times. "It is a genuinely popular movement which is sweeping him forward," observed the *Boston Journal* when the Rough Riders returned home, "and to all appearances it is as irresistible as it is spontaneous. Col. Roosevelt personally has had nothing to do with it." The eighteenth-century model of a George Washington spurning power before he could then, reluctantly, accept it had changed, it seemed, to one where the "celebrity-hero" had to embrace the popular benefits of fame without much hesitation. As cultural historians have explained, the first "new" heroes of this kind emerged following the Civil War, resulting from a democratization of popular tastes combined with the emerging mass media. As the Boston writer elaborated, "the American people love a great, strong, red blooded man who does things, [and] Mr. Roosevelt has been doing things since he was twenty years old." Another, for the *Wilkes-Barre Times*, fashioned TR's political chance, however, as a matter of cultural obligation for men of his class and level of education: "Col. Roosevelt has shown that the man of culture can wield great influence in political life; and that men of culture have as great opportunities before them in American as in European life." If men like him were to step forward more often, "it would not be so difficult to reconcile politics and the scholar in this country."[11]

By mid-August 1898, when a transport ship delivered the surviving Rough Riders to Montauk Point, Long Island, for a period of quarantine, TR himself felt a vague sense of melancholy about the war. It had been such an eerily brief experience—really only ten days of serious fighting—compared to that of the Civil War veterans he so venerated. He had no wounds to show for his service, no lasting badges of courage. Yet if he had been at all motivated by his father's choice not to serve in 1861, Roosevelt had proven all he needed to: "It makes me feel as though I could now leave something to my children which will serve as an apology for my having existed." Before seeing action, he had promised sons Ted and Kermit that, if killed in battle, he wanted them to receive his sword and revolver—again, little comfort for Edith who valued the return of her husband over having a proud name and a few war relics.[12]

By the time she finally got to see him, at Camp Wyckoff, where the regiment was demobilizing, it was obvious that life with Theodore would never be the same as before. Talk of his running for governor swirled all around, but he refused to discuss politics with reporters while still an officer in the army. Even so, political visitors surrounded him, and the same would be true, everyone quickly learned, when he got back home. Laudatory onlookers and newspaper scribes besieged him every time he went into or out of New York City, constantly inquiring when he was going to run for president. Whenever he could dodge the newsmen, TR—ever after known as "Colonel Roosevelt" or "the Colonel"—used this brief interlude to write about himself, as well as his famous regiment and the Cuban campaign. It would be a series of articles and then a book about his experience: *The Rough Riders*.[13]

In the months to come, another stream of reporters and politicians, in addition to throngs of relatives and friends, inundated Oyster Bay and set up

Roosevelt leads the charge of the Rough Riders on the cover of *Puck Magazine*, July 27, 1898. The oversize depiction of TR here typifies the media exaggeration not only of his role in the "Battle of San Juan Hill" but also of his Rough Riders. Library of Congress, LC-DIG-ppmsca-28721

camp around Sagamore Hill. TR's six children reveled in all the new attention that the Roosevelts were receiving, and when they could not find the hero himself, headline-hungry newspapermen never hesitated to approach the younger members of the family. One day, amid the regular hullabaloo, a correspondent spied 5-year-old Archie playing outdoors.

"So, where's the Colonel?" the visitor inquired.

"I don't know where the Colonel is," the little boy replied thoughtfully, eyes twinkling, "but Father is taking a bath."[14]

Heroes

On Sunday, July 31, 1898, just five days after the Spanish government requested formal peace terms, Rev. P. A. Hellman, pastor of St. Paul's English Lutheran Church in Baltimore, decided to preach a patriotic sermon on "the qualities that make the American soldier invincible." Significantly, America's newest national heroes, the Rough Riders, would serve as his case in point. The attributes that made one "a good soldier of Jesus Christ," Hellman contended, "are the same as those which make a good soldier on the battlefield—patriotism, endurance, courage, loyalty, devotion." In Cuba, as the newspapers had reported, Spanish captains had to stand over their men with drawn revolvers and compel them to fight. Not so with Roosevelt's troopers who had charged up the hills outside Santiago. "It was their patriotism"—that of ordinary Americans, especially those who had volunteered to fight—"that bore them through." The strength of its people thus had singled out America as "the nation that is to be a model for the nations of the earth." The dynasties of the Old World were "jealous of us," avowed Hellman, "because we have proven the stability of a republican form of government, and our very existence is a death thrust at the almost blasphemous assumption of the 'divine right of kings.' Royalty is trembling on its throne at the unmeasured success of the United States."[15]

A columnist for the *New York Sun* also found in the war's outcome a reassurance of the traditional republican mission of the United States. At the start of the conflict, the Spanish had fortified themselves with confidence in the "superior merit and effectiveness" of their Old World monarchy. "The honor and the nobility of Spain," the writer gloated, in retrospect, "were to be matched against the low, avaricious, shop-keeping spirit of the Yankee pigs," and the "immutable laws of strife" would guarantee a Spanish victory. In the end, the obvious one-sidedness of the American victory on both land and sea, not to mention the corruption and cruelty of Spain's governance of Cuba beforehand, had settled the question of ideological preeminence. "In America and Spain[,] we have a very healthy republic and a sadly diseased monarchy. We will leave them in that state to the political philosophers." Addressing the same concern internally, Rev. Barton O. Aylesworth, pastor of the Central Christian Church in Denver and former president of Drake University, noted the war's role in distracting Americans from the more recent, class-divisive crises at home. Just as the struggle between labor and capital "was reaching the danger line," and it seemed that "discussion would grow into bloodshed, revolution and national death, . . . relief comes in the nation's war," Aylesworth asserted. Now "both great classes" stood "side by side," with the "millionaire's son and cowboy . . . indistinguishable as 'Rough Riders.' They will never be very far apart again," he predicted, wishfully.[16]

Overblown rhetoric for sure, but it echoed a revived confidence in original ideals of the republic as well as expansionist ambition now extending far beyond American shores. The emotional intensity of war had worked a certain cultural magic. Even before they returned home, TR and the Rough Riders, once reviled as mere amateurs at war, stood in the vortex of that revival. Comparable to modern rock stars, their popularity had skyrocketed to the point that women admirers reportedly descended on Camp Wyckoff just to see the recently returned troopers, implored them for autographs or pictures, and even followed them to the laundries, poking through their soiled clothing in search of souvenirs from Santiago. Some whipped out scissors and knives to clip off buttons and cut out squares of insignia. A few even carried off dirty collars as prizes. Meanwhile, in Perry, Oklahoma, a Miss Lizzie Deleaderler, styling herself as a "cowboy young lady," had gathered together a company of forty-two young women as "feminine rough riders." Every one of these "petticoated soldiers," she claimed, "is a crack shot," and "no Spaniard could ever get within Mauser range without regretting his rashness." In mid-July, said the *New York Evening Journal*, they offered their services to McKinley to go to Cuba and "demolish" whatever remained of the enemy, promising to "do as good work at the front as their masculine namesakes."[17]

Roosevelt's volunteers had delivered a boost to stateside morale as soon as the reports of "San Juan Hill" first hit the newsstands, offsetting the "ambush" at Las Guásimas. The timing could not have been better. In most places, the Fourth of July celebrations of 1898 reflected a general feeling of reassurance that American troops had measured up to the job in Cuba. But the soldiers had proven far more than that. The future of American diplomacy, the compatibility of North and South, the strength and character of manhood, and the preservation of key values of the republic—all somehow hinged on the success of US armed forces in the war.

For the townsfolk of Salem, Oregon, it seemed there had never been a more "enthusiastic" Independence Day, complete with shouts and cheers, firecrackers, and a parade featuring the town's "military" band—all specially occasioned by news of the victory near Santiago. "It is becoming plain that the nation exists no longer for itself alone," said their featured orator, state official W. S. Duniway, "but that destiny beckons it to new duties and . . . new obligations. It must rise to the demands of the hour, or it must begin to weaken and decay." Local merchants everywhere made all they could of the moment. "With Independence, Union, Dewey, . . . Sampson, the Rough Riders[,] and all the other good things in mind, past and prospective, surely we have an abundance of reason for uncorking our patriotism" (and purchasing new attire for the occasion), proclaimed a clothing shop owner in Jackson, Michigan. In the same spirit, the millinery department at Donaldson's in Minneapolis, celebrating "the war spirit in the very air," offered a fresh assortment of military-style headgear: "Come and see our Army Hats, Rough Riders and Volunteers—these will suit you."[18]

More relevant politically, however, were the remarks of Benjamin Harrison, Republican from Indiana, former president and grandson of a former president, a confirmed nationalist though lukewarm on expansion, and guest of honor at the July Fourth meeting and banquet of the New Jersey Society of the Cincinnati. "This is not a war of conquest, but . . . of humanity. We have not struck the blow for additional territory, but for starving men and women," he declared. In case that statement landed unpersuasively, he added that the work of the Rough Riders in Santiago had "shown the country that the cowboy of Arizona and the millionaire of Fifth-ave. can rush on to victory, shoulder to shoulder, . . . that wealth does not enfeeble or sap the patriotism from the American heart." That assertion, repeated again and again in the months to come, would carry significant campaign potential for a Republican Party eager to label the Democrats and Bryan as perpetrators of division: poor opposing rich, West against East, North versus South. Further, said Harrison, the war had "demonstrated that the man who wore the gray uniform in 1862 can charge the Spanish foe with the men from New-York and Massachusetts, who wore the blue." Indeed, white southern editors often emphasized that very point. As the *Augusta Chronicle* boasted, "'Old Confederate Joe' [Wheeler] saving the military honor of the nation at Santiago and southern soldiers taking the places of stampeded regulars, northern volunteers and western Rough Riders will occupy a proud place in future annals." No longer, said the *Omaha World Herald*, could a northern politician "have the temerity to stand before an American audience and wave the 'bloody shirt,'" blaming the South for the Civil War.[19]

That theme of national unity would feature heavily as the presidential election of 1900 approached. At the first annual reunion of the Rough Riders in Las Vegas, New Mexico, Lafe Young, who had served with the regiment and now edited the *Iowa State Capital*, picked up that theme. "The Fourth of July," Young told the veterans assembled, including Roosevelt, "is our national Christmas commemorating the birth of the nation, but the Rough Riders' celebration should be its Easter, for it marked the resurrection." He recalled his pride in seeing "the sons of veterans marching beneath the flag which their fathers died to save, and the sons of confederates clothed in the same uniform, bearing the same arms and marching under the same flag." So it was, too, in the other regiments fighting beside them, "the sons of former slaves, . . . with the flag above them, and the same purpose in their hearts." Further, a host of "full-blood Indians" had aided the cause. "I made a vow to high heaven never to be a partisan again," Young confessed, "and henceforth and forever all Americans should look alike to me."[20]

Other Rough Riders made the most of their new celebrity. Buffalo Bill Cody quickly hired sixteen former troopers to reenact the "Battle of San Juan Hill" for his Wild West Show. Others, eager for employment, signed up with competing extravaganzas hailing by various names, including "the famous Teddy Roosevelt cow boy band" and the "Congress of Rough Riders and Ropers." Meanwhile, Leonard Wood, now a brigadier general, remained in Cuba after the war, serving as military governor of Santiago in 1898, then of Cuba from 1899 to 1902. While there, he tried to improve the appalling medical and sanitary conditions for the island population. Following several other prominent assignments, he would finally retire from the army as a major general in 1921, six years before his death.[21]

In the meantime, few African American subscribers of the Washington, DC, *Colored American*, could have been shocked by what they read in the October 8, 1898, issue. Page six featured a column by George W. Prioleau, chaplain of the Ninth US Cavalry, which had just returned from Cuba where its black troopers—also heroes, but *not* celebrities—had fought in the battle for the San Juan Heights. Prioleau was angry—and rightly so. Yes, "Teddy's Terrors" had shown great courage and deserved the glory that now covered them. But what about the four African American regiments—the Ninth and Tenth Cavalry along with the 24th and 25th Infantry—who had given their blood, too, in those same hours and same places? Some even said that they rescued the Rough Riders from a massacre as memorable as Custer's in 1876. "Let me inform you," insisted Prioleau, "that the history of this war will be a lie unless full credit for the victory is given the Negro regiments who played so important a part."[22]

Other African American newspapers had been saying the same, week after week, almost since the shooting stopped at San Juan Hill. "Our soldiers are wringing plaudits from those who are not our friends," one black columnist wrote on July 16, but too much of the world remained "too prejudiced or too indifferent to study the Negro's character in the proper light." Reporters for the influential New York newspapers seemed a case in point. "They miss no opportunity to glorify Roosevelt's Rough Riders or the Seventy-first New York Volunteers, . . . yet never a word about this [the 24th Infantry] regiment of colored regulars." Just a week later, the African American *Illinois Record* put it still more bitterly, noting that the Rough Riders had "experienced no feeling of prejudice as they fought side by side with the gallant boys of the Tenth [Cavalry]." Yet "when a negro steals a pair of pants or a ham; commits a rape and is lynched, the average newspapers come out with bold headlines and declare the fact that a big burly negro done so and so." Would the "white friends" of America's black community "soon forget that it was the 10th Cavalry that helped save the day" on that fateful first of July?[23]

In all, an estimated ten thousand African Americans served in one military theater or another during the Spanish-American War and its aftermath. Some of them went because of the prominent black southern leader and founder of Tuskegee Institute, Booker T. Washington, who regarded the occasion as one to express "gratitude" for past "lives laid down" for their country. Others, repeating the same miscalculation by black volunteers for Union service in the Civil War, imagined that they in turn would be recognized by a grateful nation. "Let us be men and show loyalty and we shall be rewarded," predicted a wishful columnist in the *Iowa State Bystander*. But some African American editors promised no more than conditional support for the war—only if black soldiers could serve under officers of their own race, they said, or be promoted above the rank of lieutenant.[24]

African Americans, in fact, had fought in *all* previous American wars, always with the hope of freedom, equality, citizenship, voting—the kinds of promises made in the Thirteenth, Fourteenth, and Fifteenth Amendments to the Constitution after the Civil War but forgotten, limited, or denied by whites later on. The aftermath of the Spanish-American War looked like the same old story: a hypocritical Jim Crow nation filled with bigotry and denying its own black population the same rights that many white Americans had deemed so urgently needed for the oppressed native Cubans. One African American journalist in August 1898 implored racist white Americans to "give the black soldier fair play. Judge him by his battle, not by your prejudices, and he will show you a soldier giving up his life as freely on the altar of Cuban freedom as ever a gallant white did for the honor of our flag." Further, observed another in November 1898, "that the liberty of the colored man is made a mere mockery is seen in the shameless discrimination made against him when he tries to put up at a hotel or eat at a decent restaurant."[25]

For a while, it looked to blacks as if TR's candidacy for governor of New York in the fall of 1898 might offer some hope. From his earlier political career, he had a reputation for fair-mindedness and reform. But then came the April 1899 installment of Roosevelt's articles on the Rough Riders for *Scribner's Magazine*. There, he said that black soldiers in Cuba had generally fought well but that differences existed between the races that should be weighed in deciding to use blacks on a regular basis. They had been, he said, "particularly dependent" on white officers, lacked capacity to lead, had exhibited "extraordinary panic" under fire, and had to be stopped from fleeing during battle. To that, the African American press reacted sharply—and with outrage. "We confess to a feeling of disappointment not unmixed with surprise at Colonel Roosevelt's patronizing reference to these Negro troops whom the press of the whole country and of some parts of Europe heralded as the saviors of the Rough and inexperienced Riders under his command," wrote one black editor. As TR later attempted to explain to Robert J. Fleming of the Tenth Cavalry, "I attributed the trouble to the superstition and fear of the darkey, natural in those but one generation removed from slavery and but a few generations removed from the wildest savagery." That statement, without meaning to, revealed even more his blind spot on matters of race.[26]

Not racial justice but restored sectional harmony among whites took precedence in 1898 and for many years following. This would leave African Americans once again denied fundamental rights and ignored for their contributions and achievements. Roosevelt was now partly responsible for that ongoing injustice. As historian David Blight has written, the war "served the ends of reunion by uniting North and South against a common external foe," but "it also exacerbated [further] racial antagonism." In fact, white promoters of de jure segregation in the South would seize the occasion to harden their racist system all the more and to increase their nostalgic celebration of the old "lost cause" of the Confederacy. Also in years to come, the army would revert to its former policy of keeping its regiments segregated, led entirely by whites except for just the few black officers allowed. Racial discrimination would remain the order of the day in the armed forces, just as it did in society at large. "We are a people, and have a part in the government of the army and country as well as any other race," Prioleau declared. "We belong here. It is our country." When would white Americans stop asking, "What shall we do with the Negro?"[27]

"Strenuous Life"

TR's renown as a war hero proved just barely enough for him to win the New York governorship in November 1898. Although he had campaigned tirelessly for others, especially McKinley in 1896, he had never held an elected position except for a brief period in the New York state assembly prior to his ranching days in Dakota, his only other attempt being a third-place finish for mayor of New York City in 1886. Prior to his Rough Rider days, almost all of TR's political experience had come in appointive positions. State Republican Party boss Sen. Thomas Platt disliked Roosevelt because of the Colonel's unpredictability as a loyal party man and because of his moral crusading—for Sunday saloon closings—as New York City police commissioner.

Still, it had been a propitious time to challenge for the office. TR's surge of popularity came just when incumbent governor Frank Black (also a Republican) lost credibility because of a canal-building scandal. After Roosevelt promised to tow the party mark, Platt agreed to back him, and the campaign was on, whistle-stopping all over the state, a Rough Rider veteran in the caboose sounding a bugle upon every arrival. Then, TR would pop out of the back, waving vigorously to the strains of the local band playing "There'll Be a Hot Time in the Old Town Tonight," a ragtime tune, composed by Theodore August Metz in 1896 and unofficially the regiment's favorite.[28]

But Roosevelt faced enough difficulties during his first several months in office to leave himself wishing "he were fighting Filipinos rather than Boss Platt," according to biographer Kathleen Dalton. He favored Progressive reforms in the Empire State, but the Old Guard Republican establishment there had different ideas. A more sympathetic venue would come as welcome relief, so when the invitation appeared to address an audience of city dignitaries at downtown Chicago's prestigious Hamilton Club on April 10, 1899, he leapt at the chance.[29]

In the days before radio and television, a major speech, heavily reported, would connect an aspiring politician to a national audience. Still basking in his war-hero fame, the Colonel always attracted reporters, but for this event, press attention would intensify in spades. Editors everywhere waited to print what he said, while critics of his jingoism stood ready to pounce. The list of invited guests for the evening included not just prominent men in the city but also political notables from around the country.

Roosevelt's arrival in Chicago quickly turned into a victory festival. Two months had passed since the Senate had ratified the 1899 Paris Treaty, officially transforming the United States into a transoceanic empire, reaching from Puerto Rico in the Caribbean to the Philippines in the Pacific. Now everybody wanted to see "the Hero of San Juan Hill." On the morning of April 10, a crowd gathered around the entrance of his hotel, waiting for the governor to emerge for a busy day of appearances around the city. For this trip, TR had instructed his staff to arrange meetings with groups of younger men, especially those of college age. He saw himself as representing America's future and wanted his public image to match, just as he had designed the Rough Riders to project an optimistic message about Americans and their national character. Others agreed. His well-publicized background and record of service later prompted George P. Morris of Boston to comment that Roosevelt appealed "more strongly to the men of the rising generation than any man in public life to-day." TR's "willingness to take hard knocks and give them" and his "indifference" to the opinions of those "militating against him," said Morris, ennobled him "in the eyes of men who are tired . . . of the time-serving, self-seeking policies and politicians which have had the field since reconstruction days."[30]

Onlookers cheered him along as a carriage took him to the University of Chicago campus. There a student audience treated him to "a storm of cheers and college yells" prior to his informal remarks. A few hours later, TR met with about three hundred members of the city's Harvard Club, lunching in a crimson-decorated dining room so packed that the waiters barely had enough room to serve the meal. And then, after his main speech that evening, he would head for the railroad depot for a Michigan Central train to Ann Arbor, where the next day at the University of Michigan another contingent of students would welcome him.[31]

In Chicago, the Hamilton Club catered to the city's business elite, and since its founding in 1890, the directors had brought in spokesmen for various Republican candidates, including the presidency. In this case, many suspected, they had the future nominee himself. A special printed program announced the celebratory keynote for the evening: "Appomattox Day, the First Day of Peace." The event included a magnificent banquet, featuring a procession of eighteen dishes and a main entree of tenderloin of beef, larded, *au Madère*. Afterward, in an auditorium full of six hundred members and guests, Roosevelt would give the iconic speech of his career, well-suited for the "City of the Big Shoulders."[32]

"I wish to preach, not the doctrine of ignoble ease, but the doctrine of the strenuous life," one of "toil and effort, of labor and strife," Roosevelt said. The "highest form of success" therein would come not to those desiring "mere easy peace" but to men who did "not shrink from danger" or hardship. As on previous occasions, he invoked recollection of the past—in this case, a shared northern memory of the Civil War: Lincoln and Grant, victorious armies, the "iron in the blood of our fathers," the men of 1861 who had valued Union above peace. An American society that had lost its "manly and adventurous qualities," he argued, could prove no more worthy among nations than an individual without such virtues could among the most powerful peers. All that, of course, involved choices. Like the war of 1898 against Spain, that of 1861 did not have to be fought, nor did men who served, like young Oliver Wendell Holmes Jr., have to volunteer. But to have avoided the suffering "would have shown that we were weaklings, . . . unfit to stand among the great nations of the earth."[33]

The speech, moreover, carried a message for isolationists and anti-imperialists: "We cannot sit huddled within our borders and avow ourselves merely an assemblage of well-to-do hucksters who care nothing for what happens beyond." If Americans had driven out a "medieval tyranny" (Spain) only to "make room for savage anarchy" (native Cubans and Filipinos), better not to have made the effort at all. Naval and commercial supremacy, the building of an isthmian canal, and a new "legacy of duty" toward Cuba, the Philippines, and Puerto Rico—these tasks, in the wake of victory in 1898, would test whether "we are worth our salt" as a modern civilized nation. If the United States were to avert this role, then "some stronger, manlier power" assuredly would assume its place, leaving Americans to accept the consequences of their own indecision. By the black-and-white logic TR espoused, if expansionists were "noble," "manly," and "strenuous," then their opposition had to be cowardly, effeminate, and halfhearted.[34]

Like Mahan, Roosevelt turned upside down the idea that strong military forces posed a standing threat to America's own security, arguing in Chicago, as he had before in Newport, that old-fashioned soldierly virtues would save rather than ruin the republic. "Our army has never been built up as it should be built up," he said, venturing far beyond his gubernatorial purview, and it was "puerile" to think that "a nation of seventy millions of freemen is in danger of losing its liberties" from having "an army of one hundred thousand men, three-quarters of whom will be employed in certain foreign islands, . . . coast fortresses, and on Indian reservations." Besides, as he had said before, military service built character, making Americans a better, more disciplined people. "There is no body from which the country has less to fear," he insisted, "and none of which it should be prouder, none which it should be more anxious to upbuild."[35]

On the Philippines, which had most sharply divided the Senate in the Paris Treaty ratification debate, Roosevelt took a stand that he would later reverse as president. More complicated than governing the Caribbean island of Puerto Rico, the native Filipinos presented problems of diversity and volatility, including "half caste and native Christians, warlike Moslems, and wild pagans"—in all, he declared, "utterly unfit for self-government." It would be "cowardly" to "shrink" from the supervision, "at once firm and beneficent," that in TR's mind linked to responsible parenting. To leave "savage anarchy" in place of "Spanish tyranny" could not conform to the responsibilities of "civilized" nations. Further, as he had said regarding Hawaii, "if we are too weak, too selfish, or too foolish" to take on the problem of the Philippines, then "some bolder and abler people must undertake the solution." Besides, the benefits of imperial governance would accrue to Americans at home, as in the British Empire: "England's rule in India and Egypt has been of great benefit to England, for it has trained up generations of men accustomed to look at the larger and loftier side of public life."[36]

It all sounded more like a presidential speech than it did the musings of a state governor. The Rough Riders had given him the credibility he needed for it—the "pulpit," as opposed to a voice alone, that he would transfer to the presidency.

Few, if any, of the ideas in the speech had originated with TR. Throughout his political life he used public opportunities to reflect and promote views that he favored—from Holmes's to Alfred Thayer Mahan's and those of many others. In the June 1897 number of *Atlantic Monthly,* for example, historian Henry C. Mervin had bemoaned the "over-sophisticated and effete" type of American as "a being in whom the springs of action are, in a greater or lesser degree, paralyzed or perverted by the undue prominence of the intellect." Further, "when the instinct [of pugnacity] is weakened," Mervin continued, "they hire others to fight for them, as the Romans did in their decadence." Many more readers likely encountered the lamentations of Basil Ransom, Henry James's tradition-conscious, Mississippi-born protagonist in his 1886 novel *The Bostonians*: "the whole generation is womanized; the masculine tone is passing out of the world; it's a feminine, a nervous, hysterical, chattering, canting age," full of "hollow phrases and false delicacy and exaggerated solicitudes and coddled sensibilities, which, if we don't look out, will usher in a reign of mediocrity." And the antidote? "The masculine character, the ability to dare and endure, to know and yet not fear reality, to look the world in the face and take it for what it is . . . that is what I want to preserve, or rather, as I may say, recover," says Ransom, in terms that Roosevelt would echo again and again.[37]

Perhaps because his views sounded so familiar, the governor's speech impressed many newspaper writers, especially Republican ones. When Roosevelt arrived in Ann Arbor, the local *Argus* declared him "a typical American," despite his wealth and social position, and praised the "democratic spirit" along with his courage in battle that had made him a "popular hero." If successful in the governorship of the Empire State, then "the highest position in the gift of the people is easily within his reach." The *Weekly Herald* in Phoenix, where many Rough Riders had enlisted, called the Chicago speech "an inspired address." The *Los Angeles Express* commented, "We have theorists in plenty; we have reformers who cannot reform when they have a chance; we have men apparently devoid of patriotism, selfish in money making, or in 'slothful ease,' but we have few men like the brave young Governor of New York." Whitelaw Reid's *New York Tribune* found that the speech had captured the prevailing sentiment of the country, likely to "be influential in extending and fortifying" the sentiment that the nation's "new duties" in foreign affairs "must be met."[38]

Roosevelt always branded his opponents as worse than they were—stupid, corrupt, unpatriotic, unmanly, and whatever else. As a result, they answered in force. "That his exaggerated bellicose traits of character should prove attractive to Christian ministers and editors of the religious press is perhaps the most surprising thing observed in a long while," wrote one anti-imperialist editor, who judged Roosevelt to be "medieval" because he "glorifies brute force," having "much in common with the present German emperor" (Kaiser Wilhelm II). Meanwhile, in Cambridge, William James, once Roosevelt's anatomy professor at Harvard, ridiculed him as locked in the "sturm and drang period of early adolescence." While "gushing over war as the ideal condition of human society for the manly strenuousness which it involves," the Colonel had treated peace as "a condition of blubber-like and swollen ignobility." An anti-jingo editor in Montana wrote that Roosevelt had "become the apostle of war, violence, turbulence, excitement, alarms, processions of uniformed men carrying weapons of death; gore is a pleasing sight to his eyes, the smell of new-shed human blood agreeable in his nostrils." Another, in Kansas City, thought TR a "misguided zealot," whose imploring of people to live strenuously denigrated the daily efforts of ordinary men and women who faced no choice but to work "from early morning till late at night," priding themselves only as "brave competitors in the struggle for success" and bearing the "ills and aches" of "endless attention to domestic duties."[39]

The speech also made Roosevelt a target for critics of US policy in the Philippines. His "strenuous" philosophy seemed to portend further expansion in all directions, like the British and the Germans. One editorial suggested that if the philosophy applied generally, it should encourage the Filipinos to "even more endeavor" in the struggle for freedom against the new aggressor, the Americans, than they had against the Spaniards. If TR wanted a true challenge to American strength, we ought to pick on a foreign foe our own size rather than "carry death among savage tribes." Another, in Baltimore, recalling Shakespeare, commented that the New York governor seemed unsatisfied with the "ignoble arts and pursuits of peace," preferring instead, "at all times with 'shield and sword,' to cry 'Havoc, and let loose the dogs of war.'" For a true reflection of the Philippine war and its lack of nobility, that columnist advised, consider the words, published in the *Spokane Review*, of a US army volunteer in Manila: "We burned hundreds of houses and looted hundreds more. Some of the boys made good hauls of jewelry and clothing. Nearly every man has at least two suits of clothing and our quarters are furnished in style."[40]

"Expansionists"

First had come the conquest, then the political decisions to justify it. The issue that most divided opposing sides was the continuing US war in the Philippines, which began as part of the Spanish-American War. Commodore Dewey had sunk the Spanish fleet in Manila Bay. After that, President McKinley sent in the ground forces that took the city on August 13, 1898. Then, the peace treaty with Spain, signed in December and ratified the following February, ceded the Philippines to the United States, along with other territorial gains. Thereafter, American expansionists would learn, slowly, what their European counterparts already knew: subordinated peoples wanted the modernization that advanced nations enjoyed, but they wished even more to dismiss their imperialist rulers and govern themselves.

In the midst of it all, in early fall 1900, Josiah Strong's new book, *Expansion, Under New-World Conditions*, appeared. "New responsibilities confront us, new possibilities invite us, new necessities compel us," the author declared, appealing especially to American Protestants who already shared his Anglo-Saxon, Christian-missionary view of the world. The objections of anti-imperialists notwithstanding, Strong's arguments would prove hard to refute. Few went further in gathering all the interrelated themes of American imperialism in a single place. Strong's 1885 tract, *Our Country*, had sold well, and since that time, he had become both a good friend and an ideological ally of Alfred Thayer Mahan, a matching of minds that TR had arranged.[41]

In laying out a new political economy of American empire, Strong, too, reflected others' ideas more than he originated any of his own. The book reflected major changes since 1885: the supposed "closing" of the frontier, industrial expansion, the depression of 1893, the "jingo" element in national politics, the success of the Spanish-American War, the 1899 Treaty of Paris, and the conversion of the United States from a continental empire into a transoceanic one. To that it added a heavy dose of social Darwinism combined with deep-rooted Christian belief. Mahan had read the chapters in draft form and made suggestions that Strong incorporated. The work thus reflected Mahan's later thoughts, post-1898, as it did Strong's.[42]

Both men believed that energy and capital previously devoted to developing a continent now should be "turned in other directions"—a new empire based on maritime power, like Great Britain's. While Spain's influence had plummeted, pressures of international competition still increased. The potential threat to US interests emanated from other manufacturing-based countries. In France, for example, economist Pierre Paul Leroy-Beaulieu urged that his nation grow into a great African power or else become a secondary European one. The German press increasingly amplified the drumbeat for a "Greater Germany." Expansionists in Italy, too, looked to establish a foothold in tropical parts of the world, as did those in Russia and Japan. "The greatest lines of commerce have been between the East and the West," Strong instructed. "The time is likely to come when they will run between the North and the South, the temperate regions and the tropics."[43]

As in *Our Country* and his other writings, deep racial and ethnic prejudices laced almost everything Strong wrote on imperialism. In this, he would have found few exceptions among his elite circle of acquaintances, which included Roosevelt. In the post–Civil War era, "the negro" had been "thrown into the midst of an advanced industrial system, and of matured political and religious institutions," Strong asserted, speaking for most other white people of the time. "All he can do is to accept them and to adjust himself to them in a passive spirit." By contrast, the Anglo-Saxon "race"—that is, the English-speaking peoples of the world—had long since emerged from "barbarism," developed free institutions and a "high industrial civilization," and evolved "a strength and fibre of character" not found in most other modern cultures. That assumption converted into an automatic justification for imperial domination of peoples living in tropical parts of the globe—more a matter of a white contempt for racial "inferiors" than of "taking up the white man's burden," in Kipling's phrase. "Among races, as among individuals," Strong averred, distinguishing especially between peoples of tropical and temperate zones, "there will be permanent differences of temperament and tendency, of adaption and skill."[44]

Commercially, the Panic of 1893 had shaken many Americans and sobered some. For Strong, it exposed the vulnerability of domestic manufacturers who relied too much on the home market as opposed to an expanded foreign one for the goods they produced. In the five years after the financial collapse, according to data he had gathered, the excess of US exports over imports had increased almost eightfold, and exports of manufactured goods in 1898 exceeded imports for the first time in the country's history. But would those gains continue? Not, Strong argued, without the new American empire that he and other imperialists now envisioned. For key resources of coal and iron, low labor costs, and cheap raw materials, the United States held advantages over competing industrial nations. But in years to come, America's economic prospects of empire would hinge on another essential change: the building of the shipping canal through Central America, converting a one-ocean economy into a two-ocean one and taking full advantage of the recent Pacific acquisitions, especially Hawaii and the Philippines. "We lie midway between Europe and Africa on the east and Asia and Australasia on the west, while another continent adjoins us on the south; and when the isthmian canal is cut, it will emphasize the advantages of our position." That canal, anticipated to go through Nicaragua, would reduce the distance from New York to San Francisco from 14,840 to 4,760 miles, saving 10,000 miles and fifty days of freight-steamer time, and tie the commerce of the north and south Atlantic coasts, as well as the Mississippi Valley, with that of the Pacific, reaching as far as Asia. Once the US Navy grew strong enough to protect that trade, control of markets throughout the Far East would transfer to the United States.[45]

Before 1900, the "Far East" mostly had meant the China trade. But even after the Boxer Rebellion, Strong sensed no cause for alarm. Under benign foreign influence, the western-inspired "innovations once feared and hated are already become necessities." Books and maps and matches, carriages, scientific instruments and the telegraph, nails, cotton and iron and steel, printing paper, flour and meats and butter and salt, lumber and wood products of all kinds—China offered a vast market for nearly everything. As Indiana senator Albert J. Beveridge had told the Senate during the Paris treaty debate, everything hinged on development of the Pacific empire that now lay at the feet of decision makers in Congress.[46]

Alternatively, what if no canal were built, the China trade remained as it was, and the anti-imperialists were to prevail? Then, Strong said, economic disaster would follow, along with an unraveling of values that had supported the republic. Labor strikes, radical doctrines, and violence could proliferate and become the norm. "Our cities already contain quite enough dynamite for the safety of civilization," he advised. Representative institutions might fail and be replaced by rule of force under an American tyrant. "Either some Caesar or Napoleon will seize the reins of government with a strong hand, or your republic will be as fearfully plundered and laid waste by barbarians in the twentieth century as the Roman Empire was in the fifth." But with one major difference: the "Huns and Vandals" who ravaged Rome "came from without, and . . . your Huns and Vandals will have been engendered within your own country."⁴⁷

Avoiding that fate, the Pacific Ocean could become for the United States what the Mediterranean had once been for the Romans. Others had prophesied the same. Half a century before, Prussian explorer Baron Alexander von Humboldt had predicted that the commerce of the Pacific would in time exceed that of the Atlantic. Lincoln's secretary of state, William H. Seward, who in 1867 had engineered the purchase of Alaska, believed that a transoceanic arc of empire from North America to China might one day become the central theater of world events and remain so for centuries. All the more reason, then, for the United States to keep the Philippines and its other Pacific holdings, however many "savages or semi-civilized tribes" occupied those islands. To let the Philippines go would mean to diminish the power of "Anglo-Saxon Civilization" in favor, most likely, of the most antithetical alternative: Russia, which also bordered on the Pacific, held massive geographical resources, and whose civilization depended not on civil and religious liberty but "for its very existence on the suppression of the individual."⁴⁸

So, looking ahead from 1900, as a new century dawned, Strong articulated the optimistic vision of American imperialists. The "New World" empire of the United States would offer something industrially sturdier, politically wiser, and morally better than other empires of the past. As for America's struggle to govern the Philippines and its ongoing supervision of Cuba, Strong restated the default justification that had already become US policy: "freedom is a matter of character. Men become free only so far as they learn self-government. . . . Giving a tribe independence no more confers upon it freedom than letting an anarchist out of jail confers on him a love of law." Moreover, the "civilized races" with higher "moral fiber" had the right, even the obligation, to police the supposedly less advanced ones—the exact creed that would underlie the Roosevelt Corollary to the Monroe Doctrine of 1904 and the "Big Stick" diplomacy toward Latin America to follow.⁴⁹

"Anti-Imperialists"

Let us pray: "O Lord our Father, our young patriots, idols of our hearts, go forth to battle—be Thou near them!" a stranger, suddenly replacing the regular minister, instructed the surprised congregation. "With them—in spirit—we also go forth from the sweet peace of our beloved firesides to smite the foe. O Lord our God, help us to tear their soldiers to bloody shreds with our shells; help us to cover their smiling fields with the pale forms of their patriot dead; help us to drown the thunder of the guns with the shrieks of their wounded, writhing in pain; help us to lay waste their humble homes with a hurricane of fire."

The visitor went on, his spellbound listeners still rapt in their attention, savoring every word. "Help us to wring the hearts of their unoffending widows with unavailing grief; help us to turn them out roofless with their little children to wander unfriended the wastes of their desolated land in rags and hunger and thirst."

> "Lord, blast their hopes, blight their lives, protract their bitter pilgrimage, make heavy their steps, water their way with their tears, stain the white snow with the blood of their wounded feet! We ask it, in the spirit of love, of Him Who is the Source of Love, and Who is the ever-faithful refuge and friend of all that are sore beset and seek His aid with humble and contrite hearts. Amen."

(After a pause.) "Ye have prayed it; if ye still desire it, speak! The messenger of the Most High waits!"

It was believed afterward that the man was a lunatic, because there was no sense in what he said.[50]

So wrote America's most famous man of letters, Mark Twain, in a short story mocking his country's intervention in the Philippines. Anti-imperialist groups, though never dominant, had proliferated around the country. Their perspective resembled that of the jingoes in one—perhaps *only* one—key respect: they, too, drew much of their inspiration from the early republic in American history.

Twain would serve as vice president of the American Anti-Imperialist League for most of his late life, from 1901 until 1909, the year before he died. His fame as a writer gave his voice weight in public. Under exclusive contract with Harper & Brothers, he submitted the story in 1905 to *Harper's Bazaar*, a ladies' magazine, entitling it "The War Prayer." *Harper's* rejected it as inappropriate for the female subscribers. Unsurprised, Twain remarked to his friend Daniel Carter Beard, "I don't think the prayer will be published in my time. None but the dead are permitted to tell the truth." Because the contract bound him from shopping the story elsewhere, it remained unpublished until 1923. It would be republished later, during the Vietnam War, appealing then to dissenters of another time.[51]

By 1900, the disillusioned, 65-year-old Twain had become a bitter social critic of the way that American jingoes had overreached the moral limits of imperial expansion. He had not believed so all along, however. In spring 1898, when the Spanish-American War started, he was in Vienna, Austria, on a lecture tour of Europe. Twain had long favored American control of Hawaii, and judging from media reports, he thought Dewey's triumph at Manila Bay to have been a brilliant first stroke in one the noblest wars ever fought. As he wrote to his Hartford, Connecticut, friend Rev. Joseph H. Twichell, "It is a worthy thing to fight for one's freedom; it is another sight finer to fight for another man's. And I think this is the first time it has been done." In July, he relished the reports of Admiral Sampson's annihilation of Spanish naval forces in the waters outside Santiago.[52]

But over the next few months, his opinion began to shift. A letter from another close friend, the anti-imperialist editor and novelist William Dean Howells, had suggested that America's sacrifice for "humanity" had actually changed "into war for coaling stations." Soon after, in 1899, came the Boer War in South Africa, pitting the Dutch-settled Boer—or Afrikaner—states in the interior against the English-controlled coastal provinces to the south. Along with most Americans, Twain privately sympathized with the Boers as beleaguered combatants against the imperial British. But in public, as he traveled through England early in 1900, visiting friends and reaping adulation as a celebrity, he remained noncommital.[53]

Then, when the Boxer Rebellion in China broke out in summer 1899, the famous author revealed truer feelings. The rebellion, a nationalist, anti-foreign uprising against western (and Japanese) influence, especially targeting Christian proselytizers who were equated with imperial domination, aimed at driving the intruders out of China and restoring the country's ancient traditions. In doing so, the rebels marauded over the countryside for some forty-five days, burning and slashing, mutilating and murdering the "foreign devils." By the time that armed forces sent from eight nations with commercial interests in China, including the United States, finally brought order in summer 1901, thousands of missionaries and their Chinese converts had perished. In America, however, the whole episode had raised further questions about the rightness of American imperial involvement in the Far East. "We have no more business in China than in any other country that is not ours," Twain told a *New York World* reporter in early October 1900, as he prepared to sail home. Shortly thereafter, speaking in New York City, he declared: "It is the foreigners who are making all the trouble in China. . . . The Boxer is a patriot; he is the only patriot China has, and I wish him success."[54]

Still, the issue that mattered most to Twain and most other anti-imperialists was American conduct in the Philippines. The Boers were confronting the British Empire, not an American one. US interests in China and support of Christian missionaries there represented only a part of the overall foreign incursion. But after Dewey's victory at Manila Bay and the success of American troops, twenty thousand of them, in driving the Spaniards out, the decisions regarding those South Pacific islands and their 8 million native inhabitants had been American ones. "We come, not as invaders or conquerors, but as friends to protect the natives in their homes, in their employments, and in their personal and religious rights," McKinley had proclaimed. The Filipinos were expected to accept gratefully a "benevolent assimilation" to the will of their new rulers. But in the eyes of Filipino insurgents, led by Emilio Aguinaldo, that meant only the substitution of American tyranny for that of the Spanish and, as it turned out, similarly brutal methods as well. Approached by a *New York Herald* scribe shortly after his ship arrived home, Twain said he had left New World shores at Vancouver in summer 1895 as "red-hot" as any imperialist and wanted "the American eagle to go screaming into the Pacific." But now he had read the Treaty of Paris and seen that "we do not intend to free but to subjugate[,] . . . to conquer, not to redeem." Returning home, he opposed "having the eagle put its talons on any other land."[55]

As a critic of American imperialism, the curmudgeonly Twain stood more and more in distinguished company. The number of anti-expansionist voices had been growing steadily since the anti-imperialist meeting at Faneuil Hall in June 1898. In one example, on January 16, 1899, just weeks before Senate ratification of the Paris treaty, a 59-year old Yale professor planted himself behind the podium at College Street Hall in New Haven. William Graham Sumner, a classical liberal social scientist who believed in minimal government and whose 1883 book *What Social Classes Owe to Each Other* had marked him as America's foremost social Darwinist, had been invited to address the university's Phi Beta Kappa Society. Encapsulating the anti-imperialist view, Sumner entitled his lecture "The Conquest of the United States by Spain." Imperial expansion conflicted "with the best traditions, principles, and interests of the American people," he contended, and would "plunge us into a network of difficult problems and political perils, which we might have avoided, while they offer us no corresponding advantage in return."[56]

To Sumner, the jingo arguments amounted to "delusions," the products of "partisan tactics and the strife of parties" in Washington, appealing to "national vanity" and "national cupidity." More statesmanlike leaders should be "hard-headed enough to resist them." Wars of choice, like America's of 1898, sprang from "a policy of adventure and of gratuitous enterprise." They could be expected to produce unexpected—and undesirable—consequences and, indeed, "embarrassments," such as this one now resulting "with the Philippines on our hands." The wiser foreign policy, Sumner thought, would have resonated with that of American leaders over a hundred years earlier: "What comes to us in the evolution of our own life and interests, that we must meet; what we do to seek which lies beyond that domain is a waste of our energy and a compromise of our liberty and welfare."

If the demise of Spain's empire, built on "national pride and ambition," had not been enough of a cautionary tale, Sumner told his audience, then the case of the British Empire should have been, especially for the United States. "The Phariseeism with which they [the English] correct and instruct other people has made them hated all over the globe." For that matter, he added, the French, the Germans, the Russians, and even the "Mohammedans"—all, along with the Spanish, had spoken of themselves as having a "civilizing mission." And now, Americans, in a way "grossly and obviously untrue," assumed the same regarding Cubans, Puerto Ricans, and Filipinos. "They hate our ways. . . . Our religion, language, institutions, and manners offend them. . . . [A]nd if we appear amongst them as rulers, there will be social discord. . . . The most important thing which we shall inherit from the Spaniards will be the task of suppressing rebellions."[57]

"He's Galloping"

Not since 1844, when Democratic candidate James K. Polk won a narrow victory on a platform of "Manifest Destiny," had a battle for the presidency so much involved questions of US foreign policy. That of 1900 presented the voters with fundamental choices about the character, content, and direction of American empire. Would the majority respond approvingly of the Republican incumbent, McKinley, and the jingo philosophy he had embraced, albeit gradually? Put another way, would they endorse the Republicans' expansionist faction, now spearheaded by the Rough Rider hero, Theodore Roosevelt?

The alternative was the anti-imperial vision now promulgated by the Democrats and their nominee, again William Jennings Bryan. The famous Nebraskan hoped to turn the campaign narrative, and the election, away from the jingoism of the Republicans and toward the domestic, primarily rural, issues that most concerned his Midwestern constituency. But the odds seemed to favor the Grand Old Party. The return of prosperity after the Panic of 1893, the winning of a brief war against Spain, and the addition of a major hero of that war, Roosevelt, to the Republican ticket as the vice presidential nominee would seem, in all, to favor McKinley even more than in 1896.

Roosevelt's ability as a campaigner stood well-established, as did his popular appeal. An irony of his being placed on the ticket was that the McKinley administration, if reelected, might not care to have him around. Nor did he think much of them. By summer 1899, TR had concluded that the president and Secretary of State John Hay had not been aggressive enough in suppressing the Aguinaldo rebellion in the Philippines. They had, at first, preferred diplomacy instead of the military force he believed necessary for stability and, after that, strict colonial rule for a time. "We have the wolf by the ears and we cannot let him go safely," he wrote to Baltimore banker Bartlett S. Johnston on September 4, 1899, paraphrasing the metaphor that Thomas Jefferson had employed in 1820, during the Missouri crisis, to characterize the dilemma of slaveholding.[58]

Historians telling the story of TR's nomination as McKinley's running mate have emphasized Sen. Thomas Platt's successful conniving to free the New York Old Guard from their annoying reformist governor. In that version, Roosevelt, ever loyal to his party, grudgingly accepted the role, even voting against himself at the Republican Convention. And yet some evidence supports a different interpretation: that he wanted the position, knowing that his Rough Rider reputation could win it. Republicans other than Platt thought the ticket needed some energizing, the president benefiting from the young man leading the charge. Lodge, in particular, saw his young friend as more useful not by slaying dragons in Albany but in returning to the nation's capital and taking a hand in foreign policy.[59]

True, Roosevelt felt reservations about playing second fiddle on the ticket. Historically, the vice presidency had been a political dead end, and his ambition burned for the top job, at least by 1904, before public memory of "San

Juan Hill" began to fade. Edith was happy in Albany; the governor's salary, considerably more than the vice president's, freed them from financial troubles, and she worried about the effect on him of four "comparatively inactive years" in Washington. On the other hand, everybody knew that Roosevelt craved to be the center of attention, which he would be, more so than McKinley, in the campaign to come. No question he had "Potomac fever," sought the limelight, and reveled in media coverage—all the more so after the Rough Riders had made him famous. The governorship of New York promised only a two-year term, and none of three immediate predecessors, two of them Republicans, had lasted more than one term. Reelection, if Governor Roosevelt wanted it, might be no more assured in 1900 than his narrow election, by just 17,794 votes, in 1898. Beyond all that, if anyone could transform the second-highest federal office into a stepping stone to the presidency, the charismatic TR could.[60]

If Roosevelt had been loath to take the vice presidency, his public behavior that June at the Republican National Convention in Philadelphia hardly showed it. Scribes covering the first day found the governor's theatrical appearance in the Exposition Auditorium—well-calculated, of course—to be the lead story. As one wrote, "At 12:02 [p.m.] the first pronounced demonstration in the convention occurred. Roosevelt came in through the main entrance and moved down the centre aisle. He wore the Rough Rider's hat and was instantly recognized. A deep reverberating cheer greeted him." At that moment, men jumped atop their chairs to applaud him, and women fluttered their handkerchiefs in the fashion of the day. The delegates crowded forward to see him, as if paying homage to a great conqueror. Soaking up every accolade, TR proceeded to his seat with the New York delegation, to the rear of Senator Platt and just in front of New York senator Chauncey Depew. Then, at 12:30, "the band broke into the stirring strains of 'The Star Spangled Banner.' Governor Roosevelt was the first on his feet in response to the national anthem. His Rough Rider hat came off, and he stood with head uncovered. Instantly the whole convention rose en masse." After that, convention chairman, Senator Mark Hanna of Ohio, who despised TR as much as Platt did, "faced the storm of applause with a resolute face" and gaveled the convention to order. It was "a matter of record," noted one Ohio newspaper, that Hanna was "bitterly antagonistic" to the idea of putting TR on the ticket and that he tried to smash the Roosevelt boom at the convention. "No doubt he [Hanna] foresaw the trouble that would come from the appearance of the irrepressible

Teddy as lieutenant colonel of the Republican regiment. There was danger that the lieutenant colonel would forget the colonel and the entire regiment and imagine himself 'the whole thing.' It is a way Teddy has."[61]

In all of this—the overtly dramatic entrance, the Rough Rider headgear, his conspicuous display of patriotism, his welcoming of curious onlookers, his upstaging of Hanna, and the pretense of traditional (small-r) republican restraint in declining to vote for himself—Roosevelt showed how much the job interested him. Perhaps he was only trying to register his claim to 1904. But the only real question at the 1900 convention was who would get the nomination as McKinley's running mate. TR did not refuse. More than that, he did nothing at all to dissuade popular acclaim. Of course, the nomination was his to accept all along.

That same summer, the Democrats nominated Bryan, hoping for a better result than before. The "Great Commoner" of Nebraska featured charismatic qualities of his own that the Republican incumbent lacked: youth, oratorical brilliance, a rich voice, an evangelical style, and authentic sympathy for white Americans who felt downtrodden, disillusioned, and underrepresented. But improving economic conditions worked against him this time and made it easy for Republicans to claim prosperity at home along with conquest overseas.

Adding Roosevelt, the Republican Party infused its campaign with a restless energy that perfectly counterbalanced McKinley's mellower, nonconfrontational temperament. The president had never been much of a campaigner anyway and much preferred to spend the late summer rusticating at his home in Canton, Ohio, while Roosevelt, Hanna, and others took care of reelection chores. The New York governor, by contrast, furnished hell on wheels as a stump speaker, equaling if not surpassing Bryan. In a column poking fun at McKinley's passive politicking, *Chicago Journal* pundit Finley Peter Dunne had his comical Irish bartender Mr. Dooley quip: "'Tis Tiddy alone that's running, and he ain't running, he's galloping." TR's opinion of Bryan had changed not an iota since 1896. If Roosevelt held mixed feelings about McKinley, he despised the "Boy Orator," recoiled from his religiosity, and considered him an anti-elitist demagogue of the worst kind. He regarded the Democratic Party platform of 1900, its rehash of 1890s populism, the standard promise of lower tariffs, and yet another inflationary free silver plank—all seasoned this time with an anti-imperialist condemnation of the 1899 Treaty of Paris—as "criminal," "vicious," and "fundamentally an attack on civilization."[62]

Again, Roosevelt's intemperate language made some listeners recoil even more than did his imperialist views. The campaign had just begun when one editor, though pro-Republican, took exception to an "injudicious" speech TR made in St. Paul, Minnesota, declaring that Democrats stood "for lawlessness and disorder, for dishonesty and dishonor, for license and disaster at home and cowardly shrinking from duty abroad." Could it be, asked another in the *Washington Post*, that voters' eyes would be so "dimmed by the smoke and dazzled by the glare of San Juan" that they could miss the Colonel's impulsiveness as a major flaw in a potential leader? "Roosevelt is brilliant and aggressive, earnest and eloquent, but the qualities that he most conspicuously lacks are those which come first in the equipment of a safe president of the United States in troublous times."[63]

As for Roosevelt's expansionism, especially regarding the Philippines, Illinois Democrat and former governor John Peter Altgeld called it simply a justification for "land-grabbing" and for doing the "bidding" of Great Britain. Sixto Lopez, former secretary to the Filipino commission in Washington, took angry exception to TR's comparison of the Filipino rebels to the Boxers in China and the Apache Indians of the American Southwest. Nor was it true, Lopez insisted, that the Filipino government resembled a "bloody Aguinaldoan oligarchy." Others asked whether the story of the Colonel's heroism in Cuba reflected more fraud than fact. In *The Rough Riders*, had he not admitted being uncertain of the enemy position during the Las Guásimas affair? Was it not true that his knowledge of the assault on the actual San Juan Hill (as opposed to Kettle Hill) came from long-distance observation? "Such is Roosevelt's claim to heroism and military genius as presented by himself," wrote one pro-Democratic critic. His insensitive comments about black soldiers in the April 1899 *Scribner's* article came back to haunt him, too, despite the governor's efforts to placate the African American press, belatedly calling the "Afro-American soldier . . . a first-class fighting man."[64]

At one stop that September in Victor, Colorado, pro-Bryan elements in the crowd, armed with sticks and clubs, rotten potatoes, stale eggs, and lemons, had prepared to retaliate against TR's provocative words. Scheduled to speak at the packed Armory Hall, Roosevelt had only begun when "noisy demonstrations" erupted, leading to angry exchanges with the candidate. One campaign lie he would not brook was the accusation of being cowardly under fire, and when one of the louts impugned his war record, TR retorted "you will never get near enough [to a battle] to be hit with a bullet, or within five miles of it." Afterward, as he walked back to the train, surrounded by one of many local entourages of "Rough Riders," now converted into bodyguards, one angry demonstrator got close enough to whack him across the chest. An Associated Press man on the scene reported that "the crowd began throwing stones and shouting for Bryan." A similar event occurred the following month in Elmira, New York, mostly involving rotten eggs, an assortment of vegetables, and "the vilest epithets." Recovering his composure this time, TR simply dismissed the behavior as "nasty conduct, the conduct of hoodlums."[65]

But in most of his campaign stops, TR received rousing, peaceful, and more supportive welcomes. When his midnight special train from Detroit rolled into Bay City, Michigan, at 7:00 a.m. on September 8, Roosevelt and his traveling corps, which always included several press correspondents, met his usual escort of "Rough Riders" (townsfolk volunteering on his behalf) and headed for Central Avenue Park. In his speech there, he stressed the usual Republican campaign themes of prosperity, national honor, and how the fight against Spain had tested a new generation of Americans. "You at Bay City sent your sons to the Spanish war as their fathers before them had gone to the great war. It was but a small war, but it showed the spirit of the people. It showed they had not forgotten the lesson taught in the great contest of '61 to '65."[66]

Election Day brought the predictable Republican victory—McKinley's 292 electoral votes to Bryan's 155. The "Commoner," having grossly misjudged his chances of a second go-round victory against the Ohio favorite, went away deeply disappointed. He had lost heavily in western states that the Democrats had carried four years before, including Kansas, Washington, Wyoming, Utah, South Dakota, and even his home state of Nebraska—all places where TR's western reputation and Rough Rider fame had eroded Democratic strength.

"A Dreadful Thing"

Darkening skies threatened to soak the throng of onlookers gathered at the Capitol on March 4, 1901, as William McKinley, the last Union veteran to sit in the White House, prepared to take the presidential oath of office for the second and final time. The rain in Washington had continued over much of the previous night and, despite the moderately rising temperatures of that morning, the day felt clammy, wet, and cold. It was the first presidential inauguration to be recorded in moving pictures, thanks to Thomas Edison's 1893

Kinetoscope, though the footage ran only forty-five seconds. The dignitaries present assembled on the East Portico. They included the inaugural committee of Marcus Hanna, John Spooner, and James Jones of the Senate, along with Speaker Joe Cannon, John Dalzell, and Thomas McRae of the House. Under a covered platform, rain drops spattering on the canvas above, Chief Justice Melville W. Fuller handled the swearing in: first, the new vice president, Theodore Roosevelt, then McKinley.

Attired in a black suit and black overcoat and clutching his speech in his left hand, the president had to project his voice to the crowd, as politicians did in the days before microphones. In the preceding few years, as the ledger closed on the nineteenth century, the revival of commercial and industrial profits indicated that the hard times of the mid-1890s, still evident when McKinley took office, had ended at last. Stocks soared on Wall Street. Men of wealth grew much richer while a recovering white middle class partook of heightened comforts as well. The American people, with the highest per capita income in the world, lived better than they ever had. All this despite the continuing rivalry between impoverished labor and fattened bosses that denoted further troubles to come.

Other sweeping changes had occurred in what seemed the blink of an eye. Americans felt more global, enlightened, and advanced than ever. Popular magazines now referred to exotic places like Hawaii, Guam, and the Philippines as if no reader any longer found them strange. Medical advances, such as Wilhelm Roentgen's X-ray device and Walter Reed's identification of the mosquito that transmitted yellow fever, promised a new century of improved public health. Technological progress registered everywhere, as modern machines and the proliferation of electricity revolutionized daily life. Newfangled automobiles increasingly startled wide-eyed pedestrians and carriage drivers on town streets, sending frightened chickens scurrying for safety. Modern marvels appeared even in places like William McKinley's Canton, Ohio, where the president one day enjoyed a noisy outing in a new Stanley Steamer. In all, the possibilities for progress seemed limitless, the future never brighter. And to top everything, the United States had suddenly become a world power.[67]

But the challenges of becoming a new empire had intensified divisions among lawmakers, especially in the Senate, where opinions still diverged sharply on the course of foreign policy. McKinley's Republicans, the majority party, stood united, except for a few outliers who joined the anti-imperialists.

As the inauguration had approached, McKinley and his advisers monitored anxiously both the Cuban constitutional convention in Havana, in session since November, and the situation in the Philippines. In Cuba, Governor General Leonard Wood tried to enforce a contradictory mandate: on the one hand, to guide Cuban leaders in organizing an independent republic, on the other, getting them to accept a US protective interest in both their domestic governance and their relations with other nations.

The Teller amendment, disclaiming any US intent to annex Cuba, had stipulated that political control would be left to its own people after the war, but it stated no process for doing so. With the Spanish now defeated, could American forces just withdraw without destabilizing the island and endangering American financial and strategic interests? The same question would haunt American foreign interventions for generations to come. Finally, a solution of sorts seemed to emerge when Senator Orville Platt, chairman of the Committee on Cuban Relations, and Secretary of War Elihu Root collaborated on a set of provisions to be attached to the Army Appropriations Bill. The Platt amendment, later approved on March 2, 1901, would require Cuba never to agree to a treaty with a foreign power that would impair its independence, reserving to the United States the right to intervene, if necessary.

McKinley's words on March 4 evoked patriotic celebration of the war's success but also marked a shift in the nature of the republic. He had tried "all that in honor could be done" to avert the war, the president said, truthfully. Nevertheless, "it came," and with it the "signally favorable" results now imposed on American "obligations from which we cannot escape and from which it would be dishonorable to seek escape." Those "obligations" in the Philippines would eventually require more than 126,000 American soldiers and cost over 4,000 of their lives. As he spoke, the cold drizzle increased, but the wet crowd still answered the president's pauses with hearty approval.[68]

The change, of course, had been a matter of political choices—largely *his* choices, yielding to the jingoes in the Republican Party. In no previous inaugural address had any president spoken so much of the *overseas* obligations of the United States. "Our institutions will not deteriorate by extension," McKinley proclaimed, "and our sense of justice will not abate under tropic suns in distant seas"—a remark seemingly voided by the Supreme Court's series of decisions in 1901, what would be called the Insular Cases, where the justices decreed that full constitutional rights did not apply to all places under American control, namely those acquired from the Spanish: Puerto Rico,

Guam, and the Philippines. In the speech, the words "honor," "honorably," "honorable," or "dishonorable" appeared seven times, always in relation to the war and subsequent foreign policy—a chiding of the anti-imperialists. As for the continuing Filipino insurrection, McKinley instructed the crowd, disingenuously, that "we are not waging war against the inhabitants of the Philippine Islands. A portion of them are making war against the United States."

For white Americans, however, the war had brought nation-building, or *re*building, prospects but still no end to North-South differences, not to mention class conflicts. "We are reunited. Sectionalism has disappeared," McKinley assured his listeners, apparently disregarding the electoral vote distribution in 1900, as well as ignoring questions of racial justice that most Republican leaders no longer cared to address. "Division on public questions can no longer be traced by the war maps of 1861," he exaggerated.[69]

Following the inauguration, the plan was for the president to embark on a long sojourn around the country, six weeks by rail with aides, some cabinet members, an entourage of reporters, and the physically invalid first lady, Ida McKinley. They would travel southward and then west, to the Pacific coast, then back via the Northwest. It would be, he hoped, a unifying tour, in the style of James Monroe, the fifth president. The trip was to conclude with the July 13 celebration of President's Day at the Pan-American Exposition in Buffalo, where McKinley would deliver his most important speech of the journey. But Mrs. McKinley's health—her proneness to epileptic attacks and a weakened heart—required an early return to Washington.[70]

Even so, the steamy days of summer 1901 would offer some relief from the foreign troubles that loomed over McKinley's second term. The issues that had followed the war finally seemed to be sorting themselves out. In Havana, the constitutional convention had stalemated only a few months before it ratified unconditionally the terms of the Platt amendment. In the Philippines, the capture of Aguinaldo by US troops on March 23, 1901, had temporarily taken the steam out of the insurrection, enabling a start toward Filipino "pacification." The ebbing of pressure on her husband had enabled Mrs. McKinley's health to revive. As the president spent late evenings sitting with advisers, smoking cigars and musing about tariff revision and hemispheric unity, they thought about McKinley's long-postponed trip to the Pan-American Exposition, now rescheduled for September 5.[71]

The Pan-American Exposition—a world's fair—was supposed to be the cultural highlight that summer. Congress, three years before, had pledged half a million dollars to help finance the spectacle. Scheduled to run from May 1 through November 2, the exposition covered 350 acres of Lake Erie waterfront in Buffalo, which now ranked as the eighth largest city in America, with its 350,000 people and convenient rail access for northbound travelers. McKinley looked forward to seeing the marvelous sights for himself, especially electrical engineer Henry Rustin's breathtaking light displays that reportedly surpassed even those of the 1900 Exposition Universelle in Paris. Partly in honor of the president's visit, there would be a magnificent fireworks display over Lake Erie on the evening of September 5. The next day, McKinley and his entourage would visit Niagara Falls and then return for a public reception—a round of handshaking—at the Temple of Music.[72]

Most of the plan seemed fine, but Cortelyou, the president's chief of staff, had a bad feeling about the reception. He tried to talk McKinley out of it. While pride in American progress swirled that summer, so did assassination threats against prominent world leaders. But McKinley never paid much attention to the danger. Routinely, he went strolling through the streets of Washington without bodyguards. He welcomed the crowds that traditionally descended on the White House on New Year's day and, a skilled handshaker, could pump along some 2,600 eager visitors in those three hours. His were the traditions and values of small-town, Midwestern America—those of Niles, Ohio, where he had grown up. Calm and kind, McKinley always played the role of soft-spoken conciliator. Nothing about him could seem polarizing or despicable enough to inspire a killer. "No one would wish to hurt me," he shrugged.[73]

Meanwhile, 28-year-old Leon Czolgosz, a disillusioned loner, anarchist, and owner of a .32 caliber Iver-Johnson, short-barrel revolver, waited for his perfect chance.

As rumors of plots proliferated that summer, so had actual attacks in recent years. Anarchist labor radicals targeted heads of state in particular—"propaganda by the deed," they called it. In St. Petersburg twenty years before, a member of the revolutionary "People's Will" had fatally injured Czar Alexander II of Russia by hurling a fuse-lit bomb that shattered his lower body and left dozens around him horrendously mutilated. More recently, on July 29, 1900, Italian-born Gaetano Bresci, founder of an anarchist newspaper in Paterson, New Jersey, claimed the life of Umberto I, the king of Italy, shooting him four times with a .32 caliber revolver like Czolgosz's. The news of failed attempts had been no less chilling. In Bremen, Germany, just two days after McKinley's second inauguration, an assassin's bullet had narrowly missed Kaiser Wilhelm II. Just a month later, the Prince of Wales and future King Edward VII had barely escaped when a radicalized Belgian tinsmith apprentice, Jean-Baptiste Sipido, seeking revenge for the Boer War, fired two shots into his train compartment in Brussels.[74]

On September 6, 1901, President McKinley's crowded itinerary in Buffalo had unfolded without a glitch, including a visit to Niagara Falls, then lunch and a few other stops at the exposition. The 4:00 p.m. reception at the Temple of Music also began on schedule, a large crowd already amassed for a quick handshake. Several minutes later, as McKinley greeted the visitors, Czolgosz, his right hand covered with a white handkerchief, walked toward him. Under the heat of the day, many of the men carried similar handkerchiefs, mopping their brows as they moved slowly ahead. Police and a detachment of soldiers scrutinized the line, but they somehow missed the one fateful individual. When Czolgosz's turn came, McKinley instinctively reached forward. Their eyes locked for an instant. Suddenly, two shots exploded from the white cloth. One bullet harmlessly scraped the president's rib cage, but the other penetrated deeply into his belly. It went through the stomach and nicked the pancreas before lodging somewhere in McKinley's back. Given the likelihood of infection, it was the kind of wound that in many cases would have been regarded as fatal.[75]

A team of local surgeons headed by Dr. Matthew D. Mann, who lacked experience with abdominal wounds, patched McKinley's internal organs as well as they could and then reported on the patient's prospects with undue optimism. Meanwhile, alerted amid early fears that the president might not survive, Vice President Roosevelt cut short a speaking tour in Vermont and rushed to Buffalo immediately, arriving the next day.

Soon enough, however, the outlook brightened markedly. McKinley, conscious, feeling stronger, and able to converse, seemed to be "on the highroad to recovery." For the sake of public reassurance, all agreed it would be best for TR to go ahead with plans for a long-planned family vacation deep in the Adirondacks. While feeling relieved, Roosevelt still lamented the anarchist threat of that time as an assault "in the most naked way . . . not on power, not on wealth, but simply and solely upon free government." Later, W. R. Kuylendall of Topeka, Kansas, imagined TR as fixing the terrorist problem: "Put Teddy Roosevelt in his lightning stirrups, heading his horse westward[, and] gathering his rough riders as he comes; turn them loose and in twelve months this curse of anarchy will be extirpated and national decency vindicated."[76]

Told once again that no further complications would impede McKinley's convalescence, Roosevelt boarded a train eastbound for the mountains of upstate New York on September 10. For him at that point, little more than an outdoor retreat seemed to impend. His services to the government, he assumed, would not be necessary.

Then, early in the afternoon of September 13 another bulletin came, the one most feared. The president's condition had worsened. Intensifying pain in his abdomen and an elevated heart rate signaled a spreading of gangrene along the path of the bullet and through the interior of a stomach that could no longer function. Roosevelt was to race to the nearest rail station and come at once.[77]

McKinley died at 2:15 a.m., Saturday, September 14, 1901. His vice president took the oath of office later that day in the parlor of his Buffalo friend Ansley Wilcox. The assassinated president's cabinet gathered around to witness, their faces grim. Theodore Roosevelt, colonel of the Rough Riders and the "hero of San Juan Hill," thus became the twenty-sixth president of the United States. It was the job he sought in the fullness of time—but not suddenly, not by an assassin's bullet. "It is a dreadful thing to come into the Presidency this way," he wrote to Lodge nine days later, "but . . . here is the task, and I have got to do it to the best of my ability; . . . that is all there is about it."[78]

EPILOGUE
Eclipse of Old Heroes

IN JOHN FORD'S CLASSIC 1962 FILM *The Man Who Shot Liberty Valance*, a newspaper editor in the western town of "Shinbone" interviews Senator Ransom Stoddard (played by James Stewart) to find out why the senator has just made the long journey from Washington, DC, to revisit the place where he had lived as a fledgling lawyer back in the wild frontier days. The reason, it turns out, is that he wants to attend the funeral of his old acquaintance, a local rancher, Tom Doniphon (John Wayne). Many years before, Stoddard had become a hero for having, apparently, killed in a late-night showdown the despised outlaw Liberty Valance (Lee Marvin), leader of a criminal band that had been terrorizing the townsfolk. But in reality, the shot that killed Valance had come not from Stoddard's shaking hand but from the more sure-aiming Doniphon, lurking off to the side, out of view. Afterward, Doniphon takes no credit and tells nobody except Stoddard, whose life he had saved.

As many years pass, the secret remains undivulged—until that moment, in Stoddard's confession to the stunned editor. So now the question arises: What really matters, the actual truth or what people want—perhaps *need*—to believe? After all, Valance lies in his grave, his gang has scattered and disappeared, the town has become safe and civilized, and Stoddard's reputation for virtue and public service stands well established. A journalist may not shirk his obligation, but in this case, must any more be said?

Then, a surprising thing happens. The editor abruptly tears up his notes and pitches the scraps into a wood stove.

"You're not going to use the story?" Stoddard asks, bewildered.

The veteran newspaperman replies, "No sir. This is the West, sir. When the legend becomes fact, print the legend."[1]

So it would be, in a way, with Roosevelt and the Rough Riders. Their initial identity and, later, their lasting fame, came largely from the myth-making power of the old West. Roosevelt's real courage in battle, his heroism, stands undeniable, as does Stoddard's in the film. Yet others around him, including the long-forgotten black troopers of the Ninth and Tenth regiments, helped save his life. All of them drove the fortified Spanish out of their trenches and off of those hills. They, and not TR alone, made that moment pivotal in American history. As with Stoddard, truth and legend became more and more intertwined regarding TR as the years passed. His having organized the Rough Riders as an expression of core values, and then leading them in battle, would sustain him politically for the rest of his life. The "Battle of San Juan Hill"—that name itself an invention—gave him a lasting claim to fame, a path to political glory, a chance to serve as president, and a role in shaping the imperial destiny of the United States.

Here, too, is a lesson on how our "heroes" sometimes become so. All along, there had been many Doniphons watching the Colonel's back, both in war and in politics. The Rough Riders had propelled him, and sometimes he acknowledged as much. Whenever he could, TR attended their annual reunions. Even after he became president, he threw open his doors to them. Sure enough, former troopers, ranging from grubby, unlettered cowpokes to urbane graduates of fine eastern colleges, showed up at Sagamore Hill and even the White House. One Washington scribe, observing these arrivals with trepidation— their ragged attire, rowdy manners, and possession of weapons—protested that the president was welcoming "thugs and assassins" to the capital. One time, after a skeptical White House sentry refused entry to a scraggly looking cowboy friend, TR intervened personally. "The next time they don't let you in, Sylvane," the president announced loudly, "you just shoot through the windows!"[2]

Did the Colonel extend the same offer to the African American heroes who fought beside the Rough Riders? Did he throw open his doors to them

Eclipse of Old Heroes   161

President Roosevelt "Arrives in 'San Antone' to Attend a Reunion of the Rough Riders," 1904. TR attended the annual reunions of his old regiment whenever he could. On occasions when he did, of course, the Colonel became the center of press coverage. Library of Congress. LC-USZ62-34276

or promote their reunions? Sadly, no. One can only imagine how the white newspaper writers might have howled if *those* veterans, too, had started to appear at the White House, expecting to see the president. Roosevelt did host the African American leader Booker T. Washington for dinner on one occasion but afterward suffered vilification in many newspapers, especially southern ones, for doing so. His reputation among blacks eroded further when in 1906 he peremptorily discharged, without honor (and without evidence), 167 African American soldiers for their alleged role in shooting up the town of

Brownsville, Texas. Six of the men dismissed were Congressional Medal of Honor winners, including one for heroism in the Spanish-American War.[3]

Otherwise, however, Roosevelt would go on to influence American political culture in the ways he long had sought. In shaping the expansionist policies of the 1890s, as well as domestic politics, he went on to emphasize the traditional themes of *citizenship* and pursuit of the *common good* as the highest principles in American life. Those themes would echo in the Progressive reform movement that highlighted Roosevelt's presidency from 1901 to 1909—and beyond. Concerned about imperial Japan's growing power and influence in the Pacific, President Roosevelt continued to work toward American naval dominance. In building the Panama Canal, TR's sense of national interest overcame the greatest of New World geographical barriers, the land mass itself, effectively creating the long-sought water passage from Atlantic to Pacific. Completion of the canal in 1914 made the US naval fleet freer to roam both oceans and connected the two newly established American spheres of influence: the Caribbean and the Pacific.

As for the Rough Riders, perhaps only because they and their colonel traveled that misty trail from real life into the stranger realms of symbol and legend does anyone still care about them long afterward. Their story does not quite end with that, however. Another episode, less known, would unfold later as a bizarre finale to Roosevelt's lifelong military obsession.

Beginning in July 1915, the former president tried to raise *another* group of volunteer cavalry, and other specialized units, to fight in World War I. Imagine TR, by then in his late-fifties, much overweight, blind in one eye from a boxing accident in the White House, tormented by rheumatism and occasional malaria, indifferent to modern technology and tactics, but still eager for one more heroic charge—right into the deadly maw of German machine-gun fire.[4]

To some at the time, the idea seemed almost that crazy. In July 1916, a columnist in the *New York Call*, an antiwar socialist daily in New York City, likened the scheme to some newfangled circus—and more: "There is to be a bit of everything, flying machines, cavalry, mounted infantry, artillery scouts, rough riders of the Wild West variety, rough necks, red necks, bums, college sports[men], millionaires' sons, trench diggers from the subway, and so on." And directing the whole show would be Roosevelt, who had fought in just two battles eighteen years before and "devoted about one-twentieth of his spare time since then to military affairs—if that much. . . . Sure, he is just the man to be a Major General, right off the bat." Other critics considered the Rough Rider concept itself to be hopelessly obsolete. "We yield to none in our admiration for Col. Theodore Roosevelt," commented the *Boston Journal* on April 12, 1917, but "when we fight on the side of the Allies, let us fight as a nation, not as a group of daredevils." Long past were the days of "half-trained men rushing to battle for a cause, and better able to exercise emotion than marksmanship."[5]

And yet the notion of returning to the battlefield had interested TR for some time. In 1908, while still president, he told the Englishman John St. Loe Strachey that "if a war should occur while I am still physically fit, I should certainly try to raise a brigade, and, if possible a division, of cavalry." He actually had offered as much when trouble brewed on the Mexican border during President William Howard Taft's administration. Then, on July 10, 1915, less than a year after World War I broke out in Europe and a month after the *Lusitania* disaster, Roosevelt announced his intention to ask War Department permission to raise four brigades of cavalry, each containing two regiments, one or two pioneer battalions, a field battalion of signal troops, a regiment or battalion of machine gun troops, plus supply and sanitation trains. TR also started selecting prospective officers and staff members, many of them West Pointers and veterans of the 1898 war, including a few former Rough Riders. He planned to include his four sons, Theodore Jr., Archie, Kermit, and Quentin—all then occupied in preliminary training at the military preparedness camp in Plattsburg, New York.[6]

Still smarting from his 1912 presidential election defeat to Woodrow Wilson, Roosevelt thought the Wilson administration had failed to prepare the nation sufficiently for war. The United States should already have a standing army of 200,000 men, TR told a large crowd at the Panama-Pacific Exposition in San Diego on July 29, 1915. "If after his Gettysburg address Lincoln had listened to those who said that war is the worst of all evils," as President Wilson apparently believed, "we would not be here tonight. . . . And we remember those apostles of peace now by the name copperheads." A year later, during the campaign of 1916, TR set aside his own reservations about Charles Evans Hughes, the Republican nominee, and launched a merciless attack on the Democratic incumbent, especially his neutrality policy and promises to keep the United States out of the war. "Instead of speaking softly and carrying a big stick," Roosevelt snorted, "Wilson spoke bombastically and carried a dishrag."[7]

By the end of the first week of February 1917, the United States had broken off diplomatic relations with Germany as a result of their resumption of unrestricted submarine warfare. Meanwhile, TR had begun correspondence with Secretary of War Newton Diehl Baker on the raising of his new, improved, and expanded version of the Rough Riders. Baker, a lawyer by training, had never served in the military, nor had President Wilson. "Mr. Baker is an amiable pacifist, who, I do not doubt, could render respectable service along other lines," Roosevelt told a crowd in New Mexico, "but he is exquisitely unfit for his present position."[8]

To friends, privately, the Colonel expressed his mounting frustration, also reminiscent of his 1898 impatience with the McKinley administration. Wilson lacked manliness and resolve—"very cold & selfish . . . a very timid man when it comes to dealing with physical danger," he informed California governor Hiram Johnson on February 17. Now running the country, he thought, was the living antithesis of the strenuous life. "I don't think he is capable of understanding the emotion of patriotism, or the emotion of real pride in one's country." As for whether the United States would ever go to war against Germany, he added, "Heaven only knows, and certainly Mr. Wilson doesn't."[9]

In truth, Wilson and Baker had no time for the romanticized heroes of past wars. Even in 1898, horse soldiering was "fast becoming useless," or so said at least one military critic at that time. It seemed all the more so now that armies faced a new, more modern, and more horrible fight, featuring all the weapons that recent military ingenuity could devise: submarines, bombs, tanks, air power, advanced machine guns, and deadly gas. "The business now at hand," Wilson said, "is undramatic, practical and of scientific definiteness and precision." There were to be no more "Charge[s] of the Light Brigade." Even so, the president had to be somewhat careful because, unlike the assortment of Indian fighters, Texas Rangers, and "southern colonels" whose applications for commission also crowded his desk, TR was still a Republican leader and rival political voice.[10]

Baker answered politely that the Colonel's "patriotic spirit" and offers to serve were "cordially appreciated." Others appreciated them far more, however. News of TR's intentions had stimulated the same kind of groundswell that the Rough Riders had in 1898. By the end of March, droves of volunteers were contacting Roosevelt's headquarters at 753 Fifth Avenue in New York City—so many that more than one division would be needed to hold them. Now widely publicized, the "Roosevelt Division" had become a kind of national cause célèbre. Just two weeks later, Sloan Simpson, who had been recruiting for TR in Dallas, would report that he had tentatively enlisted a thousand men there alone. One California volunteer, Dave W. Dobbins of San Jose, gushed that he was sure Roosevelt's new army force "would outshine anything ever accomplished in the history of American arms." More than even that, wrote Henry Watterson in the Louisville Courier-Journal, "the appearance of an ex-President of the United States leading American soldiers to the battle front" would "electrify the world."[11]

Wilson's war message on April 2, 1917, marked the governmental commitment TR had waited for. "The world must be made safe for democracy," the president avowed. The right words but about two years late in coming, Roosevelt thought. Congress declared war on Germany three days later, and, as in 1898, TR wasted no time. On April 9, he went to visit Wilson in Washington. Perhaps a personal appeal could move the president where arguments and letters to the War Department had failed. Their conference lasted about forty-five minutes, according to Joseph P. Tumulty, Wilson's private secretary. Both men behaved cordially, exchanging stories and anecdotes, and then each stated his view on the use of volunteer forces in the war.[12]

But none of that changed anything. Even after the Conscription Bill passed, authorizing the raising of some volunteer regiments, the answer to Roosevelt remained flatly negative. Baker, who had tried gradually to deflate TR's hopes, finally punctured them on April 13. His War Department letter stated the president's decision that "partially trained" troops could not be sent to France and that Roosevelt could now be of better service at home than as part of the Expeditionary Forces. In this war, the American army had to have the "the most experienced military leadership available[,] . . . men who have devoted their lives to the study and pursuit of military matters." In a private letter to Alvin Johnson, however, Baker would divulge the more frank opinion circulating in Wilson's War Department: "We could not risk a repetition of the San Juan Hill affair, with the commander rushing his men into a situation from which only luck extricated them."[13]

For the most part, Congress agreed. On April 27, the House rejected 170-to-106 the amendment that would have authorized TR's division, with most of the Democrats voting against. More than a hundred of the slim 216-to-214 majority of Republicans at the time refrained from voting, perhaps sympathizing with Roosevelt but fearful that further encouragement of volunteer regiments might undercut public support for conscription. Even Henry Cabot

Lodge thought so; in an April 20 letter to Winthrop Chanler, he wrote that along with a draft policy, "you cannot very easily have also a proposition for volunteers, and we all have to stand by the conscription, including Theodore himself."[14]

Still, the government's final decision embittered the former president. TR brooded for a week before answering, and when he did, on April 23, he gave the war secretary—and historians—a large piece of his mind. The letter, filling eighteen typewritten pages, lectured Baker on what a "capital mistake" it was not to allow volunteers to choose for themselves their leaders for battle. As for the lack of proper training and leadership, he reminded the secretary that the Rough Riders had been criticized on the same grounds twenty years before yet had performed superbly. "I believe I can appeal to the natural fighting men of this country," he insisted. It would be a good lesson for those who subscribed to "prosperity-at-any-price, peace-at-any-price, safety-first instead of duty-first, the love of soft living, and the get-rich-quick theory of life." Any volunteers who could distinguish themselves in battle would help to restore the sagging "morale" of the country and prove that Americans had not really lost their frontier fiber. "It is an ignoble thing," Roosevelt declared, "for us not to put our men into the fighting line at the earliest possible moment. Such a failure will excite derision and may have a very evil effect upon our national future."[15]

In the end, the aging warrior sat behind, watching all four sons go to war instead. One, Quentin, the youngest, died in aerial combat over France on July 14, 1918—two German shots through the head. Heartbroken, Edith faced the news bravely: "You cannot bring up boys as eagles and expect them to turn out sparrows." But Theodore nearly broke down. "To feel that one has inspired a boy to conduct that has resulted in his death, has a pretty serious side for a father," he wrote. Yet "it would have been far worse if he had lived at the cost of the slightest failure to perform his duty." Quentin fell in battle—a "good death" for a man of action—just as his father might have wanted for himself: leading from the front, never flinching. Battling grief, TR resorted to convictions he had espoused, at times uncritically, throughout his life: "Unless men are willing to fight and die for great ideals, including love of country," he concluded, "ideals will vanish, and the world will become one huge sty of materialism . . . filled by the spawn of the unfit."[16]

With that old belief, passed down from earlier generations, the old Rough Rider would leave a legacy—and a legend—of his own.

ACKNOWLEDGMENTS

To start, I owe heavy professional and personal debts to Robert J. Brugger, long-time friend and former senior history editor at Johns Hopkins University Press. Thanks also to Bob's successor at the Press, Elizabeth Sherburn Demers, to the Witness to History series editors Peter C. Hoffer of the University of Georgia and Williamjames H. Hoffer of Seton Hall University, and to several anonymous readers for their helpful suggestions.

As a historian of the nineteenth century, I am grateful to the members of the Society for Historians of the Early American Republic (SHEAR) for enriching my understanding of that period over the course of my career. Thanks especially to Jim Broussard and the SHEAR "poker group," not just for including me at cards but also for being such great friends. One of that group, Gene Smith, while visiting at our summer home in Northampton, Massachusetts, provided valuable insight on questions of imperial expansion and naval policy.

Many people at the Brunswick School, in Greenwich, Connecticut, have encouraged me in this project. That group includes, above all, John Pendergast, Brian Freeman, Paul Withstandley, Kristine Brennan, Stephen Duennebier, Robert Taylor, John Booth, Steve Mandes, Andy Riemer, Tom Philip, Rick Beattie, Mike Hannigan, and Will Casertano. Many thanks, as well, to my map artist Margot Beattie and technology genius Sunil Gupta. My brother, Matthew Van Atta, a freelance editor in Decatur, Georgia, took expert care of the indexing. I am particularly grateful, once again, to Glenn Perkins for his excellent job of copyediting. Various personal friends in Greenwich, especially Katie Sokoloff and Connie Rooney, supplied kind words and listened, I hope not painfully, to parts of the manuscript.

Robert E. Kennedy, S.J., has been for many years my second father and the best of spiritual guides. I dedicate this book, however, as I have all my previous ones, to the *two* Lucys in my life, wife and daughter.

NOTES

Abbreviations

ANB *American National Biography*, ed. John A. Garraty and Mark C. Carnes, 24 vols. (New York, 1999)
LTR *The Letters of Theodore Roosevelt*, ed. Elting E. Morison et al., 8 vols. (Cambridge, MA, 1951–1954)
WTR *The Works of Theodore Roosevelt*, ed. Hermann Hagedorn, 20 vols. (New York, 1926)

Prologue. Old Values, New Challenges

1. TR to Henry Cabot Lodge, July 19, 1898, in *LTR*, 2:851–53, quotation on 853. Mark Lee Gardner, *Rough Riders: Theodore Roosevelt, His Rough Rider Regiment, and the Immortal Charge Up San Juan Hill* (New York, 2016), 158–59; Dale L. Walker, *The Boys of '98: Theodore Roosevelt and the Rough Riders* (New York, 1998), 212–13.

2. Roosevelt possibly knew the expression "crowded hour" from Sir Walter Scott, who quoted the stanza at the beginning of chapter 13 of his novel *Old Mortality* (1816), attributing it to an "anonymous" source. Nowadays, scholars credit the verse to Thomas Osbert Mordaunt (1730–1809), a British army officer and poet, who was a contemporary of Scott's. Both of the stanzas quoted here appeared in his poem "The Call." For the poem in its entirety, see https://en.wikisource.org/wiki/The_Call_(Mordaunt).

3. For an eyewitness description of Spanish fire that day as a "hail storm" of bullets, see "From Capt. M'Clintock," *Weekly Phoenix Herald*, July 28, 1898. James H. McClintock, aged 38, was a Rough Rider volunteer from Phoenix. A full roster of Roosevelt's regiment appears as an appendix in Virgil Carrington Jones, *Roosevelt's Rough Riders* (New York, 1971), 282–340. Also, "Roosevelt Said 'Watch Me,'" *Kansas Semi-Weekly Capital* (Topeka), Aug. 12, 1898; [Travis], *Topeka Weekly Capital*, Aug. 16, 1898.

4. On the fragility of republics, see, for example, Drew R. McCoy, *The Elusive Republic: Political Economy in Jeffersonian America* (Chapel Hill, NC, 1980), 5, 13–47.

5. Anonymous reviewer of James Redpath's "The Public Life of Captain John Brown," *Atlantic Monthly* 5 (Mar. 1860), 378–81, quotation on 380; Lincoln quoted in Michael Burlingame, *Abraham Lincoln: A Life*, 2 vols. (Baltimore, 2008), 1:719.

See also Dorothy Ross, "The Liberal Tradition Revisited and the Republican Tradition Addressed," in *New Directions in American Intellectual History*, ed. John Higham and Paul K. Conkin (Baltimore, 1979), 116–31.

6. G. Stanley Hall, *Adolescence: Its Psychology and Its Relations to Physiology, Anthropology, Sociology, Sex, Crime, Religion, and Education*, 2 vols. (New York, 1904), 1:202; Gail Bederman, *Manliness and Civilization: A Cultural History of Gender and Race in the United States, 1880–1917* (Chicago, 1995), 92–94.

7. See Karl-Friedrich Walling, *Republican Empire: Alexander Hamilton on War and Free Government* (Lawrence, KS, 1999), 69–70, 96–97, 279–80. On Revolutionary Americans' recognition of the fragility of republics, including their own, see Gordon S. Wood, *The Creation of the American Republic 1776–1787* (Chapel Hill, NC, 1969), 66, 92, 123, and Gerald Stourzh, *Alexander Hamilton and the Idea of Republican Government* (Stanford, CA, 1970), 63–70. On Washington's role as a nation-builder, see Edward J. Larson, *George Washington, Nationalist* (Charlottesville, VA, 2016), 31–33.

8. Alexander Hamilton, in the initial number of *The Federalist Papers*, written in 1788, may have been the first American to refer to the young United States as an "empire," its fate being "in many respects the most interesting in the world." One reason for that might have been, as historian Bethel Saler has said, that the early nation struggled between dual identities as both a westward-expanding "post-colonial republic" and as a "contiguous domestic empire," composed of entangled—and often conflicting—cultural and political interests. See Saler, *The Settlers' Empire: Colonialism and State Formation in America's Old Northwest* (Philadelphia, PA, 2015), 1–2.

9. "Washington's Forgotten Maxim" [Naval War College Address], June 2, 1897, in *WTR*, 13:182–99, quotations on 184, 186–87, 188.

10. On fairness in interpreting TR, see Kathleen Dalton, "Theodore Roosevelt: A Personal and Political Story," *Journal of the Gilded Age and Progressive Era* 6 (Oct. 2007): 363–83.

11. On military history as reflecting culture, see John Shy, "The Cultural Approach to the History of War," *Journal of Military History* 57 (Oct. 1993): 13–26, and Akira Iriye, "Culture," *Journal of American History* 77 (June 1990): 99–107.

12. George M. Frederickson, *The Inner Civil War: Northern Intellectuals and the Crisis of the Union* (New York, 1965), 219. For cultural angles taken on the Rough Riders, see Gary Gerstle, *American Crucible: Race and Nation in the Twentieth Century* (Princeton, NJ, 2001), chap. 1; Sarah Watts, *Rough Rider in the White House: Theodore Roosevelt and the Politics of Desire* (Chicago, 2003), chaps. 4–5; and John Pettegrew, *Brutes in Suits: Male Sensibility in America, 1890–1920* (Baltimore, 2007), 218–42.

CHAPTER ONE. Legacies

1. Kathleen Dalton, *Theodore Roosevelt: A Strenuous Life* (New York, 2002), 34.
2. "'Past and Present,' Address Delivered at Chicago, on Jubilee Day, by Rev. R. C. Ransom," *Freeman* (Indianapolis), Nov. 5, 1898.

3. TR to Corinne Roosevelt Robinson, June 15, 1898, in *LTR*, 2:843–45, esp. 843. Among studies that have emphasized the cultural implications of the Spanish-American War, see especially Kristin L. Hoganson, *Fighting for American Manhood: How Gender Politics Provoked the Spanish-American and Philippine-American Wars* (New Haven, CT, 1998), and, for TR, Gary Gerstle, "Theodore Roosevelt and the Divided Character of American Nationalism," *Journal of American History* 86 (Dec. 1999): 1280–1307.

4. Theodore Roosevelt, *An Autobiography* (New York, 1913), 11–13, 7–8.

5. Ibid., 94; TR to Anna Roosevelt, May 15, 1886, in *LTR*, 1:100.

6. "Address to Citizens of Dickinson," Dakota Territory, July 4, 1886, www.theodore-roosevelt.com/images/research/txtspeeches/dickinson4july1886speech.pdf, p. 2 (accessed Aug. 9, 2016).

7. "The Duties of American Citizenship," address to the Liberal Club, Buffalo, NY, Jan. 26, 1893, www.theodore-roosevelt.com/images/research/txtspeeches/783.pdf, pp. 1, 7 (accessed Aug. 9, 2016).

8. H. W. Brands, *TR: The Last Romantic* (New York, 1997), 3–18; see also Kathleen Dalton, "Why America Loved Teddy Roosevelt: Or, Charisma Is in the Eyes of the Beholders," in *Our Selves / Our Past: Psychological Approaches to American History*, ed. Robert J. Brugger (Baltimore, 1981), 269–91.

9. For Holmes at Ball's Bluff, see G. Edward White, *Justice Oliver Wendell Holmes: Law and the Inner Self* (New York, 1993), 51–52; Casper Crowninshield to Harriet Sears Crowninshield (his mother), Oct. 22, 1861, Charles Pickering Putnam Papers, Massachusetts Historical Society, www.masshist.org/online/civilwar/index.php?entry_id=633 (accessed Apr. 3, 2015).

10. Mark Twain and Charles Dudley Warner, *The Gilded Age: A Tale of To-day* (Hartford, CT, 1874), 168; Dalton, *Theodore Roosevelt*, 166, 291.

11. Louis Menand, *The Metaphysical Club: A Story of Ideas in America* (New York, 2001), 3–4; Michael C. C. Adams, *Living Hell: The Dark Side of the Civil War* (Baltimore, 2014), 130.

12. Quotation in Adams, *Living Hell*, 130.

13. Sheldon M. Novick, "Holmes, Oliver Wendell," in *ANB*, 11:87–93.

14. Hoganson, *Fighting for American Manhood*, 24–25.

15. "Memorial Day—An Address Delivered May 30, 1884, at Keene, N.H., before John Sedgwick Post No. 4, Grand Army of the Republic," in *The Essential Holmes: Selections from the Letters, Speeches, Judicial Opinions, and Other Writings of Oliver Wendell Holmes, Jr.*, ed. Richard A. Posner (Chicago, 1992), 80–87, quotations on 81–82, 85, 86.

16. Hoganson, *Fighting for American Manhood*, 26, 28–29.

17. "The Soldier's Faith—An Address Delivered on Memorial Day, May 30, 1895, at a Meeting Called by the Graduating Class of Harvard University," in Posner, *Essential Holmes*, 87–93, quotations on 88, 89, 91.

18. Henry Cabot Lodge, ed., *Selections from the Correspondence of Theodore Roosevelt and Henry Cabot Lodge, 1884–1918*, 2 vols. (New York, 1925), 1:146.

19. Porter quoted in George M. Frederickson, *The Inner Civil War: Northern Intellectuals and the Crisis of the Union* (New York, 1965), 222; David W. Blight, *Race and Reunion: The Civil War in American Memory* (Cambridge, MA, 2001), 242, 206–7, Higginson quoted at 206; Adams, *Living Hell*, 110, 211.

20. Brooks Adams, *The Law of Civilization and Decay: An Essay on History* (New York, 1896), x–xi, 37, 337, 362–63, 370; Roosevelt to Cecil Arthur Spring-Rice, Aug. 5, 1896, in *LTR*, 1:553–56, quotation on 554. Roosevelt, "The Law of Civilization and Decay," *Forum* 22 (Jan. 1897): 575–89, quotation on 587–88. See also Frederickson, *Inner Civil War*, 166–80, and T. J. Jackson Lears, *No Place of Grace: Antimodernism and the Transformation of American Culture, 1880–1920* (Chicago, 1981), 132–36.

21. C. P. Selden, "The Rule of the Mother," *North American Review* 161 (Nov. 1895): 637–40, esp. 639; Joseph F. Kett, *Rites of Passage: Adolescence in America, 1790 to the Present* (New York, 1977), 215–16, 232–33, 222–23; Thomas J. Schlereth, *Victorian America: Transformations in Everyday Life, 1876–1915* (New York, 1991), 274, 276–77, 247–49; David I. Macleod, *Building Character in the American Boy: The Boy Scouts, YMCA, and Their Forerunners, 1870–1920* (Madison, WI, 1983), 32, emphasis in original.

22. Kett, *Rites of Passage*, 233–34; Gail Bederman, *Manliness and Civilization: A Cultural History of Gender and Race in the United States, 1880–1917* (Chicago, 1995), 84–88.

23. Schlereth, *Victorian America*, 217–19; John Higham, "The Reorientation of American Culture in the 1890's," in *Writing American History: Essays on Modern Scholarship*, ed. John Higham (Bloomington, IN, 1970), 73–102, esp. 87–88; E. Anthony Rotundo, *American Manhood: Transformations in Masculinity from the Revolution to the Modern Era* (New York, 1993), 240. For evidence of the Rough Riders' influence on arguments for expanded college and school athletics programs, see, for example, "The Dudes in War," *Grand Forks (ND) Daily Herald*, July 23, 1898, and "Summer Games for Boys," *New York Tribune*, July 25, 1898. On TR's struggles as police commissioner, see Richard Zacks, *Island of Vice: Theodore Roosevelt's Quest to Clean Up Sin-Loving New York* (New York, 2012).

24. Waldo H. Sherman, "The Boy Scouts 300,000 Strong," *World's Work* 22 (Sept. 1911): 14859–72, esp. 14865–66; Mahan quoted in Edward J. Renehan, *The Lion's Pride: Theodore Roosevelt and His Family in Peace and War* (New York, 1998), 25; Michael Kimmel, *Manhood in America: A Cultural History* (New York, 1998), 127–29, 167–71, esp. 168; Rotundo, *American Manhood*, 233–234. On Roosevelt's impact as a symbol of American manliness, see Richard Slotkin, *Gunfighter Nation: The Myth of the Frontier in Twentieth-Century America* (New York, 1992), 51–62; also Bederman, *Manliness and Civilization*, 170–215.

25. See John Higham, *Strangers in the Land: Patterns of American Nativism, 1860–1925* (New York, 1972), 68–105.

26. See George M. Fredrickson, *The Black Image in the White Mind: The Debate on Afro-American Character and Destiny, 1817–1914* (New York, 1971), chap. 8.

27. Josiah Strong, *The New Era; or, The Coming Kingdom* (New York, 1893), 80.

On Strong in relation to other Social Gospel leaders of his time, see Matthew Bowman, "Sin, Spirituality, and Primitivism: The Theologies of the American Social Gospel, 1885–1917," *Religion and American Culture: A Journal of Interpretation* 17 (Winter 2007): 95–126.

28. On the Social Gospel movement generally, see Sidney E. Ahlstrom, *A Religious History of the American People* (New Haven, CT, 1972); and Susan Curtis, *A Consuming Faith: The Social Gospel and Modern American Culture* (Baltimore, 1991).

29. On Strong's imperialism, see Walter LaFeber, *The New Empire: An Interpretation of American Expansion, 1860–1898* (Ithaca, NY, 1963), 72–80, 95–101. See also Dorothea R. Muller, "Josiah Strong and American Nationalism: A Reevaluation," *Journal of American History* 53 (Dec. 1966): 487–503, and William H. Berge, "Voices for Imperialism: Josiah Strong and the Protestant Clergy," *Border States: Journal of the Kentucky-Tennessee American Studies Association* (1973), https://spider.georgetowncollege.edu/htallant/border/bsd1/berge.htm (accessed Apr. 27, 2015).

30. Gary Scott Smith, "Strong, Josiah," in *ANB* 21:44–46.

31. Strong, *Our Country: Its Possible Future and Its Present Crisis* (New York, 1885), 160; Patrick Egan in the *New York Journal*, quoted in the *Denver Post*, June 14, 1898. See also Martin E. Marty, *Righteous Empire: The Protestant Experience in America* (New York, 1970), 155–56.

32. Strong, *Our Country*, 173; Emily S. Rosenberg, *Spreading the American Dream: American Economic and Cultural Expansion, 1890–1945* (New York, 1982), 28–31.

33. David McCullough, *Mornings on Horseback* (New York, 1981), 316–20.

34. Frederick Jackson Turner, "The Significance of the Frontier in American History," in *The Turner Thesis: Concerning the Role of the American Frontier in American History*, ed. George Rogers Taylor (Lexington, MA, 1956), 27.

35. Theodore Roosevelt to Frederick Jackson Turner, Apr. 26, 1895, Theodore Roosevelt Collection, Houghton Library, Harvard University, www.theodorerooseveltcenter.org/Research/Digital-Library/Record.aspx?libID=0282383 (accessed Jan. 3, 2014).

36. Robert Seager II, "Mahan, Alfred Thayer," in *ANB*, 14:336–38.

37. Roosevelt to Alfred Thayer Mahan, May 12, 1890, in *LTR*, 1:221–22; Roosevelt, "The Influence of Sea Power upon History," *Atlantic Monthly*, 66 (Oct. 1890), 563–67, quotation on 567.

38. See R. R. Palmer and Joel Colton, *A History of the Modern World*, 6th ed. (New York, 1984), 608–15.

39. Rosenberg, *Spreading the American Dream*, 16, 18, 25.

40. See Jon Tetsuro Sumida, *Inventing Grand Strategy and Teaching Command: The Classic Works of Alfred Thayer Mahan Reconsidered* (Baltimore, 1999), and Benjamin F. Armstrong, ed., *21st Century Mahan: Sound Military Conclusions for the Modern Era* (Annapolis, MD, 2013).

41. Alfred Thayer Mahan, "The United States Looking Outward," *Atlantic Monthly*, Dec. 1890, reprinted in Mahan, *The Interest of America in Sea Power, Present and Future* (Boston 1917), 16, 25–27.

42. Rosenberg, *Spreading the American Dream*, 50–51; Niall Ferguson, *Colossus: The Rise and Fall of the American Empire* (New York, 2004), 42–43.

43. Alfred Thayer Mahan, "Hawaii and Our Future Sea Power," *Forum*, Mar. 1893, reprinted in Mahan, *Interest of America in Sea Power*, 50, 35–36; Mahan, "The Future in Relation to American Naval Power," *Harper's New Monthly Magazine*, Oct. 1895, reprinted, ibid., 171.

44. Alfred Thayer Mahan, "A Twentieth-Century Outlook," *Harper's New Monthly Magazine*, Sept. 1897, reprinted in Mahan, *Interest of America in Sea Power*, 232–33, 237–38, 245–46, 252–53, 267; Mahan, "The Isthmus and Sea Power," *Atlantic Monthly*, Sept. 1893, reprinted, ibid., 95; Mahan, "Preparedness for Naval War," *Harper's New Monthly Magazine*, Mar. 1897, reprinted, ibid., 177–78, 191; Mahan, "Twentieth Century Outlook," ibid., 232–33, 268. See also Mahan, "Possibilities of an Anglo-American Reunion," *North American Review*, Nov. 1894, reprinted, ibid., 119–20.

45. On the question of "imperialism," the Latin word *imperium* refers to absolute rule, a sphere of power or dominion, as in the Roman Empire. On modern empire-building, see esp. Niall Ferguson, *Colossus: The and Fall of the American Empire* (New York, 2004) and *Empire: How Britain Made the Modern World* (London, 2003). See also Ian Tyrrell, *Transnational Nation, United States History in Global Perspective since 1789* (New York, 2007), and Frank Ninkovich, *The United States and Imperialism* (Malden, MA, 2001).

46. Alfred Thayer Mahan, *Lessons of the War with Spain and Other Articles* (Boston, 1899), 298.

CHAPTER TWO. Jingo Doctrines

1. "Soldier Athletes Show Their Skill," *New York American*, Mar. 15, 1898; "The Soldiers' Carnival," *New York Tribune*, Mar. 15, 1898.

2. Kristin L. Hoganson, *Fighting for American Manhood: How Gender Politics Provoked the Spanish-American and Philippine-American Wars* (New Haven, CT, 1998), 7–13; John Shy, "The Cultural Approach to the History of War," *Journal of Military History* 57 (Oct. 1993): 24–26.

3. On western dime novels, see Christine Bold, *Selling the Wild West: Popular Western Fiction, 1860–1960* (Bloomington, IN, 1987), and Daryl Jones, *The Dime Novel Western* (Bowling Green, OH, 1978).

4. On the cultural significance of Buffalo Bill's Wild West, see Richard White, "Frederick Jackson Turner and Buffalo Bill," in *The Frontier in American Culture*, ed. Richard White and Patricia Nelson Limerick (Berkeley, CA, 1994), 6–65, esp. 27–45.

5. Mark Twain, *Roughing It* (Hartford, CT, 1872), 415. See also Joseph L. Coulombe, *Mark Twain and the American West* (Columbia, MO, 2003), 56.

6. On the impact of Wister and others, see Kristine Bold, *The Frontier Club: Popular Westerns and Cultural Power, 1880–1924* (New York, 2013).

7. David McCullough, "Remington, the Man," in *Frederic Remington, the Masterworks*, ed. Michael E. Shapiro and Peter H. Hassrick (New York, 1988), 14–37, esp. 19–20; Ben M. Vorpahl, *Frederick Remington and the West* (Austin, TX, 1978), 79–83; Peter H. Hassrick, *Remington, Russell and the Language of Western Art* (Washington, DC, 2000), 14–19, 76.

8. McCullough, "Remington, the Man," 26; Phillip Drennon Thomas, "Remington, Frederic," in *ANB*, 18:333–34.

9. Remington quoted in McCullough, "Remington, the Man," 29; *Frederic Remington—Selected Letters*, ed. Allen P. Splete and Marilyn D. Splete (New York, 1988), 171, 212.

10. TR to Anna Roosevelt, May 15, 1886, in *LTR*, 1:100–101.

11. TR to Charles Henry Pearson, May 11, 1894, ibid., 376–78, quotation on 377.

12. TR to Osborne Howes, May 5, 1892, *LTR*, 1:278–80, quotation on 279; TR to Henry Childs Merwin, Dec. 18, 1894, ibid., 412–17, quotation on 412; TR to Henry Cabot Lodge, Dec. 27, 1895, ibid, 503–4, quotation on 504.

13. Remington to Wister, early November, 1895, in Splete and Splete, *Remington—Selected Letters*, 214; TR to Henry Cabot Lodge, Dec. 20, 1895, in *LTR*, 1:500–501, quotation on 500.

14. John A. Garraty, "Lodge, Henry Cabot," in *ANB*, 13:811–13; Henry Cabot Lodge, "Our Blundering Foreign Policy," *Forum* 19 (Mar. 1895): 8–17, quotation on 17.

15. TR to Henry Cabot Lodge, July 14, 1896, in *LTR*, 1:547–48, quotation on 547. On the election of 1896, see R. Hal Williams, *Realigning America: McKinley, Bryan, and the Remarkable Election of 1896* (Lawrence, KS, 2010).

16. Kathleen Dalton, *Theodore Roosevelt: A Strenuous Life* (New York, 2002), 163.

17. Preface to the third edition, in Theodore Roosevelt, *The Naval War of 1812* (1883; reprint, New York, 1999), xxviii.

18. TR to Edith Roosevelt, Sept. 9, 1897, quoted in Dalton, *Theodore Roosevelt*, 167.

19. US Naval War College (Newport, RI), www.usnwc.edu/About/History.aspx (accessed Aug. 5, 2016).

20. "Washington's Forgotten Maxim" [Naval War College Address], June 2, 1897, in *WTR*, 13:182, 185, 183; Roosevelt to J. M. Wall, June 7, 1897, in *LTR*, 1:621–22.

21. Ferguson, *Colossus*, 46–48.

22. Alfred Thayer Mahan, "Hawaii and Our Future Sea Power," *Forum*, Mar. 1893, reprinted in Mahan, *The Interest of America in Sea Power, Present and Future* (Boston 1917), 48–49.

23. Ferguson, *Colossus*, 45–46.

24. Ibid., 46.

25. Ibid., 46–47.

26. TR to Alfred Thayer Mahan, June 9, 1897, in *LTR*, 1:622–23; *Gunton's Magazine* article quoted in Frederick Merk, *Manifest Destiny and Mission in American History* (Cambridge, MA, 1963), 256.

27. Louis A. Pérez Jr., *The War of 1898: The United States and Cuba in History and Historiography* (Chapel Hill, NC, 1998), 3–5.

28. On the cultural origins of the Spanish-American War, see Hoganson, *Fighting for American Manhood*, 1–14.

29. Ibid., chap. 2.

30. Pérez, *War of 1898*, 7–22.

31. Weyler quoted in Douglas Allen, *Frederic Remington and the Spanish-American War* (New York, 1971), 5. See also A. O. Hagen and E. B. Kaufman, *Cuba at a Glance* (New York, 1898), 94–96.

32. Allen, *Frederic Remington and the Spanish-American War*, 11.

33. Explanations as to why the United States went to war in 1898 vary widely. For an excellent discussion, see Hoganson, *Fighting for American Manhood*, 210–14.

34. Lewis L. Gould, *The Presidency of William McKinley* (Lawrence, KS, 1980), 64–66.

35. Ibid., 64, 66, 88–90. For the Republican and Democratic Party platforms of 1896, see "Republican Party Platform of 1896," June 16, 1896, and "1896 Democratic Party Platform," July 7, 1896, in Gerhard Peters and John T. Woolley, *The American Presidency Project*, www.presidency.ucsb.edu/ws/?pid=29629 and www.presidency.ucsb.edu/ws/?pid=29586 (accessed Aug. 8, 2016).

36. TR to Anna Roosevelt Cowles, Jan. 2, 1897, in *LTR*, 1:573–74.

37. Gould, *Presidency of William McKinley*, 66–68, quotation on 67.

38. Ibid., 68.

39. See McKinley's First Annual Message, Dec. 6, 1897, in *Messages and Papers of the Presidents, 1789–1897*, comp. James D. Richardson, 10 vols. (Washington, DC, 1899), 10:127–136.

40. Gould, *Presidency of William McKinley*, 70–71, Crowninshield quotation on 71.

41. TR to French Ensor Chadwick, Nov. 4, 1897; TR to John Hay, Nov. 4, 1897; TR to William Wirt Kimball, Nov. 19, 1897; TR to William Astor Chanler, Dec. 23, 1897, in *LTR*, 1:706, 707, 716–177, 746–47.

42. Gould, *Presidency of William McKinley*, 71–72.

43. Ibid., 72. For official information on the USS *Maine*, see US Navy, *Report of the Secretary of the Navy*, Nov. 26, 1890 (Washington, DC, 1890), 7.

44. Gould, *Presidency of William McKinley*, 73–74.

45. For a gripping account of the *Maine* disaster, see David Traxel, *1898: The Tumultuous Year of Victory, Invention, Internal Strife, and Industrial Expansion that Saw the Birth of the American Century* (New York, 1998), chap. 4.

46. Ibid., 100–104.

47. Ibid., 102–3.

48. For the official casualty report, see US Navy, *Report of the Surgeon-General, U.S. Navy, Oct. 1, 1898* (Washington, DC, 1898), 173–74. On the black victims, Reese Turner, "The Black Soldier," *Broad Ax* (Salt Lake City, UT), Aug. 13, 1898.

49. David Nasaw, *The Chief: The Life of William Randolph Hearst* (New York, 2000), 125–42, 131.

50. On the power and methods of yellow journalism, see ibid., 108, 132–33, and Traxel, *1898*, 82–84, 111–12.

51. Dickens, quoted in Gould, *Presidency of William McKinley*, 74.

52. On the proliferation of the media in the late nineteenth century and its increased focus on the White House, see Stephen Ponder, *Managing the Press: Origins of the Media Presidency, 1897–1933* (New York, 1998).

53. TR to John Davis Long, Feb. 16, 1898, in *LTR*, 1:773–74, quotation on 773; TR to Benjamin Harrison Dib[b]lee, Feb. 16, 1898, ibid., 774–75, quotation on 775. Today, few would accept the conclusions of the official 1898 investigation. More recent examination suggests that a spontaneous fire in a coal bunker must have ignited the ship's ammunition supply. Naval vessels of that era burned bituminous coal, which burns at high temperatures and releases firedamp, a gas prone to spontaneous explosions. Thus it is much more likely that an internal coal fire caused an explosion that would blow outward from the ship, not inward as in the case of an external Spanish mine. For a good brief discussion of modern findings, see www.loc.gov/law/help/usconlaw/pdf/Maine.1898.pdf (accessed June 11, 2015).

54. Allen, *Frederic Remington and the Spanish-American War*, 24.

55. Frederic Remington, "With the Fifth Corps," *Harper's New Monthly Magazine*, Nov. 1898, 962–75, quotation on 962.

56. Thomas, "Remington," 333–34.

57. McCullough, "Remington, the Man," 17–19; Thomas, "Remington," 333.

58. Remington to Poultney Bigelow, July 27, 1894; Remington to Owen Wister, early April 1896 and June 1898, in Splete and Splete, *Frederic Remington—Selected Letters*, 211–12, 216–17, 223–24.

59. Roosevelt to Remington, Sept. 15, 1897, in Splete and Splete, *Frederic Remington—Selected Letters*, 221; Ben Merchant Vorpahl, *My Dear Wister—The Frederic Remington-Owen Wister Letters* (Palo Alto, CA, 1972), 215.

60. On the emotional and psychological impact of the *Maine* explosion, see David F. Trask, *The War with Spain in 1898* (New York, 1981), xii–xiv, 58–59.

61. Theodore Roosevelt, "Social Evolution," in *WTR*, 13:233, 231; Douglas Brinkley, *The Wilderness Warrior: Theodore Roosevelt and the Crusade for America* (New York, 2009), 317. See also David H. Burton, "Theodore Roosevelt's Social Darwinism and Views on Imperialism," *Journal of the History of Ideas* 26 (Jan.–Mar. 1965), 103–18, esp. 107.

62. For a piercing indictment of many traditional arguments on 1890s imperialism, see James A. Field Jr., "American Imperialism: The Worst Chapter in Almost any Book," *American Historical Review* 83 (June 1978): 644–68.

63. Hoganson, *Fighting for American Manhood*, 88–106, esp. 91.

64. Warren quoted in Gould, *Presidency of William McKinley*, 77.

65. Ibid., 79–81.

66. William McKinley, "To the Congress of the United States," Apr. 11, 1898, in Richardson, *Messages and Papers of the Presidents*, 10:139–50, esp. 147.

67. Dalton, *Theodore Roosevelt*, 169.

68. Ferguson, *Colossus*, 48–52. The many important studies on the America war, and later governance, in the Philippines include Hoganson, *Fighting for American Manhood*, chaps. 6–7, and Frank Ninkovich, *The United States and Imperialism* (Malden, MA, 2001), chap. 2. See also Alfred W. McCoy, "Policing the Imperial Periphery: Philippine Pacification and the Rise of the U.S. National Security State"; Owen J. Lynch, "The U.S. Constitution and Philippine Colonialism: An Enduring and Unfortunate Legacy"; and Brian McAllister Linn, The Impact of the Philippine Wars (1898–1913) on the U.S. Army," all in *Colonial Crucible: Empire in the Making of the Modern American State*, ed. Alfred W. McCoy and Francisco A. Scarano (Madison, WI, 2009), 106–15, 353–64, 460–72.

69. For Dewey's personal account of the battle, see www.wtj.com/archives/dewey2.htm.

70. [Walter Hines Page], "The War with Spain and After," *Atlantic Monthly* 81 (June 1898): 721–27, quotation on 725.

71. In western civilization, theological definitions of a "just war"—divided into two catagories, *jus ad bellum* and *jus in bello*—go back to the writings of St. Augustine in the fourth century and St. Thomas of Aquinas in the thirteenth. For nineteenth-century applications in American history, see James McPherson, "A Just War?" in *The War That Forged a Nation: Why the Civil War Still Matters* (New York, 2015), 32–45, and Harry S. Stout, *Upon the Alter of the Nation: A Moral History of the Civil War* (New York, 2006), 13.

CHAPTER THREE. Teddy's Terrors

1. John D. Long, *The Journal of John D. Long*, ed. Margaret Long (New York, 1956), 224.

2. Chanler quoted in Sylvia Jukes Morris, *Edith Kermit Roosevelt* (New York, 1980), 172; Evan Thomas, *The War Lovers: Roosevelt, Lodge, Hearst, and the Rush to Empire, 1898* (New York, 2010), 8.

3. Proctor's recollection in "Roosevelt in Earnest," *Kalamazoo (MI) Gazette*, July 16, 1898.

4. TR to William Sturgis Bigelow, Mar. 29, 1898, in *LTR*, 2:801–3, quotation on 803. (Perhaps Roosevelt was thinking more specifically of his father as he composed the final lines of this letter: "Moreover, it seems to me that it would be a good deal more important from the standpoint of the nation as a whole that men like myself should go to war than that we should stay comfortably in offices at home and let others carry on the war that we have urged. This doesn't apply to a man in very high civic position. It does apply to men in low civic position." While perhaps motivated politically in doing so, he stated the same public service reason in the first paragraph of *The Rough Riders*, published in 1899. TR's sisters Bamie and Corinne and his daughter Alice believed he wanted to compensate for his father's decision not to enlist.) Further, see TR to Alexander Lambert, Apr. 1, 1898; TR to Douglas Robinson Apr. 2, 1898; TR to Paul Dana, Apr. 18, 1898, in *LTR* 2:807–9, 809, 816–18. For

alternative perspectives, see especially David McCullough, *Mornings on Horseback* (New York, 1981), 54–58; Sarah Watts, *Rough Rider in the White House: Theodore Roosevelt and the Politics of Desire* (Chicago, 2003), 199–200; Edward J. Renehan, *The Lion's Pride: Theodore Roosevelt and His Family in Peace and War* (New York, 1998), 24; Thomas, *War Lovers*, 22.

    5. Watts, *Rough Rider in the White House*, 123; John Pettegrew, *Brutes in Suits: Male Sensibility in America, 1890–1920* (Baltimore, 2007), 218–42.

    6. TR to Henry Cabot Lodge, Aug. 10 and Aug. 20, 1886, in *LTR*, 1:108–9.

    7. Kathleen Dalton, *Theodore Roosevelt: A Strenuous Life* (New York, 2002), 113–15. Also see Morris, *Edith Kermit Roosevelt*, 168–72 and, for the "deathbed" quotation, 172–73.

    8. TR to Anna Roosevelt Cowles, Jan. 17, Feb. 23 and 25, Mar. 7 and 16, 1898, in *LTR*, 1:765, 783, 785, 786, 790, 796.

    9. TR to William Sheffield Cowles, Feb. 23, 1898; TR to Douglas Robinson, Mar. 3 and 6, 1898; TR to Brooks Adams, Mar. 21, 1898, in *LTR*, 1:781, 787–88, 789, 797–98.

    10. TR to Corinne Roosevelt Robinson, May 5, 1898, *LTR*, 2:823–24, quotation on 824.

    11. Kathleen Dalton, "Why America Loved Teddy Roosevelt: Or, Charisma Is in the Eyes of the Beholders," in *Our Selves/Our Past: Psychological Approaches to American History*, ed. Robert J. Brugger (Baltimore, 1981), 269–91, esp. 271.

    12. *Springfield (MA) Republican*, June 3, 1898. On the Rough Riders as an "all-American" regiment, see excerpts from Roosevelt's farewell remarks to his troops in Virgil Carrington Jones, *Roosevelt's Rough Riders* (New York, 1971), 277–78. For the most recent full-length study of the Rough Riders, see Mark Lee Gardner, *Rough Riders: Theodore Roosevelt, His Rough Rider Regiment, and the Immortal Charge Up San Juan Hill* (New York, 2016). See also, Jon A. Knokey, *Theodore Roosevelt and the Making of American Leadership* (New York, 2015).

    13. "American Adaptability," *New Mexican* (Santa Fe), July 6, 1898. For a detailed roster of the regiment, see Jones, *Roosevelt's Rough Riders*, 282–340.

    14. "The Rough Riders," from the *New York Advertiser*, quoted in the *Dallas Morning News*, Aug. 21, 1898; "American Patriotism Aroused," *St. Louis Republic*, reprinted in *Minneapolis Journal*, May 27, 1898.

    15. "Editorial Comment," *Denver Rocky Mountain News*, June 1, 1898.

    16. Graham A. Cosmas, *An Army for Empire: The United States in the Spanish-American War*, 2nd ed. (College Station, TX, 1994), 326; David F. Trask, *The War with Spain in 1898* (New York, 1981), 86. See also Edward M. Coffman, *The Regulars: The American Army, 1898–1941* (Cambridge, MA, 2004), 3–26.

    17. Cosmas, *Army for Empire*, 85–86.

    18. "Mr. Roosevelt; Lieutenant-Colonel Roosevelt," *Springfield (MA) Republican*, Apr., 27, 1898; George B. Duncan, "Reasons for Increasing the Regular Army," *North American Review* 166 (Apr. 1898): 448–60 (quotations on 453).

    19. Duncan, "Reasons for Increasing the Regular Army," 453; Cosmas, *Army for Empire*, 88–89, 92–93.

20. *Philadelphia Enquirer* and *Buffalo Commercial*, quoted in "The American Soldier," *Augusta (GA) Chronicle*, July 7, 1898. On traditional fears of a professional standing army in Anglo-American culture, see J. G. A. Pocock, *The Machiavellian Moment: Florentine Political Thought and the Atlantic Republican Tradition* (Princeton, NJ, 1975), chaps. 12 and 15.

21. "Formal Declaration of War by Congress," *Columbus (GA) Daily Enquirer*, Apr. 26, 1898.

22. "No Sectional Lines Now," *New York Tribune*, May 11, 1898; "The Honors of the War," *Charleston (SC) News and Courier*, Aug. 20, 1898; Cosmas, *Army for Empire*, 142–43.

23. See Edward G. Longacre, *Fitz Lee: A Military Biography of Major General Fitzhugh Lee, C.S.A.* (Cambridge, MA, 2005).

24. John P. Dyer, *"Fightin' Joe" Wheeler* (Baton Rouge, LA, 1941), 327–35, quotation on 331. For a colorful description of Wheeler, see *New York Tribune*, May 13, 1898.

25. "A Regiment of 'Rough Riders,'" *Parsons (KS) Weekly Blade*, Mar. 26, 1898; Middleton quoted in "These Western Men Would Help Cuba," *St. Louis Republic*, Apr. 3, 1898; "Dr. Powell Raising Troops," *Elkhart (IN) Daily Review*, Apr. 4, 1898; "Cow Boys Want to Go," *Daily Register Gazette* (Rockford, IL), Mar. 25, 1898; "Politician Resigns to Fight against Spain," *St. Louis Republic*, Apr. 24, 1898.

26. "Grigsby Would Fight," *Aberdeen (SD) Daily News*, Mar. 28, 1898; "Cowboys Want to Fight," *Kansas City Star*, Apr. 27, 1898.

27. McCord quotation in Dale L. Walker, *Rough Rider: Buckey O'Neill of Arizona* (Lincoln, NE, 1997; originally published as *Death Was the Black Horse* [Austin, TX], 1975), 122.

28. "Roosevelt's Rough Riders," *Idaho Falls (ID) Times*, May 19, 1898.

29. Benjamin F. Alexander, *Coxey's Army: Popular Protest in the Gilded Age* (Baltimore, 2015), 32–33. See also Harold U. Faulkner, *Politics, Reform, and Expansion, 1890–1900* (New York, 1959), 141–62, esp. 141–42, and, generally, Douglas W. Steeples and David O. Whitten, *Democracy in Desperation: The Depression of 1893* (Westport, CT, 1998).

30. Alexander, *Coxey's Army*, 38.

31. See Christina Romer, "Spurious Volatility in Historical Unemployment Data," *Journal of Political Economy* 94 (1986): 1–37.

32. Dalton, *Theodore Roosevelt*, 171–72.

33. "Dr. Wood's History," *Daily Oklahoman* (Oklahoma City), May 7, 1898; reference to Geronimo in the *Denver Rocky Mountain News*, May 22, 1898. On Roosevelt's admiration for Wood, see Theodore Roosevelt, *The Rough Riders* (New York, 1899), 7–9, quotation on 8.

34. TR to Brooks Brothers, May 2, 1898; TR to Paul Dana, Apr. 18, 1898, in *LTR*, 2:822, 816–18, quotation on 817.

35. Jones, *Roosevelt's Rough Riders*, appendices, 282–343. On the feeling for war in the West, see Roosevelt, *Rough Riders*, 7.

36. Roosevelt, *Rough Riders*, 13; TR to John William Fox, Apr. 25, 1898, in *LTR*, 2:820–21 (Fox would further his journalistic reputation as a war correspondent in Cuba, working for *Harper's Weekly* and covering the Rough Riders); TR to William Austin Wadsworth, Apr. 25, 1898, ibid., 821 (Wadsworth was a fellow Harvard graduate, class of 1870, and a longtime friend of Roosevelt's and a fellow hunting enthusiast).

37. TR to Guy Murchie, May 2, 1898, in *LTR*, 2:822; TR to Joseph Lincoln Steffens, May 4, 1898, ibid., 823; TR to Corinne Roosevelt Robinson, May 5, 1898, ibid., 823–24, quotation on 824; TR to Fitzhugh Lee, May 6, 1898, ibid., 824. (William Sloan Simpson, a young Texan and a relative of Lee's, was one of the Harvard students who left college to serve with the Rough Riders.)

38. "Leaders of Rough Riders," from the *Chicago Record*, reported in the *Dallas Morning News*, Aug. 14, 1898.

39. Ibid. On Wood generally, see Jack McCallum, *Leonard Wood: Rough Rider, Surgeon, Architect of American Imperialism* (New York, 2006).

40. "Roosevelt's Troopers: College Men and Cow Punchers Serve Together," *Washington Post*, quoted in the *Evening Post* (Charleston, SC), May 9, 1898; "Roosevelt's Cowboys," *Saginaw (MI) News*, May 11, 1898; "Fighting Millionaires," *Indianapolis Freeman*, June 4, 1898; *Fresno (CA) Republican Weekly*, May 13, 1898.

41. "Likes to Bully Millionaires," *Kansas City Star*, June 4, 1898; "Uniforms for Rough Riders," ibid., May 15, 1898; "Rough Riders Gathering," *Dallas Morning News*, May 11, 1898; *Butte (MT) Weekly Miner*, June 2, 1898.

42. Howard P. Chudacoff, *The Age of the Bachelor: Creating an American Subculture* (Princeton, NJ, 1999), 40–44; Richard Zacks, *Island of Vice: Theodore Roosevelt's Quest to Clean Up Sin-Loving New York* (New York, 2012), 134.

43. McCullough, *Mornings on Horseback*, 198–99.

44. Thomas, *War Lovers*, 30; McCullough, *Mornings on Horseback*, 328–29.

45. Roosevelt, *Rough Riders*, 17–19.

46. Ibid., 18.

47. *Beeville (TX) Bee*, May 20, 1898; *Cincinnati Post*, June, 11, 1898; "Two Sets of Rough Riders," *St. Louis Republic*, June 12, 1898.

48. "Teddy's Terrors," *Boston Journal*, May 27, 1898; "Commanded by Dudes," *Daily Oklahoman* (Oklahoma City), May 27, 1898; "Rough Riders Bowl Up," *Omaha World Herald*, May 27, 1898; "Teddy's Riders Raise Cain," *Denver Rocky Mountain News*, May 27, 1898; "Rough Riders on the Way," *Trenton (NJ) State Gazette*, June 2, 1898. Regarding Jones, see "The Roosevelt Regiment," *New York Tribune*, June 4, 1898. On Redmond, see "Murderer Among the Rough Riders," *Wilkes-Barre (PA) Times*, Aug. 20, 1898; "Suddenly Disappeared," *Albuquerque Citizen*, Aug. 20, 1898; and "Found and Lost," *Emporia (KS) Gazette*, Aug. 20, 1898.

49. Roosevelt, *Rough Riders*, 68; "How He [O'Neill] Came to Arizona," *Weekly Phoenix Herald*, July 21, 1898; Walker, *Rough Rider*, 5, 7, 8–11, 15–17, 19, 23, 33, 34–35, 54–55.

50. Walker, *Rough Rider*, 50, 38–39.

51. "A Gallant Soldier," *San Jose (CA) Evening News*, July 9, 1898; "Adventurous Capt. O'Neill," *Baltimore Sun*, July 4, 1898; "Arizona Miner, Scout, Judge, Sheriff, Mayer, Gambler, Dead Shot, Soldier, Hero and All-Round Good Fellow," *Denver Post*, July 17, 1898; Walker, *Rough Rider*, 47–52, 67–75.

52. "The Man for Cuba," *Oregonian* (Portland), May 5, 1898; "Roosevelt's Rough Riders *Dallas Morning News*, May 15, 1898.

53. "All Are Democrats," *Omaha World Herald*, June 13, 1898; "Cowboy Fighters," *Minneapolis Journal*, May 11, 1898.

54. "Don't Call Them Rough Riders," *New York Tribune*, May 13, 1898; "Don't Like Being Called 'Rough Riders,'" *Kansas City Star*, June 9, 1898; "Roosevelt Gets All the Fame," *Sioux City (IA) Journal*, June 10, 1898.

CHAPTER FOUR. Crowded Hour

1. On the "Immunes," see Edward M. Coffman, *The Regulars: The American Army, 1898–1941* (Cambridge, MA, 2004), 11, 14; Graham A. Cosmas, *An Army for Empire: The United States in the Spanish-American War*, 2nd ed. (College Station, TX, 1994), 127; "Latter Day Reasoning," *Indianapolis Freeman*, Aug. 20, 1898.

2. McKinley quoted in Evan Thomas, *The War Lovers: Roosevelt, Lodge, Hearst, and the Rush to Empire, 1898* (New York, 2010), 287.

3. "Sombrero Hats the Latest Very Correct New Fashion," *Philadelphia Inquirer*, May 18, 1898.

4. Sylvia Jukes Morris, *Edith Kermit Roosevelt* (New York, 1980), 178.

5. "The American Policy Outlined," *Springfield (MA) Republican*, July 23, 1898. On the anti-imperialists, see Robert L. Beisner, *Twelve against Empire: The Anti-Imperialists, 1898–1900* (New York, 1968), esp. 215–39; E. Berkeley Tompkins, *Anti-Imperialism in the United States: The Great Debate, 1890–1920* (Philadelphia, 1970); and Michael Patrick Cullinane, *Liberty and American Anti-Imperialism, 1898–1909* (New York, 2012).

6. David F. Trask, *The War with Spain in 1898* (New York, 1981), chap. 6.

7. For Shafter's Cuban strategy, see Thomas, *War Lovers*, 298–99; Cosmas, *Army for Empire*, 204–6

8. Theodore Roosevelt, *The Rough Riders* (New York, 1899), 12; Dale L. Walker, *The Boys of '98: Theodore Roosevelt and the Rough Riders* (New York, 1998), 108; Mark Lee Gardner, *Rough Riders: Theodore Roosevelt, His Rough Rider Regiment, and the Immortal Charge Up San Juan Hill* (New York, 2016), 26; Stanhope Sams, "The Krag-Jorgensen Gun . . . Inferior in Many Respects to the Mauser Used by the Spanish," *New York Times*, Aug. 16, 1898. See also Arcadi Gluckman, *United States Muskets, Rifles, and Carbines* (Buffalo, NY, 1948).

9. On the history of smokeless powder, see Tenney L. Davis, *The Chemistry of Powder and Explosives* (Los Angeles, 1943), chap. 6; Louis Médard, "The Scientific Work of Paul Vieille" [in French], *Revue d'histoire des sciences* 47 (July–Dec. 1994): 381–404.

10. "Troops with Springfield Rifles," *New York Tribune*, July 1, 1898; "The Fight at Siboney," *Flint (MI) Journal*, July 19, 1898.

11. On the Mauser rifle as compared to the Krag, see Sams, "Krag-Jorgensen Gun," and, generally, Ludwig Elmer Olson, *Mauser Bolt Rifles* (Aberdeen Proving Ground, MD, 1950).

12. "The Fighting at Siboney," *New York Tribune*, July 9, 1898; "Freaks of Bullets," *New York Journal*, reprinted in the *Kalamazoo (MI) Gazette*, July 23, 1898; "Hospital Scenes," *Jackson (MI) Citizen Patriot*, July 19, 1898.

13. "Lining Up for Battle," *American* (Coffeyville, KS), July 2, 1898.

14. Thomas, *War Lovers*, 160. See also "Yellow Fever," World Health Organization, www.who.int/mediacentre/factsheets/fs100/en/ (accessed July 15, 2015).

15. Douglas Brinkley, *The Wilderness Warrior: Theodore Roosevelt and the Crusade for America* (New York, 2009), 322.

16. See above, chapter 1. For alternative perspectives, see Sarah Watts, *Rough Rider in the White House: Theodore Roosevelt and the Politics of Desire* (Chicago, 2003), 212–13, and John Pettegrew, *Brutes in Suits: Male Sensibility in America, 1890–1920* (Baltimore, 2007), 223–24.

17. Roosevelt, *Rough Riders*, 79–80. On the backgrounds of Capron and Fish, see also Walker, *Boys of '98*, 94, 115, 110, 173, and Gardner, *Rough Riders*, 52–53, 126.

18. Roosevelt, *Rough Riders*, 80.

19. "Led into Ambush," *Baltimore Sun*, June 27, 1898; "Hooper Adams Talks of the War," *Age-Herald* (Birmingham, AL), July 19, 1898.

20. Thomas, *War Lovers*, 301–3; Stephen Crane to the *New York World*, reprinted as "Stephen Crane's Story," in the *Kansas City Star*, July 10, 1898.

21. Crane to the *New York World*; Roosevelt, *Rough Riders*, 86; "Our Rough Riders," *Kalamazoo (MI) Gazette*, July 20, 1898.

22. [Lovelace], "From the Rough Riders," *Dallas Morning News*, July 9, 1898; Gardner, *Rough Riders*, 113–15, 125. On the symbolic importance of Fish's death, see "The Society Soldier," *Omaha World Herald*, June 26, 1898, and "The American as a Soldier," *Philadelphia Inquirer*, June 26, 1898.

23. TR to Corinne Roosevelt Robinson, [started on] June 15, 1898, in *LTR*, 2:843–45, quotation on 845.

24. [Freeman], "From the Field of Glory," *Michigan Argus* (Ann Arbor), July 8, 1898; Roosevelt, *Rough Riders*, 73–111; Gardner, *Rough Riders*, 105–29; Walker, *Boys of '98*, 174–81; Thomas, *War Lovers*, 301–15; Cosmas, *Army for Empire*, 209.

25. For vivid accounts of the Battle of Las Guásimas, see "Yankee Grit," *Plain Dealer* (Cleveland), June 27, 1898, "Battle at El Caney," *Topeka Weekly Capital*, Aug. 16, 1898; and Richard Harding Davis's narrative, printed in many newspapers around the country, as in "Great Odds against the Rough Riders," *St. Louis Republic*, June 26, 1898.

26. "Gen. N. A. M. Dudley" and "Col. Wood and Lieut. Col. Roosevelt the New Heroes," both in *Boston Journal*, June 25, 1898.

27. "Friday's Unnecessary Sacrifice," *Philadelphia Inquirer*, June 27, 1898; "The

Chief Danger of Recklessness in War," *Philadelphia Inquirer*, June 28, 1898; Richard Harding Davis, "Rough Riders Advanced under Decimating Fire," *St. Louis Republic*, June 28, 1898.

28. Roosevelt, *Rough Riders*, 106.

29. [Thomas], "Fighting of Rough Riders," *Sioux City (IA) Journal*, July 18, 1898; [White], "Wildest Country I Ever Saw," *Boston Journal*, July 9, 1898; [Bull], "Horrors of War," *San Jose (CA) Evening News*, July 19, 1898; [Cash], "A Rough Rider's Story," *New York Tribune*, July 12, 1898.

30. "Let Us Be Fair," *Boston Journal*, June 29, 1898; "The Soldier of 1898," from the *Minneapolis Journal*, quoted in *Grand Forks (ND) Daily Herald*, June 29, 1898; "Note and Comment," *Springfield (MA) Republican*, June 29, 1898.

31. Davis, quoted in Virgil Carrington Jones, *Roosevelt's Rough Riders* (New York, 1971), 213; "Dudes," *Weekly Phoenix Herald*, July 28, 1898. For similar testimony of a wounded Rough Rider volunteer from Milwaukee, see "Roosevelt and His Dudes," *Kalamazoo (MI) Gazette*, Aug. 10, 1898.

32. Gardner, *Rough Riders*, 147–49; Walker, *Boys of '98*, 202-04; Evans, *War Lovers*, 312–15.

33. Walker, *Boys of '98*, 206–9; Gardner, *Rough Riders*, 208.

34. Cosmas, *Army for Empire*, 210–15.

35. Ibid., 216–17; Frederic Remington, "With the Fifth Corps," *Harper's New Monthly Magazine* Nov. 1898, 962–75, 972.

36. [Reubelt], "Shot in Battle," *Plain Dealer* (Cleveland), July 30, 1898; Remington, "With the Fifth Corps," 968.

37. Walker, *Boys of '98*, 171–72; Gardner, *Rough Riders*, 126, 132–33.

38. [Van Treese], "Bravest Men Fell," *Cincinnati Post*, July 9, 1898; [Mitchell], "With the Riders," *Boston Daily Advertiser*, July 22, 1898; TR to Lodge, July 3, 1898; July 5, 1898, in *LTR*, 2:846, 849, quotation on 846; Walker, *Rough Rider*, 172. See James M. McPherson, *For Cause and Comrades: Why Men Fought in the Civil War* (New York, 1997).

39. [Larned], "Rough Rider's Experience," *New York Tribune*, July 21, 1898; Walker, *Rough Rider*, 173.

40. Roosevelt, *Rough Riders*, 122; Walker, *Rough Rider*, 172–73.

41. Morris, *Edith Kermit Roosevelt*, 180–81; Kathleen Dalton, *Theodore Roosevelt: A Strenuous Life* (New York, 2002), 90, 550 n41.

42. TR, quoted in Morris, *Edith Kermit Roosevelt*, 179–80.

43. Roosevelt, *Rough Riders*, 123–24, 126–27.

44. TR to Henry Cabot Lodge, July 19, 1898, in *LTR*, 2:851–53, quotation on 853.

45. [Brown], "Some Personal Observations," *Weekly Journal Miner* (Prescott, AZ), Aug. 24, 1898; "A Pen Picture of 'Teddy,'" *Augusta (GA) Chronicle*, Aug. 12, 1898; "Wounded Men's Stories, A Rough Rider's Admiration of Colonel Roosevelt's Bravery," *New York Tribune*, Aug. 12, 1898; [Chilcoot], "Western Rough Rider Praises Eastern Tenderfeet," *Boston Journal*, Aug. 23, 1898.

46. Davis's account for the *New York Journal* appeared in many newspapers

around the country within weeks after the battle. See, for example, "Roosevelt's Ride at San Juan," *Age-Herald* (Birmingham, AL), July 17, 1898, and "The Rough Riders, Their Famous Charge Up San Juan Heights to Victory," *Albuquerque Citizen*, July 19, 1898.

47. [Laird], "Seen by a Private," *Weekly Phoenix Herald*, Aug. 11, 1898. On the importance of the "Buffalo Soldiers" at Kettle Hill and, later, San Juan Hill, see Edward Van Zile Scott, *The Unwept: Black Soldiers and the Spanish American War* (Montgomery, AL, 1996).

48. [Dame], "From the Front," *New Mexican* (Santa Fe), July 27, 1898.

49. [Hughes] "Battle of Santiago," *Albuquerque Citizen*, July 20, 1898; [Robinson], "Praise for Negro Soldiers," *Beeville (TX) Bee*, July 22, 1898; [Roberts], "Modest Tale of the Lieutenant," *Daily Illinois State Journal* (Springfield), July 21, 1898; [Larned], "Rough Rider's Experience"; "The Black Regiment," *Plain Dealer* (Cleveland), July 6, 1898.

50. "Description of the Battle," *Dallas Morning News*, July 3, 1898; "Story of the Fight," *Trenton State Gazette*, July 4, 1898. See also Gardner, *Rough Riders*, 159, 170; Walker, *Boys of '98*, 213; and Thomas, *War Lovers*, 322, 323–24.

51. "The Rough Riders," *San Antonio Express*, July 7, 1898; "Llewellyn's Letter," *New Mexican* (Santa Fe), July 22, 1898 (Llewellyn, aged 45, had been a lawyer in New Mexico before volunteering for Rough Riders duty; on Llewellyn's background as a frontier lawman before the war, see "Life of Bold Adventure," *Sioux City [IA] Journal*, July 17, 1898); "Dudley Dean Writes of the Rough Riders' Skirmish," *Boston Journal*, July 20, 1898; "Heroic Rough Riders," *Kalamazoo (MI) Gazette*, July 19, 1898; [Honeyman], "From the Front," *San Antonio Express*, July 28, 1898; "Swept up the Hill Like a Hurricane," *Omaha World Herald*, July 3, 1898; "Told by a Topekan," *Kansas Semi-Weekly Capital* (Topeka), July 22, 1898. See also "An American Quality," *Kansas Semi-Weekly Capital* (Topeka), Aug. 2, 1898. Private Sherman M. Bell of Colorado Springs later revealed that "[w]e had it agreed between us westerners that we would never retreat and would never individually or otherwise be taken prisoners by the Spaniards." See "From Santiago's Field of Battle," *Colorado Springs Gazette*, Aug. 16, 1898.

52. TR to Leonard Wood, July 4, 1898; TR to Henry Cabot Lodge, July 19, 1898; TR to Douglas Robinson, July 19, 1898, in *LTR*, 2:846–49, 851–53, 854–56; Roosevelt, *Rough Riders*, 130–31; [Andrews], "San Juan Hill Battle," *Kalamazoo (MI) Gazette*, July 30, 1898; [Carr], "A Rough Riders Story," *Columbus (GA) Daily Enquirer*, July 27, 1898; Gardner, *Rough Riders*, 171–76.

53. Roosevelt, *Rough Riders*, 132–33; [Carr], "Rough Rider's Story"; Frank N. Schubert, "Buffalo Soldiers at San Juan Hill" (paper presented at the Conference of Army Historians, Bethesda, MD, 1998), www.history.army.mil/documents/spanam/bssjh/Shbrt-bssjh.htm (accessed Aug. 20, 2016).

54. Roosevelt, *Rough Riders*, 133–34. See John H. Parker, *History of the Gatling Gun Detachment Fifth Army Corps, at Santiago* (Kansas City, MO, 1898), 18–20, and, on the Rough Riders, 178–84.

55. Remington, "With the Fifth Corps," 975, 970; [Gilbert], "War's Horrors Made Vivid," *Sioux City (IA) Journal*, July 27, 1898; Margherita Arlina Hamm, "As It Appears to a Woman," *Sioux City (IA) Journal*, Aug. 14, 1898.

56. Cosmas, *Army for Empire*, 218, 225; Roosevelt, *Autobiography*, 265–67.

57. Trask, *War with Spain*, 261–69.

58. Cosmas, *Army for Empire*, 227, 231, 243.

59. On the Spanish strategy at Santiago and Linares's decisions, see Trask, *War with Spain*, 201–2, 238–39, 245–46.

60. "Rough Riders' Good Example," from the *New York Commercial Advertiser*, reprinted in the *Oregonian* (Portland), July 7, 1898; "The 'Rough Riders,'" from the *New York Times*, reprinted in the *New Mexican* (Santa Fe), July 6, 1898; Trask, *War with Spain*, 243, 247–48.

61. Trask, *War with Spain*, 245.

62. Roosevelt, *Rough Riders*, 104; [Tallman], "Wounded in Battle," *Topeka Weekly Capital*, Aug. 12, 1898. See also Lt. William Wallace, 7th Infantry, "Night in the Trenches," *Indiana State Journal* (Indianapolis), Aug. 17, 1898.

63. On Faneuil Hall, see Abram English Brown, *Faneuil Hall and Faneuil Hall Market, or Peter Faneuil and His Gift* (Boston, 1901).

64. Tompkins, *Anti-Imperialism*, 120–23, quotation on 123.

65. Ibid., 123–25, quotations on 124, 125. See also, *Anti-Imperialist Speeches at Faneuil Hall, Boston, June 15, 1898* (Boston, 1898).

66. "Some Events of Fourth," *Springfield (MA) Republican*, July 5, 1898; "No Policy Formulated," *Dallas Morning News*, July 21, 1898; "What Should We Do," *Helena (MT) Independent*, Aug. 4, 1898.

67. Tompkins, *Anti-Imperialism*, 127, 139, 295.

68. Silvana Siddali, "Boutwell, George Sewall," in *ANB* 3:260–61. See also Thomas H. Brown, *George Sewall Boutwell: Human Rights Advocate* (Groton, MA, 1989).

69. George S. Boutwell, *Reminiscences of Sixty Years in Public Affairs*, 2 vols. (New York, 1902), 2:324; see generally 323–44.

70. *Weekly Journal Miner* (Prescott, AZ), July 6, 1898.

71. Ibid.; "Women's Relief Corps," *Weekly Phoenix Herald*, July 7, 1898; Rudyard Kipling, "Recessional" (1898), www.poetryfoundation.org/poems-and-poets/poems/detail/46780 (accessed Aug. 16, 2016).

72. Pauline O'Neill to the *San Francisco Examiner*, quoted in "The Sacrifices of War: A Tribute to 'Buckey' O'Neill," Sharlot Hall Library and Archives, Prescott, AZ, www.sharlot.org/library-archives (accessed Aug. 21, 2015); from the *New York Journal*, reprinted in the *Denver Rocky Mountain News*, July 17, 1898; "Capt. O'Neill of Arizona," *Augusta (GA) Chronicle*, July 7, 1898.

73. "Captain O'Neill," *Weekly Phoenix Herald*, July 14, 1898; "Capt. W. O. O'Neill" and "Our Nation's Honor," ibid., July 7, 1898.

74. "Arizona; Capt. O'Neill," *Afro-American Sentinel* (Omaha, NE), Sept. 3, 1898.

75. Buckey O'Neill Statue / Rough Rider Monument, Digital Photographs, Shar-

lot Hall Library and Archives, Prescott, AZ, http://sharlot.org/archives/photographs (accessed Aug. 31, 2015).

CHAPTER FIVE. New Empire

1. "Artists Inspired by War," *Philadelphia Inquirer*, Feb. 26, 1899; Alexander Nemerov, *Frederic Remington and Turn-of-the-Century America* (New Haven, CT, 1995), 87.

2. The painting is part of the collection at the Frederic Remington Art Museum, Ogdensburg, NY; see www.fredericremington.org.

3. TR to Frederic Remington, Nov. 29, 1895, in *LTR*, 1:497–98, quotation on 497; TR to Bradley Tyler Johnson, July 31, 1899, ibid., 2:1042. Remington, quoted in David McCullough, "Remington, the Man," in *Frederic Remington, the Masterworks*, ed. Michael E. Shapiro and Peter H. Hassrick (New York, 1988), 14–37, esp. 30. See also Ben M. Vorpahl, *Frederick Remington and the West* (Austin, TX, 1978), *Remington and the West*, 240, 244, 249.

4. Nemerov, *Frederic Remington*, 87–94.

5. On the Treaty of Paris, see David F. Trask, *The War with Spain in 1898* (New York, 1981), 445–72, esp. 468–72.

6. *Dallas Morning News*, July 26, 1898; "Past and Present," *Freeman* (Indianapolis, IN), Nov. 5, 1898. See Lewis L. Gould, *The Presidency of William McKinley* (Lawrence, KS, 1980), chap. 6.

7. Graham A. Cosmas, *An Army for Empire: The United States in the Spanish-American War*, 2nd ed. (College Station, TX, 1994), 255–56; Nell Irvin Painter, *Standing at Armageddon: The United States, 1877–1919* (New York, 1987), 157.

8. TR to Henry Cabot Lodge, July 3, 1898; TR to Russell Alexander Alger, July 23, 1898, in *LTR*, 2:846, 859–60. See also TR to Lodge, July 5, 1898, July 7, 1898, July 10, 1898, July 19, 1898, and TR to Corinne Roosevelt Robinson, July 19, 1898, ibid., 849, 850, 850–51, 851–53, 855–56.

9. "With the Rough Riders," *New York Sun*, reprinted in the *Minneapolis Journal*, July 20, 1898; "Teddy," *Springfield (MA) Republican*, Aug. 19, 1898.

10. "Colonel Theodore Roosevelt," *New Haven (CT) Register*, Aug. 22, 1898; [Dixon], "Tribute to Roosevelt," reported in the *Tacoma (WA) Daily News*, Aug. 15, 1898; Kathleen Dalton, *Theodore Roosevelt: A Strenuous Life* (New York, 2002), 174–75.

11. "Theodore Roosevelt," *Boston Journal*, Aug. 23, 1898; "Typical American," *Wilkes-Barre (PA) Times*, Aug. 9, 1898. On the shift toward the celebrity-hero in American culture, see generally Richard Schickel, *Intimate Strangers: The Culture of Celebrity* (Garden City, NY, 1985), and P. David Marshall, *Celebrity Power: Fame in Contemporary Culture* (Minneapolis, 2004). On the democratization of hero worship, see especially Edward Tabor Linenthal, *Changing Images of the Warrior Hero in America: A History of Popular Symbolism* (New York, 1982), 1–18.

12. TR to Douglas Robinson, July 27, 1898, in *LTR*, 2:860–61, quotation on 860; Dalton, *Theodore Roosevelt*, 176–77.

13. [Roosevelt], *Argus and Patriot* (Montpelier, VT), Aug. 24, 1898; Dalton, *Theodore Roosevelt*, 177–78.

14. Hermann Hagedorn, *The Roosevelt Family of Sagamore Hill* (New York, 1954), 60.

15. "The American Soldier," *Baltimore Sun*, Aug. 1, 1898.

16. "Monarchy vs. Republic; a Study for the Political Philosophers," from the *New York Sun*, in the *Topeka (KS) Weekly Capital*, July 19, 1898; Rev. Barton O. Aylesworth, "A Sword: A Sunday Morning Breakfast Sermon," *Denver Rocky Mountain News*, Aug. 7, 1898.

17. "'Rough Riders' Last Charge," *Kansas City Star*, Aug. 21, 1898; "Young Women Who Want to Be Rough Riders," *New York Evening Journal*, July 18, 1898.

18. "Day in Two States," *Oregonian* (Portland), July 5, 1898; advertisement in *Jackson (MI) Citizen Patriot*, June 30, 1898; advertisement in *Minneapolis Journal*, July 8, 1898.

19. "Harrison to the Cincinnati," *New York Tribune*, July 5, 1898; "The South's Opportunity," *Augusta (GA) Chronicle*, Aug. 16, 1898; "American Citizenship a Splendid Privilege," *Omaha (NE) World Herald*, Aug. 14, 1898. On Harrison's politics, see Robert L. Beisner, *Twelve against Empire: The Anti-Imperialists, 1898–1900* (New York, 1968), 187–93.

20. "Rough Riders' Great Day," *State Ledger* (Topeka, KS), July 8, 1899.

21. Mark Lee Gardner, *Rough Riders: Theodore Roosevelt, His Rough Rider Regiment, and the Immortal Charge Up San Juan Hill* (New York, 2016), 261–62; Jack C. Lane, "Wood, Leonard," *ANB*, 23:767–68.

22. George W. Prioleau, "An Impartial View of the American Negro," *Colored American* (Washington, DC), Oct. 8, 1898; "Promote Sergeants of 10th Cavalry," *Illinois Record* (Springfield), Aug. 20, 1898.

23. "The Light Turned On," *Colored American*, July 16, 1898; "A Soldier's Recognition," *Illinois Record*, July 23, 1898.

24. David W. Blight, *Race and Reunion: The Civil War in American Memory* (Cambridge, MA, 2001), 348–49.

25. "The Black Soldier," *Broad Ax* (Salt Lake City, UT), Aug. 13, 1898; "Peril in Negro Wrongs," *Iowa State Bystander* (Des Moines), Nov. 25, 1898.

26. Theodore Roosevelt, "The Rough Riders," *Scribner's Magazine*, 25 (Apr. 1899), 420–40, esp. 435–36; TR to Robert J. Fleming, May 21, 1900, in *LTR*, 2:1304–6, quotation on 1305; "Deliver Us from Our Friends," *Washington (DC) Bee*, Apr. 8, 1899; Thomas G. Dyer, *Theodore Roosevelt and the Idea of Race* (Baton Rouge, LA, 1980), 100.

27. Blight, *Race and Reunion*, 351–52, quotation on 351; Prioleau, "Impartial View of the American Negro"; Cosmas, *Army for Empire*, 131–32.

28. Dalton, *Theodore Roosevelt*, 178–80; Gardner, *Rough Riders*, 60; "A Hot Time in the Old Town," lyrics by Joe Hayden, music by Theodore A. Metz (sheet music, New York, 1896).

29. Dalton, *Theodore Roosevelt*, 185.

30. "Observe Appomattox Day," *Daily Illinois State Register* (Springfield), Apr. 11, 1899.

31. "Gov. Roosevelt at Ann Arbor," *New York Tribune*, Apr. 12, 1899; George P. Morris, letter to the editor, *Springfield (MA) Republican*, Apr. 20, 1899.

32. *Hamilton Club of Chicago* (Chicago, 1913), University of Illinois at Chicago Archives, https://archive.org/details/hamiltonclubofchoohami (accessed Apr. 3, 2016), 9–12; Evening Program, Hamilton Club of Chicago, Apr. 10, 1899, menus.nypl.org/menus/24073 (accessed Apr. 3, 2016); "Face the Issues Like Brave Men," *Philadelphia Inquirer*, Apr. 11, 1899; "The Strenuous Life—Roosevelt's Speech at the Hamilton Club, in Chicago," *Oregonian* (Portland), Apr. 11, 1899; "Listened to Roosevelt," *Bismarck Tribune*, Apr. 12, 1899; Carl Sandburg, "Chicago," *Poetry, a Magazine of Verse* 6 (Mar. 1914): 190–91.

33. Theodore Roosevelt, "The Strenuous Life," in *WTR*, 20:319–31, quotations on 319, 321.

34. Ibid., 323–24, 324.

35. Ibid., 326–27.

36. Ibid., 329, 328–29, 330.

37. Henry C. Merwin, "On Being Civilized Too Much," *Atlantic Monthly* 79 (June 1897): 838–46, esp. 839; Henry James, *The Bostonians* (1886), in *Henry James, Novels, 1881–1886* (New York, 1985), 1111; Clifford Putney, *Muscular Christianity: Manhood and Sports in Protestant America, 1880–1920* (Cambridge, MA, 2001), 26–27, 221n, 44, 45, 62. See also David Shi, *Facing Facts: Realism in American Thought and Culture, 1850–1920* (New York, 1995), 212–22.

38. *Daily Argus* (Ann Arbor, MI), Apr. 11, 1899; "An Inspired Address," *Weekly Phoenix Herald*, Apr. 20, 1899; "New Occasions and New Duties," *New York Tribune*, Apr. 12, 1899. Reid, a prominent Republican, had served on President McKinley's commission to negotiate peace with Spain after the war.

39. "War and Roosevelt Again," *Springfield (MA) Republican*, Apr. 20, 1899; James, quoted in "The Strenuous Life," *Helena (MT) Independent*, Apr. 24, 1899; "Strenuous Life," *Kansas City Star*, Apr. 11, 1899.

40. "Applied Strenuosity," *Daily Illinois State Register* (Springfield), Apr. 22, 1899; "An American D'Artagnan," *Baltimore Sun*, Apr. 12, 1899.

41. Josiah Strong, *Expansion, under New World Conditions* (New York, 1900), 19; Martin E. Marty, (New York, 1970), 198.

42. Strong, *Expansion*, 10, 238–39.

43. Ibid., 19, 21, 27–28, 29, 31–32, 34.

44. Ibid., 37, 38–39, 41.

45. Ibid., 45–48, 64, 141, 149.

46. Ibid., 104n, 117, 132–33. See also Beveridge, speech in the Senate, *Congressional Record*, 56th Cong., 1st sess., 704–12.

47. Strong, *Expansion*, 91, 99, 100.

48. Ibid., 183, 184, 180, 247, 185, 201, 190–91, 212. On Seward, see Walter LaFeber, *The New Empire: An Interpretation of American Expansion, 1860–1898* (Ithaca, NY, 1963), 24–32, 5, 311, 417.

49. Strong, *Expansion*, 216, 223–24, 274–75, 282, 279, 284–85, 296–98.

50. Mark Twain, "The War Prayer," in *The Writings of Mark Twain*, ed. Albert Bigelow Paine, 37 vols. (New York, 1922–25), 29:394–98.

51. Justin Kaplan, *Mr. Clemens and Mark Twain: A Biography* (New York, 1966), 367. See also Andrew Hoffman, *Inventing Mark Twain: The Lives of Samuel Langhorne Clemens* (New York, 1997), 432–37.

52. Philip McFarland, *Mark Twain and the Colonel: Samuel L. Clemens, Theodore Roosevelt, and the Arrival of a New Century* (Lanham, MD, 2012), 47; see also Kaplan, *Mr. Clemens and Mark Twain*, 362.

53. McFarland, *Mark Twain and the Colonel*, 48. On American sympathy for the Boers, see Peter Duignan and L. H. Gann, *The United States and Africa, a History* (London, 1984), 159–60.

54. McFarland, *Mark Twain and the Colonel*, 50–52, quotation on 51.

55. Ibid., 51–54, quotation on 54.

56. Robert C. Bannister, "Sumner, William Graham," in *ANB*, 21:147–49.

57. William Graham Sumner, "The Conquest of the United States by Spain," *Yale Law Journal* 8 (Jan. 1899): 168–93, esp. 188, 168–69, 169–70, 172–73.

58. Dalton, *Theodore Roosevelt*, 189–90.

59. Ibid., 189–91.

60. Ibid., 191, 180; Sylvia Jukes Morris, *Edith Kermit Roosevelt* (New York, 1980), 186–87, 202–3.

61. "Convention in Session," *St. Albans (VT) Daily Messenger*, June 19, 1900; "Hanna 'Hammers' Roosevelt," *Plain Dealer* (Cleveland), Aug. 3, 1900.

62. McFarland, *Mark Twain and the Colonel*, 59–60.

63. "Hanna 'Hammers' Roosevelt," *Plain Dealer*, Aug. 3, 1900; "If Roosevelt Should Be President," quoted from *Washington Post*, ibid., June 28, 1900.

64. "Altgeld's Reply to Roosevelt," *Irish World* (New York), Aug. 11, 1900; "Filipino Answers Roosevelt," *Irish World*, Sept. 1, 1900; "The Hero of San Juan Hill Was Not in the Fight," *Helena Independent*, Sept. 18, 1900; "Roosevelt as a Soldier Reviewed," *Butte (MT) Weekly Miner*, Sept. 20, 1900; "The Brave Black Men," *Recorder* (Indianapolis), Oct. 20, 1900.

65. Associated Press report, "A Gang of Pluguglies," in *Morning Herald* (Lexington, KY), Sept. 27, 1900; "Gov. Roosevelt Rotten-Egged on His Visit to Elmira," *Augusta (GA) Chronicle*, Oct. 30, 1900.

66. "Roosevelt in Michigan," *Emporia (KS) Gazette*, Sept. 8, 1900.

67. For vivid description of McKinley's second inauguration and the events immediately preceding it, see Margaret Leech, *In the Days of McKinley* (New York, 1959), 563–75.

68. Ibid., 574–75; Gould, *Presidency of William McKinley*, 240–41; Kristin L.

Hoganson, *Fighting for American Manhood: How Gender Politics Provoked the Spanish-American and Philippine-American Wars* (New Haven, CT, 1998), 133.

69. Second Inaugural Address of William McKinley, Mar. 4, 1901, the Avalon Project, Documents in Law, History and Diplomacy, http://avalon.law.yale.edu/19th_century/mckin2.asp (accessed Dec. 28, 2015).

70. Leech, *Days of McKinley*, 576.

71. Ibid., 581–84.

72. See Walter H. Page, "The Pan-American Exposition," *World's Work* 2 (Aug. 1901): 1015–48.

73. Leech, *Days of McKinley*, 584.

74. Scott Miller, *The President and the Assassin: McKinley, Terror, and Empire at the Dawn of the American Century* (New York, 2011), 105–13, 97–98, 247–49; Eric Rauchway, *Murdering McKinley: The Making of Theodore Roosevelt's America* (New York, 2003), 17–18.

75. Leech, *Days of McKinley*, 594–95; Miller, *President and the Assassin*, 300–301, 313.

76. TR to Albert Baird Cummins, Sept. 7, 1901; TR to Lodge, Sept. 9, 1901, in *LTR*, 3:140, 141–43 (quotation on 141); Kuylendall, "Exterminate the Anarchist," *Plaindealer* (Topeka, KS), Oct. 43, 1901; Miller, *President and the Assassin*, 312–14, 316–17; Leech, *Days of McKinley*, 596; Dalton, *Theodore Roosevelt*, 200.

77. Leech, *Days of McKinley*, 600; Dalton, *Theodore Roosevelt*, 200.

78. TR to Lodge, Sept. 23, 1901, in *LTR*, 3:150; Miller, *President and the Assassin*, 320, 331; Dalton, *Theodore Roosevelt*, 200–201.

Epilogue. Eclipse of Old Heroes

1. *The Man Who Shot Liberty Valance*, directed by John Ford (1962, Paramount Pictures). The parallels in the film between the fictional story of Ransom Stoddard and the real-life one of Theodore Roosevelt may not have been entirely coincidental. See Charles J. Maland, "From Aesthete to Pappy," in *John Ford Made Westerns: Filming the Legend in the Sound Era*, ed. Gaylyn Studlar and Matthew Bernstein (Bloomington, IN, 2001), 224.

2. Edmund Morris, *The Rise of Theodore Roosevelt* (New York, 1979), 15.

3. Kathleen Dalton, *Theodore Roosevelt: A Strenuous Life* (New York, 2002), 215–17, 229, 260–62, 321–22. On Brownsville, see also John D. Weaver, *The Brownsville Raid* (New York, 1970).

4. For varying accounts, see Patricia O'Toole, *When Trumpets Call: Theodore Roosevelt after the White House* (New York, 2005), chap. 16; Edmund Morris, *Colonel Roosevelt* (New York, 2010), 475–78, 483–99; William H. Harbaugh, *Power and Responsibility: The Life and Times of Theodore Roosevelt* (New York, 1961), 469–74; Edward J. Renehan, *The Lion's Pride: Theodore Roosevelt and His Family in Peace and War* (New York, 1998), 127–34; Dalton, *Theodore Roosevelt*, 474–78.

5. "Now He's the Gin'ral of Our Armee," from the *New York Call*, reprinted in *Truth* (Erie, PA), July 22, 1916; "A Wilson Army First," *Boston Journal*, Apr. 12, 1917.

6. Frederick S. Wood, *Roosevelt as We Knew Him* (Philadelphia, 1927), 419–20; TR to Frank Ross McCoy, July 10, 1915 and TR to Arthur Hamilton Lee, Sept. 2, 1915, in *LTR*, 8:947–48, 966–71, esp. 970.

7. "Urges for Preparedness," *Idaho Register* (Idaho Falls), July 30, 1915; *Boston Post*, Oct. 19, 1916. TR made the widely reported "dishrag" comment in Louisville, KY, on Oct. 18, 1916.

8. "Roosevelt Sizes Up War Secretary as Exquisitely Unfit," *Philadelphia Inquirer*, Oct., 24, 1916; TR to Baker, Feb., 2 1917 and Feb. 7, 1917, in *LTR*, 8:1149–50, 1151; Baker to TR, Feb. 9, 1917, *LTR*, 8:1151n. On Baker, see Douglas B. Craig, *Progressives at War: William G. McAdoo and Newton D. Baker, 1863–1941* (Baltimore, 2013).

9. TR to Hiram Warren Johnson, Feb. 17, 1917, *LTR*, 8:1153–56, esp., 1153–54.

10. "Passing of the Cavalry," *New Haven (CT) Register*, July 5, 1898; Harbaugh, *Power and Responsibility*, 471.

11. "Regiment about Organized," *Dallas Morning News*, Apr. 7, 1917; "Dave W. Dobbins Will Join Teddy Regiment," *San Jose Mercury News*, May 5, 1917; Watterson, quoted in Harbaugh, *Life and Times of Theodore Roosevelt*, 471–72. See also Henry Cabot Lodge, ed., *Selections from the Correspondence of Theodore Roosevelt and Henry Cabot Lodge, 1884–1918*, 2 vols. (New York, 1925), 2:505; TR to Lodge, Mar. 22, 1917, in *LTR*, 8:1165. For the exchange between Roosevelt and Baker, see TR to Baker, Mar. 23, 1917, and Baker's reply, in *LTR*, 8:1166, 1166n.

12. Joseph P. Tumulty, *Woodrow Wilson as I Knew Him* (Garden City, NY, 1924), 285, 287–88, 286.

13. Baker to TR [excerpts], Apr. 13, 1917, in *LTR*, 8:1174–75n; Baker, quoted in Alvin Johnson, *Pioneer's Progress: An Autobiography* (New York, 1952), 253. See also *LTR*, 8:1184n.

14. "T.R. Not Allowed to Raise Division," *Oregonian* (Portland), Apr. 28, 1917; O'Toole, *When Trumpets Call*, 318.

15. TR to Baker, Apr. 23, 1917, in *LTR*, 8:1176–84, esp. 1182, 1176–77.

16. TR to Mary L. Brown, July 26, 1918; TR to Edith Newbold Jones Wharton, Aug. 15, 1918, in *LTR*, 8:1355, 1363; Sylvia Jukes Morris, *Edith Kermit Roosevelt* (New York, 1980), 423; Dalton, *Theodore Roosevelt*, 505.

ESSAY ON SOURCES

In a broad sense, this book looks into historical forces that underlay American empire-building at the end of the nineteenth century. The literature on that subject is much too vast to be covered adequately in the preceding pages and in the short space provided here, but many of the following titles do contain extensive bibliographies and historiographical discussions. In one way, however, this study reflects a significant advantage over many previous ones in that the massive digital archiving now available online has given scholars instant access to a far greater wealth of newspaper and magazine resources for nineteenth-century America than ever before.

Theodore Roosevelt

For Roosevelt material, in addition to the extensive TR collections at the Library of Congress and Harvard University, see *The Almanac of Theodore Roosevelt* at www.theodore-roosevelt.com/trscholar.html and the digital collections at the Theodore Roosevelt Center at Dickinson State University, www.theodorerooseveltcenter.org/. Among TR's massive writings, see especially *The Letters of Theodore Roosevelt*, ed. Elting E. Morison et al., 8 vols. (Cambridge, MA, 1951–54), and *The Works of Theodore Roosevelt*, ed. Hermann Hagedorn, 20 vols. (New York, 1923). Of particular relevance to the present study, see also Theodore Roosevelt, *The Naval War of 1812* (New York, 1883); *The Winning of the West*, 4 vols. (New York, 1889–96); *American Ideals and Other Essays, Social and Political* (New York, 1897); *The Rough Riders* (New York, 1899); and *An Autobiography* (New York, 1913).

The most comprehensive and balanced of the scholarly biographies of Roosevelt is Kathleen Dalton's *Theodore Roosevelt: A Strenuous Life* (New York, 2002). See also Dalton, "Why America Loved Teddy Roosevelt; or, Charisma Is in the Eyes of the Beholders," in *Our Selves/Our Past: Psychological Approaches to American History*, ed. Robert J. Brugger (Baltimore, 1981), 269–91, and "Finding Theodore Roosevelt: A Personal and Political Story," *Journal of the Gilded Age and Progressive Era* 6 (Oct. 2007): 363–84. For an interesting recent study of TR's image in American life since his death, see Michael Patrick Cullinane, *Theodore Roosevelt's Ghost: The History and Memory of an American Icon* (Baton Rouge, LA, 2017). Among other prominent biographical works, beginning with the most recently published, see Douglas Brinkley, *The Wilderness Warrior: Theodore Roosevelt and the Crusade for America* (New York, 2009); Patricia O'Toole, *When Trumpets Call: Theodore Roosevelt after the White House*

(New York, 2005); Sarah Watts, *Rough Rider in the White House: Theodore Roosevelt and the Politics of Desire* (Chicago, 2003); Louis Auchincloss, *Theodore Roosevelt* (New York, 2002); H. W. Brands, *T. R.: The Last Romantic* (New York, 1997); Nathan Miller *Theodore Roosevelt: A Life* (New York, 1992); John Milton Cooper, *The Warrior and the Priest: Woodrow Wilson and Theodore Roosevelt* (Cambridge, MA, 1985); Edmund Morris, *The Rise of Theodore Roosevelt* (New York, 1979), followed by his *Theodore Rex* (New York, 2001), and *Colonel Roosevelt* (New York, 2010); John M. Blum, *The Republican Roosevelt* (Cambridge, MA, 1967); G. Wallace Chessman, *Governor Theodore Roosevelt: The Albany Apprenticeship, 1898–1900* (Cambridge, MA, 1965); William H. Harbaugh, *Power and Responsibility: The Life and Times of Theodore Roosevelt* (New York, 1961); Edward Wagenknecht, *The Seven Worlds of Theodore Roosevelt* (New York, 1958); Richard Hofstadter, "Theodore Roosevelt: The Conservative as Progressive," in *The American Political Tradition and the Men Who Made It* (New York, 1948), 206–37; and Henry F. Pringle, *Theodore Roosevelt: A Biography* (New York, 1931).

On TR's family life, see especially Edward J. Renehan, *The Lion's Pride: Theodore Roosevelt and His Family in Peace and War* (New York, 1998); Sylvia Morris, *Edith Kermit Roosevelt: Portrait of a First Lady* (New York, 1980); and Hermann Hagedorn, *The Roosevelt Family of Sagamore Hill* (New York, 1954). Regarding Roosevelt's childhood and life as a young man, see David McCullough, *Mornings on Horseback* (New York, 1981), and Carleton Putnam, *Theodore Roosevelt: The Formative Years, 1858–1886* (New York, 1959).

My study differs from others on the Rough Riders by viewing them much more from a cultural perspective than from a military one, while still blending the two approaches. Other book-length works include Mark Lee Gardner, *Theodore Roosevelt, His Cowboy Regiment, and the Immortal Charge Up San Juan Hill* (New York, 2016); Jon Knokey, *Theodore Roosevelt and the Making of American Leadership* (New York, 2015); Dale L. Walker, *The Boys of '98: Theodore Roosevelt and the Rough Riders* (New York, 1999); Peggy Samuels and Harold Samuels, *Teddy Roosevelt at San Juan* (College Station, TX, 1997); Virgil Carrington Jones, *Roosevelt's Rough Riders: The Saga of the Most Unusual American Regiment and its Role in the Spanish-American War* (Garden City, NY, 1971); and Henry Castor, *Theodore Roosevelt and the Rough Riders* (New York, 1954).

The Turn of the Century

On jingoism in addition to TR's, see Evan Thomas, *The War Lovers: Roosevelt, Lodge, Hearst, and the Rush to Empire, 1898* (New York, 2010). On Alfred T. Mahan, see Jon Tetsuro Sumida, *Inventing Grand Strategy and Teaching Command: The Classic Works of Alfred Thayer Mahan Reconsidered* (Baltimore, 1997); and Richard W. Turk, *The Ambiguous Relationship: Theodore Roosevelt and Alfred Thayer Mahan* (Westport, CT, 1987). For Frederic Remington, see *Frederic Remington: The Masterworks*, ed. Michael Edward Shapiro and Peter H. Hassrick (New York, 1988); Ben Merchant Vorpahl, *Frederic Remington and the West: With the Eye of the Mind* (Austin, TX, 1977); and Douglas Allen, *Frederic Remington and the Spanish-American War* (New York, 1971).

Regarding Henry Cabot Lodge, see William C. Widenor, *Henry Cabot Lodge and the Search for an American Foreign Policy* (Berkeley, CA, 1980). On Albert J. Beveridge, see John Braemen, *Albert J. Beveridge: American Nationalist* (Chicago, 1971). For William Randolph Hearst, there is David Nasaw, *The Chief: The Life of William Randolph Hearst* (New York, 2000). And on Richard Harding Davis, see Arthur Lubow, *The Reporter Who Would Be King: A Biography of Richard Harding Davis* (New York, 1992), and Davis's own *Notes of a War Correspondent* (New York, 1910).

On William McKinley and his administration, see especially Lewis L. Gould, *The Presidency of William McKinley* (Lawrence, KS, 1980), which highlights changes his administration brought to the presidency. More critical of McKinley is John Dobson, *Reticent Expansionism: The Foreign Policy of William McKinley* (Pittsburgh, 1988). Also see H. Wayne Morgan, *William McKinley and His America* (rev. ed., Kent, OH, 2003); and Margaret Leech, *In the Days of McKinley* (New York, 1959). H. W. Brands, *The Reckless Decade: America in the 1890s* (Chicago, 1995), offers a readable overview of the period. Much older but still of value is Harold U. Faulkner, *Politics, Reform and Expansion* (New York, 1959).

For the impact of the Civil War on American thought and popular attitudes of the late nineteenth century, see especially David W. Blight, *Race and Reunion: The Civil War in American Memory* (Cambridge, MA, 2001); David E. Shi, *Facing Facts: Realism in American Thought and Culture, 1850–1920* (New York, 1995); and George M. Frederickson, *The Inner Civil War: Northern Intellectuals and the Crisis of the Union* (New York, 1965).

For studies of the changing cultural meaning of manhood, see Kevin P. Murphy, *Political Manhood: Red Bloods, Mollycoddles, and the Politics of Progressive Era Reform* (New York, 2008); John Pettegrew, *Brutes in Suits: Male Sensibility in America, 1890–1920* (Baltimore, 2007); Amy S. Greenberg, *Manifest Manhood and the Antebellum American Empire* (London, 2005); Clifford Putney, *Muscular Christianity: Manhood and Sports in Protestant America, 1880–1920* (Cambridge, MA, 2001); Michael Kimmel, *Manhood in America: A Cultural History* (New York, 1996); E. Anthony Rotundo, *American Manhood: Transformations in Masculinity from the Revolution to the Modern Era* (New York, 1993); Mark C. Carnes, *Secret Ritual and Manhood in Victorian America* (New Haven, 1989); David Leverenz, *Manhood and the American Renaissance* (Ithaca, NY, 1989); David I. Macleod, *Building Character in the American Boy: The Boy Scouts, YMCA, and Their Forerunners, 1870–1920* (Madison, WI, 1983); and Joseph F. Kett, *Rites of Passage: Adolescence in America, 1790 to the Present* (New York, 1977).

As for the influence of the frontier and westward expansion on American cultural attitudes of the 1890s and early 1900s, Richard White's "Frederick Jackson Turner and Buffalo Bill," in *The Frontier in American History*, ed. James R. Grossman (Berkeley, 1994), 6–65, offers an engaging starting place. On the regenerative potential of the frontier, see Richard Slotkin, *Regeneration Through Violence: The Mythology of the American Frontier, 1600–1860* (Norman, OK, 1973), and his *Gunfighter Nation: The Myth of the Frontier in Twentieth Century America* (New York, 1992). See also Michael L. Collins, *That Damned Cowboy: Theodore Roosevelt and the American West, 1883–1898*

(New York, 1989); Richard Drinnon, *Facing West: The Metaphysics of Indian-Hating and Empire Building* (Minneapolis, 1980); and G. Edward White, *The Eastern Establishment and the Western Experience: The West of Frederic Remington, Theodore Roosevelt, and Owen Wister* (New Haven, 1968). Also, on the evolution of the cowboy myth and its staying power in American popular culture, Alf H. Walle's *The Cowboy Hero and Its Audience: Popular Culture as Market Derived Art* (Bowling Green, OH, 2000), merits attention.

The Spanish-American War

Historians have found all kinds of reasons for the US decision to go to war in 1898. Some of the best recent works have stressed themes of gender, race, and the reasserting of traditional white Anglo-Saxon notions of manhood in 1890s America. These include Eric T. Love, *Race over Empire: Racism and US Imperialism, 1865–1900* (Chapel Hill, 2004), and Kristin L. Hoganson, *Fighting for American Manhood: How Gender Politics Provoked the Spanish-American and Philippine-American Wars* (New Haven, CT, 1998). More broadly, see Lewis L. Gould, *The Spanish-American War and President McKinley* (Lawrence, KS, 1982); H. Wayne Morgan, *America's Road to Empire: The War with Spain and Overseas Expansion* (New York, 1965); and Walter LaFeber, *The New Empire: An Interpretation of American Expansion, 1860–1898* (Ithaca, NY, 1963). Of special interest is Richard Hofstadter's "Cuba, the Philippines, and Manifest Destiny," in *Essays in American Diplomacy*, ed. Armin Rappaport (New York, 1967), 149–70, which argued that a "psychic crisis" in American culture, spurred by several factors, including the Panic of 1893, social turmoil, and the closing of the frontier, made a foreign war in 1898 seem attractive.

On the war itself, see particularly Graham A. Cosmas, *An Army for Empire: The United States Army in the Spanish-American War*, 2nd ed. (College Station, TX, 1994); and David F. Trask, *The War with Spain in 1898* (New York, 1981). Also of note are Robert B. Edgerton, *"Remember the Maine, To Hell with Spain": America's 1898 Adventure in Imperialism* (Lewiston, NY, 2004); Edward J. Marolda, *Theodore Roosevelt, the US Navy and the Spanish-American War* (London, 2001); Ivan Musicant, *Empire by Default: The Spanish-American War and the Dawn of the American Century* (New York, 1998); John L. Offner, *An Unwanted War: The Diplomacy of the United States and Spain over Cuba, 1895–1898* (Chapel Hill, NC, 1992); Louis A. Pérez, *Cuba under the Platt Amendment, 1902–1934* (Pittsburgh, 1986) and *Cuba between Empires, 1878–1902* (Pittsburgh, PA, 1983); Gould, *Spanish-American War and President McKinley*; Gerald Linderman, *The Mirror of War: American Society and the Spanish-American War* (Ann Arbor, MI, 1974); Philip S. Foner, *The Spanish-Cuban-American War and the Birth of American Imperialism, 1895–1902*, 2 vols. (New York, 1972); and Frank Freidel, *The Splendid Little War* (Boston, 1958).

Regarding African American soldiers in the Spanish-American War, see Edward Van Zile Scott, *The Unwept: Black Soldiers and the Spanish American War* (Montgomery, AL, 1996); Bernard C. Nalty, *Strength for the Fight: A History of Black Americans in the*

Military (New York, 1986); Willard B. Gatewood Jr., *"Smoked Yankees" and the Struggle for Empire: Letters from Negro Soldiers, 1898–1902* (Urbana, IL, 1971) and *Black Americans and the White Man's Burden* (Urbana, IL, 1975); William H. Leckie, *The Buffalo Soldiers: A Narrative of the Negro Cavalry in the West* (Norman, OK, 1967); Theophilus G. Steward, *The Colored Regulars in the United States Army* (1904; reprint, New York, 1969); Edward A. Johnson, *History of Negro Soldiers in the Spanish-American War, and Other Items of Interest* (1899; reprint, New York, 1970); and Hershel V. Cashin et al., *Under Fire with the Tenth Cavalry* (1899; reprint, New York, 1970).

As for the war in the Philippines, good places to start include Stuart Creighton Miller, *"Benevolent Assimilation": The American Conquest of the Philippines, 1899–1903* (New Haven, CT, 1982); Brian McAllister Linn, *The Philippine War, 1899–1902* (Lawrence, KS, 2000); David J. Silbey, *A War of Frontier and Empire: The Philippine-American War, 1899–1902* (New York, 2007); and Gregg Jones, *Honor in the Dust: Theodore Roosevelt, War in the Philippines, and the Rise and Fall of America's Imperial Dream* (New York, 2012). On the role of imagery in the forming of American perceptions of the Philippines, see David Brody, *Visualizing American Empire: Orientalism and Imperialism in the Philippines* (Chicago, 2010).

Among the best recent titles on American imperialism are Frank Ninkovich, *The Global Republic: America's Inadvertent Rise to World Power* (Chicago, 2014) and *The United States and Imperialism* (Malden, MA, 2001); Ian Tyrrell, *Transnational Nation: United States History in Global Perspective since 1789* (New York, 2007); and Niall Ferguson, *Colossus: The Rise and Fall of the American Empire* (New York, 2004).

For works focusing more on specific aspects of American empire building, see Mark Zwonitzer, *The Statesman and the Storyteller: John Hay, Mark Twain, and the Rise of American Imperialism* (Chapel Hill, NC, 2016); Matthew F. Jacobson, *Barbarian Virtues: The United States Encounters Foreign Peoples at Home and Abroad, 1876–1917* (New York, 2000); David Traxel, *1898: The Birth of the American Century* (New York, 1998) and *Crusader Nation: The United States in Peace and the Great War, 1898–1920* (New York, 2006); J. Michael Hogan, *The Panama Canal in American Politics: Domestic Advocacy and the Evolution of Policy* (Carbondale, IL, 1986); Richard H. Collin, *Theodore Roosevelt, Culture, Diplomacy, and Expansion: A New View of American Imperialism* (Baton Rouge, LA, 1985); and Emily S. Rosenberg, *Spreading the American Dream: American Economic and Cultural Expansion, 1890–1945* (New York, 1982). David H. Burton's *Theodore Roosevelt: Confident Imperialist* (Philadelphia, 1968) interestingly finds TR's beliefs not to be consistent with social Darwinism. See also Burton, "Theodore Roosevelt's Social Darwinism and Views on Imperialism," *Journal of the History of Ideas* 26 (Jan.–Mar. 1965): 103–18, and "Theodore Roosevelt: Confident Imperialist," *Review of Politics* 23 (July 1961): 356–77. See, in addition, William Appleman Williams's new left classics, *The Roots of the Modern American Empire: A Study of the Growth and Shaping of Social Consciousness in a Marketplace Society* (New York, 1969) and *The Tragedy of American Diplomacy* (Cleveland, 1959). Also among classic works, see Frederick Merk, *Manifest Destiny and Mission in American History: A Reinterpretation* (New York, 1963), and Howard K. Beale, *Theodore Roosevelt and the Rise of America to World Power*

(Baltimore, 1956). In addition to these studies, two anthologies of value are *Colonial Crucible: Empire in the Making of the Modern American State*, ed. Alfred W. McCoy and Francisco A. Scarano (Madison, WI, 2009) and *The Cultures of United States Imperialism*, ed. Amy Kaplan and Donald E. Pease (Durham, NC, 1993).

For the anti-imperialists, see Michael Patrick Cullinane, *Liberty and American Anti-Imperialism, 1898–1909* (New York, 2012); Robert L. Beisner, *From the Old Diplomacy to the New, 1865–1900* (Arlington Heights, IL, 1986) and *Twelve against Empire: The Anti-Imperialists, 1898–1900* (New York, 1968); Richard E. Welch Jr., *Response to Imperialism: The United States and the Philippine-American War, 1899–1902* (Chapel Hill, NC, 1979); and E. Berkeley Tompkins, *Anti-Imperialism in the United States: The Great Debate, 1890–1920* (Philadelphia, 1970).

War and Culture

The "cultural approach" of this book emphasizes motivating belief systems, patterns of tradition, and uses of language and imagery that influenced various sorts of people to think and behave as they did. For elaboration on these elements and application in military studies, see Akira Iriye, "Culture," *Journal of American History* 77 (June 1990): 99–107, and John Shy, "The Cultural Approach to the History of War," *Journal of Military History* 57 (Oct. 1993): 13–26. Recent studies that have approached the Spanish-American War from a cultural perspective, in addition to Hoganson's *Fighting for American Manhood*, include Amy Kaplan, *The Anarchy of Empire in the Making of US Culture* (Cambridge, MA, 2002); Bonnie M. Miller, *From Liberation to Conquest: The Visual and Popular Culture of the Spanish-American War of 1898* (Amherst, MA, 2011); and Matthew McCullough, *The Cross of War: Christian Nationalism and US Expansion in the Spanish-American War* (Madison, WI, 2014). See also Bonnie Miller's "Remember the Alamo to Remember the Maine: The Visual Ideologies of the Mexican and the Spanish American Wars," in *The Martial Imagination: Cultural Aspects of American Warfare*, ed. Jimmy L. Bryan Jr. (College Station, TX, 2013).

On the making of "heroes" in American culture, see Edward Tabor Linenthal, *Changing Images of the Warrior Hero in America: A History of Popular Symbolism* (New York, 1982); Marshall William Fishwick, *American Heroes: Myth and Reality* (Westport, CT, 1975); and Dixon Wecter, *The Hero in America: A Chronicle of Hero-Worship* (1941; reprint, New York, 1972). For interesting observations on how the celebration of Roosevelt differed from traditional hero appreciation in American history, see Lori Bogle, "The Spanish American War's 'Most Durable Hero': Admiral Pasquale Cervera and Popular Heroic Values in the United States, 1898–1909," *War and Society* 20 (May 2017): 1–22.

Among many broader studies of late-nineteenth-century American culture and intellectual life, see Louis Menand, *The Metaphysical Club: A Story of Ideas in America* (New York, 2001); Gary Gerstle, "Theodore Roosevelt and the Divided Character of American Nationalism," *Journal of American History* 86 (Dec. 1999): 1280–1307; Alan Trachtenberg, *The Incorporation of America: Culture and Society in the Gilded Age* (New

York, 1982); and Richard Hofstadter, *Social Darwinism in American Thought* (Boston, 1944).

Regarding questions of ethnicity and race, see Gary Gerstle, *American Crucible: Race and Nation in the Twentieth Century* (Princeton, NJ, 2001); Gail Bederman, *Manliness and Civilization: A Cultural History of Gender and Race in the United States, 1880–1917* (Chicago, 1995); Arnaldo Testi, "The Gender of Reform Politics: Theodore Roosevelt and the Culture of Masculinity," *Journal of American History* 81 (Mar. 1995): 1509–33; Alexander Saxton, *The Rise and Fall of the White Republic: Class Politics and Mass Culture in Nineteenth-Century America* (New York, 1990); Reginald Horsman, *Race and Manifest Destiny: The Origins of American Racial Anglo-Saxonism* (Cambridge, MA, 1981); Thomas G. Dyer, *Theodore Roosevelt and the Idea of Race* (Baton Rouge, 1980); Ronald Takaki, *Iron Cages: Race and Culture in Nineteenth-Century America* (Berkeley, 1971); and John Higham, *Strangers in the Land: Patterns of American Nativism, 1860–1925* (Brunswick, NJ, 1955). Cecilia Elizabeth O'Leary, *To Die For: The Paradox of American Patriotism* (Princeton, NJ, 1999), addresses the question of ethnicity as part of her study of the shaping of American patriotic rituals and symbols between the Civil War and World War I. Alexander Aleinikoff's *Semblances of Sovereignty: The Constitution, the State, and American Citizenship* (Cambridge, MA, 2002) explores the issue of American citizenship for peoples of the new US overseas possessions. Marilyn Lake and Henry Reynolds, *Drawing the Global Color Line* (Cambridge, 2008), examine the exportation of white supremacist ideas in the late 1800s.

Regarding the republican tradition and its connection to military values, see Karl Friedrich Walling, *Republican Empire: Alexander Hamilton on War and Free Government* (Lawrence, KS, 1999), and, much more broadly, J. G. A. Pocock, *The Machiavellian Moment: Florentine Political Thought and the Atlantic Republican Tradition* (Princeton, NJ, 1975). On the fragility of republics and how early Americans thought to preserve theirs, see Drew R. McCoy, *The Elusive Republic: Political Economy in Jeffersonian America* (Chapel Hill, NC, 1980); Gerald Stourzh, *Alexander Hamilton and the Idea of Republican Government* (Stanford, CA, 1970); and, above all, Gordon S. Wood, *The Creation of the American Republic, 1776–1787* (Chapel Hill, NC, 1969). For late-nineteenth-century applications and permutations of republicanism, see T. J. Jackson Lears, *No Place of Grace: Antimodernism and the Transformation of American Culture, 1880–1920* (New York, 1981); Dorothy Ross, "The Liberal Tradition Revisited and the Republican Tradition Addressed," in *New Directions in American Intellectual History*, ed. John Higham and Paul K. Conkin (Baltimore, MD, 1979); and John R. Kasson, *Civilizing the Machine: Technology and Republican Values in America, 1776–1900* (New York, 1976). On beliefs regarding the obligations of American citizenship, see Rogers M. Smith, *Civil Ideals: Conflicting Visions of Citizenship in US History* (New Haven, 1997). And on the tradition of citizen soldiering in the early republic, see Ricardo A. Herrera, *For Liberty and the Republic: The American Citizen as Soldier, 1775–1861* (New York, 2015); Lorien Foote, *The Gentlemen and the Roughs: Violence, Honor, and Manhood in the Union Army* (New York, 2010); and Caroline Cox, *A Proper Sense of Honor: Service and Sacrifice in George Washington's Army* (Chapel Hill, NC, 2004).

INDEX

Adams, Brooks, 18, 19, 37, 66
Adams, Charles Francis, 115
Adams, John Quincy, 44
African Americans: as cowboys, 75; equality for, 117; and notion of ideal manhood, 21; in Rough Riders, 67; among victims of *Maine* disaster, 52
African American soldiers, 106, 107, 131, 132, 160–61; aftermath of Spanish-American War, 133; and continued segregation in the military, 67, 134; given credit by individual Rough Riders, 108; lack of credit received for service, 131–33; patronized by TR, 133. *See also* Buffalo Soldiers
Aguinaldo, Emilio, 60, 146, 155; rebellion led by, 148
Alabama, state of, 72
Albuquerque, New Mexico, 108
Aldrich, Nelson W., 46
Alger, Russell A., 64, 76, 124
Altgeld, John Peter, 151
American Anti-Imperialist League, 116, 144
Andersson, Alfred O., 87
Andrews, J. E. (sergeant, Third Cavalry), 110
anti-imperialism, 148
anti-imperialists, 24, 61, 115–17, 142, 153, 155; meeting at Faneuil Hall, 89, 115, 146; objection to Treaty of Paris, 123, 150; opposed to overseas frontier, 124; on TR, 139; supported by Twain, 143–47
Arizona Territory, 74, 77, 85, 117, 119; Rough Riders from, 84–85, 86
Art Students League, 55
Atlantic Monthly, 4, 27, 29, 38, 60, 138
Aylesworth, Barton O., 129
Aztec, New Mexico, 2

Baden-Powell, Robert, 20
Baker, Newton Diehl, 164, 165, 166
Ball's Bluff, battle of, 14, 16
Baltimore, Maryland, 128, 139, 148
Barton, Clara, 111
"Battle of San Juan Hill," 3, 29, 113, 114, 121, 127, 129, 131; invention of name, 2, 160
Beard, Daniel Carter, 144
Beveridge, Albert J., 142
Bigelow, Poultney, 56
"Big Stick" diplomacy, 143
Black, Frank, 134
black powder, 91–92
Blight, David, 133
Boas, Franz, 23
Boer War, 145, 146, 157
Bohemian Club, 80
Borglum, Solon, 120
Boston, Massachusetts, 15, 16, 80, 89, 100, 109, 115, 116, 126, 135
Bostonians, The (James), 138
Boston Journal, 83, 98, 125, 163
Boutwell, George S., 116–17
Boxer Rebellion, 142, 145–46, 151
Boy Scout movement, 20
Bradford, Gamaliel, 115
Britain. *See* Great Britain
Brodie, Alexander O., 74, 84
Brown, John, 4
Bryan, William Jennings, 39, 71, 130, 148, 150, 151, 152
Buffalo Bill. *See* Cody, William F.
Buffalo Bill's Wild West Show, 34, 35, 131
Buffalo Soldiers, 88, 106, 107, 108, 110
Bull, Charles C., 100

California, state of, 42, 89
"Call, The" (Mordaunt), 2
Campos, Arsenio Martínez, 45
Camp Wyckoff, 126, 129
Cannon, Joe, 153
Cánovas de Castillo, Antonio, 48
Capron, Allyn, 94–95, 97, 99, 100, 109
Carow, Charles, 104
Carr, Joseph A., 110
Cash, Walter S., 100
"celebrity-hero" concept, 125–26
Century Club, 80
Cerrillos, New Mexico, 107
Cervera, Pascual de, 90, 112
Chamberlain, Joshua Lawrence, 18
Chanler, William Astor, 50
Chanler, Winthrop, 24, 62, 166
charging, in battle: depicted by Remington, 121–22; desired by TR, 162; as military concept, 109; by Rough Riders, 1, 2, 106, 107, 108, 110, 113, 114, 115, 121, 127, 128
Chicago Journal, 150
Chicago World's Fair of 1893, 24, 75
Chilcoot, Fred, 106
China, 27, 49, 59, 142, 143; Boxer Rebellion in, 142, 145–46, 151; US interests in, 142
citizen soldiers, 1, 80; celebrated as concept, 70–71, 100, 113, 119; concerns about, 70, 98; Rough Riders as, 66–72
Civil Rights Act of 1875, 116
Civil War veterans, celebrated, 16, 17, 126
Cleveland, Grover, 16, 38, 39, 47, 50, 56, 72, 75
Cleveland Plain Dealer, 108
Cody, William F. ("Buffalo Bill"), 34, 35, 73, 131
Colorado, state of, 74
Colorado Springs, Colorado, 100
Confederacy, "lost cause" of, 16, 134
Congress, US. *See* US Congress
Congress of Rough Riders of the World. *See* Buffalo Bill's Wild West Show
"Conquest of the United States by Spain, The" (W. G. Sumner), 146–47
Cortelyou, George, 54, 89, 156
Cosmas, Graham, 69
Coville, Allen M., 109
cowboys, 32; admired by TR, 12, 82–83, 86; African Americans as, 75; golden age of, in the West, 75; myth of, 75; TR reinventing himself as, 12, 13; among Rough Riders, 67, 109, 129, 130. *See also* West, American
Crane, Stephen, 96, 97, 99, 109
Cripple Creek, Colorado, 76
Crowninshield, Arent S., 49–50
Crowninshield, Casper, 14
Cuba: constitutional convention in, 154, 155; insurrectionists in, 46, 50, 51, 58; native population, 136; radicalism in, 44, 45; rebellion in, 47, 48, 50, 74; rural population, 45; under Spanish rule, 41, 44, 47, 48, 128; and Teller Amendment, 154; US interests in, 43, 44, 47, 143, 154
Cuba libre movement, 44, 45–47, 56, 74; supported by TR, 47
Czolgosz, Leon, 156, 157

Daiquirí, Cuba, 88, 90, 94
Dakota Territory, 12, 13, 37, 64, 65, 81, 86, 134. *See also* South Dakota, state of
Dalton, Kathleen, 134
Dalzell, John, 153
Dame, William E., 107
Davis, Richard Harding, 2, 46, 97, 99, 107, 113
defensive perimeter, US, 42–45
Deleaderler, Lizzie, 129
Democratic Party, 39, 150
Dewey, Commodore George, 59, 60, 113, 130, 140; and victory at Manila Bay, 116, 145, 146
Dibblee, Benjamin Harrison, 54
Dickens, Commander D. W., 53
Dixon, Thomas F., 125
Dobbins, Dave W., 165
Dorst, Joseph H., 105
Dudley, Nathan, 98, 99
Duncan, George B., 70
Duniway, W. S., 130
Dunn, George, 84
Dunne, Finley Peter, 150
Dupuy de Lôme, Enrique, 45, 51

Edison, Thomas, 152
Edmunds, George F., 116
El Caney, Cuba, 95, 101, 102, 114
Eliot, Charles, 38

empire, American, 60, 140, 142, 147. *See also* imperial expansion; imperialism
Endicott, William, 64
expansion, American, 123–24; and efforts to acquire Cuba, 43–44; in the Pacific, 89, 116. *See also* imperial expansion; "Large Policy"
Expansion, Under New-World Conditions (Strong), 140
expansionism, American, 22, 27, 129, 151. *See also* imperial expansion; imperialism; "Large Policy"
expansionists: in European countries, 41, 141; and policies of 1890s, 162; TR on, 137, 148; in United States, 5, 19, 26–27, 31, 42, 43, 124, 140. *See also* "Large Policy"

Faneuil Hall, 89, 115, 146
"feminine rough riders," 129
field hospitals, 100, 111
Fifteenth Amendment, 133
First United States Volunteer Cavalry, 7, 76, 87, 90, 101, 111, 113. *See also* Rough Riders
Fish, Hamilton (Grant's secretary of state), 42–43
Fish, Hamilton (Rough Rider), 94, 95, 97, 100
Fleming, Robert J. (Tenth Cavalry), 133
Florida, 88, 90
Florida Keys, 43
Forum, 19, 30, 38
Fourteenth Amendment, 133
Fox, John William, 78
France, 26, 141, 165, 166
Freeman, Will, 98
"frontier thesis," 25
Fuller, Melville W., 153

Galapagos Islands, 29
Gatling guns, 32, 110, 111
Georgia, state of, 11, 72
Germany, 27, 49, 50, 51, 141, 164, 165
Gibbon, Edward, 18
Gilbert, Horace, 111
Grant, Ulysses S., 18, 42, 125, 136
Great Britain, 20, 29, 51; and Anglo-Saxon heritage, 23; close to war with United States, 38; culture of, 57; and imperial expansion, 26, 27, 151; missionary activity, 23; naval power of, 38, 40–41, 141; size of army compared to United States', 69
Greene, Francis V., 64
Grey, Zane, 36
Grigsby, Melvin, 73; troop-raising by, 74, 83
Grimes, George, 102
Guam, 123, 153, 155
Guantánamo, 96
Gulf and Inland Waters, The (Mahan), 26

Hale, Eugene, 123
Hall, G. Stanley, 4
Hamilton, Alexander, 5
Hamilton Club, 136
Hamm, Margherita Arlina, 111
Hanna, Mark, 39, 46, 149–50, 153
Harper's, 30, 38, 55, 56, 124
Harper's Bazaar, 144
Harper's Ferry, raid on, 4
Harrison, Benjamin, 130
Harvard Club, 80, 135
"Harvard Regiment," 14, 15
Havana, Cuba, 33, 47, 88, 90, 119; Cuban constitutional convention in, 154, 155; and *Maine* disaster, 50–54
Hawaii, 28, 31, 153; annexation of, 39, 42–44, 50, 88, 122, 142, 145; opposition to annexation of, 88–89, 116
Hawkins, Hamilton, 110
Hay, John, 50, 148
Hearst, William Randolph, 46, 51, 53, 55; and *New York Journal*, 102
Hellman, P. A., 128
Higginson, Henry Lee, 18
Hoar, George Frisbie, 123
Holmes, Oliver Wendell, Jr., 7, 14–18, 22, 136; ideas of, favored by TR, 18, 138; injuries of, in Civil War, 14, 15; Memorial Day speech, 17–18; on military virtues, 7; "Soldiers' Faith," 41
Homer, Winslow, 55
Honeyman, J. D., 109
Hood, John, 52
Howells, William Dean, 145
Howze, Robert D., 103
Hughes, Charles Evans, 163
Hughes, Garfield, 108

Index 203

Idaho, state of, 74
Idaho Falls Times, 75
imperial expansion: advocates of, 4, 22, 26; critics of, 30–31, 116, 145, 146–47. *See also* anti-imperialism; "Large Policy"
imperialism, 27, 30; in America, 31, 33, 60, 124, 140, 143, 160; and American involvement in Far East, 145; and building a canal, 31, 39, 136, 142; causes of, 46; contrast with European colonialism, 31; economic arguments for, 141–42; fit with American traditions, 116, 146–47; moral limits of, 145; naval, 40; opposition to, 117, 146; racial and ethnic prejudices in, 141; TR on benefits of, 137; and subordinated peoples, 140. *See also* jingoes/jingoism; "Large Policy"
Indian Territory, 68, 77, 83
Influence of Sea Power upon History, The (Mahan), 26, 27
Insular Cases, 154–55
insurrectionists: in Cuba, 46, 50, 51, 58; in the Philippines, 60, 146, 148, 155
Iowa State Bystander, 132
Iowa State Capital, 131
Isbell, Thomas, 99–100

James, Frank, 73
James, Henry, 138
James, Jesse, 73
James, William, 89, 90, 115, 139
Japan, 27, 29, 41, 42, 43, 141, 162
Jefferson, Thomas, 10, 44, 86, 148
jingoes/jingoism, 6, 33, 148, 194; in American politics generally, 140; criticisms of, 89, 135, 139, 145, 147; doctrines of, 32–59; embraced by McKinley, 59, 147, 154; in foreign policy, 38; and intervention in Cuba, 44, 57; and "Large Policy," 59; of Lodge, 116; and occupation of Philippines, 59; of Remington, 56; of Republicans, 46, 51, 115, 148, 154; of TR, 6–7, 34, 40, 41, 63, 135; as source of inspiration, 144; spread of, 57; and war as necessary tonic, 53. *See also* expansionism, American; imperialism; "Large Policy"; Lodge, Henry Cabot; Mahan, Alfred Thayer; Remington, Frederic; Roosevelt, Theodore, Jr.

Johnston, Bartlett S., 148
Johnston, Joseph E., 72
Jones, James, 153
Jones, Levi, 83
Jordan, David Starr, 115

Kane, Woodbury, 103, 122
Kansas, state of, 75, 152
Kansas City, 84, 139
Kansas Pacific Railroad, 34
Kentucky, state of, 78
Kettle Hill, 110, 113, 118, 151; map of, 112; O'Neill killed at, 103–4; Rough Riders' charge up, 1, 2, 101, 102, 105, 107; Rough Riders' individual accounts of, 106–7
Key West, Florida, 49, 102
Kipling, Rudyard, 118
Knickerbocker Club, 78, 80, 100–101
Krag-Jørgensen bolt-action carbine, 91–92, 102, 111; compared with Mauser rifles, 92

Laird, Thomas J., 107
Langdon, Jesse, 103
"Large Policy," 28, 30, 39–42, 59, 122
Larned, William A., 103, 108
Las Guásimas, 103; "ambush" view, 99; casualties at, 98; fighting at, 1, 95–98, 103, 104, 105, 118, 119, 129, 151; newspaper assessments of Rough Riders in, 98–101; TR's account of, to Edith, 104–5
Las Vegas, New Mexico, 131
Lawton, H. W., 94, 95, 101
Lee, Alice Hathaway, 11–12
Lee, Fitzhugh, 72, 78
Lee, "Light Horse Harry," 72
Lee, Robert E., 72
Leroy-Beaulieu, Pierre Paul, 141
Lewis, Diocletian, 20
Liliuokalani (queen of Hawaii), 43
Linares (y Pombo), Arsenio, 96, 101, 112, 113
Lincoln, Abraham, 4, 5, 6, 9–10, 71, 136, 163
Little Texas (TR's horse), 2, 110
Llewellyn, William, 109
Lodge, Henry Cabot, 24, 30, 33, 38, 40, 62, 64, 103, 116, 124, 125, 148, 158, 166; on America becoming an imperialist power, 39
Long, John Davis, 49, 50, 53, 54, 59, 62

Lopez, Sixto, 151
Los Angeles Express, 138
Louisville Courier-Journal, 165
Lovelace, Carl, 97
Lowell, Charles Russell, 17
Luce, Stephen B., 26

Macfadden, Bernarr, 20
Mahan, Alfred Thayer, 33, 42, 43, 137; argument for imperial expansion, 27–29; childhood, 25; on Hawaii's value to United States, 28, 42, 43; influence on American expansionists, 26; influence on TR, 26–27, 30, 138; influence on Strong, 22, 140; naval career, 26; on need for powerful navy, 29, 31, 39, 40, 41, 47; on war as "necessary evil," 21
Maine. *See* USS *Maine*
manhood: concept of, 1, 3, 60, 64, 68; concern about decline of, 4, 18; exemplified by westerners, 35, 82, 86; as hallmark of western civilization, 30; TR on, 4, 11, 14–21, 68, 82; symbolized by Rough Riders, 95, 129; xenophobia and, 21
Manifest Destiny, 24, 27, 124, 147; embraced by TR, 5
Manila Bay, 59–61; blockade of, 60; Dewey's victory at, 60, 116, 140, 145, 146
Mann, Matthew D., 157
Man Who Shot Liberty Valance, The (film), 159–60
Marshall, Edward, 96, 97, 99, 103
Massachusetts, state of, 98, 115, 116, 123, 130
Mauser rifles, 92–93, 97, 102, 104; compared with Krag carbines, 92
McClellan, George B., 14
McClintock, James, 74
McCord, Myron H., 74
McKinley, Ida, 155
McKinley, William, 6, 10, 16, 39, 49; and annexation of conquered territory, 124; call for volunteers, 71; campaign for president (1896), 39, 40, 134; campaign for president (1900), 147–48, 149, 150, 152; death, 157–58; efforts to avoid war, 57, 58; foreign policy, 46, 47, 48, 50, 116, 154; military appointments by, 72; naming TR assistant secretary of navy, 40; and North-South reconciliation, 71–72, 155; on Pacific expansion, 89; perceived as weak by Spanish, 51; as president, 33, 61, 62, 152, 153; pursuing neutral policy toward Spain, 41, 44, 47, 49; recommending military action to Congress, 58–59, 66; response to *Maine* disaster, 53–54; TR's disagreements with, 148, 164; and Spanish request for peace, 113; tariff of 1890, 43; and US control in the Philippines, 140, 146, 154, 155; visit to Pan-American Exposition, 155, 156–57; and volunteer cavalry, 72, 76
McKinley tariff, 43
McPherson, James M., 103
McRae, Thomas, 153
Meriwether, Walter Scott, 52
Merritt, Wesley, 60, 113
Mervin, Henry C., 138
Metropolitan Club, 80
Metz, Theodore August, 134
Mexican-American War, 69, 72
Middleton, "Doc," 73
Miles, Nelson A., 64
military tactics, changes in, 70, 106
missionary activity, 23, 140
Mississippi Valley, 5, 142
Missouri, state of, 73, 75; and 1820 crisis, 148
Missouri Labor Bureau, 73
Mitchell, Mason, 103
"Model of Christian Charity" (Winthrop), 21
Monroe, James, 44, 155
Monroe Doctrine, 38, 41, 49, 61; Roosevelt Corollary to, 143
Montana, 74, 139
Montauk Point, 126
Moody, Dwight L., 23
Mordaunt, Thomas Osbert, 2
Morgan, J. P., 24
Morris, George P., 135
Morton, Levi P., 64
Murchie, Guy, 78

Naval War College, 6, 26, 41, 58
Naval War of 1812, The (TR), 11, 40
Navy Bill (1890), 29
Nebraska, state of, 106, 150, 152

neurasthenia, 19; antidote to, 94
Nevada, 35
New Gymnastics for Men, Women, and Children (Lewis), 20
New Hampshire, state of, 76
Newlands resolution, 88
New Mexico, 68, 77, 164
Newport, Rhode Island, 6, 26, 41
New York, city of, 121, 125, 126
New York, state of, 125
New York Call, 162
New York Evening Journal, 129
New York Herald, 146
New York Sun, 128
New York Times, 113
New York Tribune, 138
New York World, 146
Ninth (US) Cavalry regiment, 88, 114; in assault on Kettle Hill, 106, 107, 108, 110; ignored by white Americans, 131–32, 160; praise of, by Rough Riders, 108
North-South sectional differences, 3, 10, 67, 155; continued reconciliation of, 17, 71–72, 125, 133
novels, dime, 34
Nuttall, G. P., 92

Oklahoma Territory, 77, 83, 94
O'Neill, John, 85, 104
O'Neill, Pauline Marie Schindler, 85
O'Neill, William Owen ("Buckey"), 74, 85-86, 103-4, 119; death of, 104, 105, 108, 118; legend of, 85, 119
Ord, Jules Garesche, 110
Ostend Manifesto, 44
Our Country: Its Possible Future and Its Present Crisis (Strong), 22, 23, 140–41
overseas frontier, 124
Oyster Bay, New York, 104

Page, Walter Hines, 38, 60–61
Panama Canal, 123, 162
Pan-American Exposition (1901), 155–56
Panic of 1893, 27, 46, 71, 74, 75, 141, 148; recovery from, 153
Parker, John H., 110; and Gatling guns, 111
Parkman, Francis, 24
Pearson, Charles Henry, 37

Pennsylvania, state of, 69
Pershing, John J. ("Black Jack"), 108, 114
Philippines, 135, 136, 137, 139, 140, 142, 153; acquired by United States, 59, 60, 113, 116, 117; and Aguinaldo rebellion, 148, 155; ceded by Spain to United States, 123, 140; insurgency in, 41, 116, 146; under Spanish rule, 41, 58, 59; US intervention in, 33, 122, 140, 143, 144, 146, 147, 151, 154
Pierce, Franklin, 44
Pinchot, Gifford, 24
Platt, Orville H., 46, 154
Platt, Thomas, 134, 148, 149
Platt amendment, 154, 155
Polk, James K., 44, 147
Pollock, William J., 109
Powell, D. Frank, 73
Prescott, Arizona, 74, 85, 86, 106, 107, 117–20
presidential election: of 1896, 39–40, 47, 71; of 1900, 131, 147–52; of 1912, 163
Prioleau, George W., 131–32, 134
Proctor, Redfield, 58
professionalized military: arguments against, 70; arguments for, 69–70
Puerto Rico, 123, 135, 136, 137, 154
Pulitzer, Joseph, 46, 53
Pullman Strike, 56, 75

racism, 21, 132, 133, 141
radicalism, 21, 44-45, 60, 85, 142, 156-57
ranchers, 34, 37, 67; TR as, 12, 13
Ranch Life and the Hunting Trail (TR), 36
Ransom, C. M., 9
"Recessional" (Kipling), 118
reconcentrado (Cuba), 45
regeneration, of core values, 3–4, 11, 23, 25; power of the West in, 4, 36, 37, 75, 82
Reid, Whitelaw, and *New York Tribune*, 138
"Remember the *Maine*," 53
Remington, Frederic, 12; admired by TR, 122; art depicting Old West, 36–37, 55; art depicting Spanish-American War, 121–22; bigotry of, 56; jingoism of, 56; and reports from Cuba, 46, 56, 102
Remington, Seth Pierre, 55
Republican Party, 9, 71, 116, 117, 130, 134, 150, 154
Reubelt, George, 102

Riders of the Purple Sage (Grey), 36
Rittenhouse Club, 80
Roberts, Tom, 108
Robinson, Kenneth, 108
Roosevelt, Anna (Bamie), 12, 47, 65
Roosevelt, Archie, 66, 104, 127–28, 163
Roosevelt, Corinne (Robinson), 65, 66, 78
Roosevelt, Edith Carow, 9, 41, 65, 89, 104, 105, 126; health issues, 65–66, 77, 149; on son Quentin's death, 166
Roosevelt, Kermit, 66, 104, 126, 163
Roosevelt, Martha Bulloch, 11
Roosevelt, Quentin, 65, 163, 166
Roosevelt, Ted, 65, 89, 126
Roosevelt, Theodore, Jr. (TR): and American manhood, 5, 95; as assistant secretary of navy, 6, 39, 40, 59, 125; becoming president, 158; blind spot on racial matters, 133; candidacy for New York governor, 125, 126, 133, 134; childhood, 11–12; and commitment to civic values, 1, 64; in command of First Volunteer Cavalry, 101; corollary to Monroe Doctrine, 143; in Dakota Territory, 12, 13, 37, 64, 65, 81, 86, 134; efforts to raise volunteer cavalry for World War I, 162–63, 164, 165, 166; experience in the West, impact of, 13, 37; and father's decision not to fight in Civil War, 11, 63, 126; as governor of New York, 138; heroism in Cuba questioned, 151; jingoism of, 6, 40, 41, 135; leadership qualities, 66–67, 98, 151; lessons of citizenship, 11–13; on manhood, 4, 11, 14–21, 68, 82; on Manifest Destiny, 5; message for isolationists and anti-imperialists, 136–37; on military service, 137; as naval imperialist, 40; *The Naval War of 1812*, 11, 40; and notion of struggle for fitness, 6, 13, 21, 71, 94; as NYC police commissioner, 12, 20, 64, 134; as NYS assemblyman, 11, 81, 134; opinion of Bryan, 150; opinion of McKinley as president, 50, 54, 58, 148; personality, 79, 81; on the Philippines, 137; physical characteristics, 78–79; political ambition, 64, 113, 125; proclaimed "Hero of San Juan Hill," 2, 135, 158; as Progressive reformer, 134, 162; reaction to son Quentin's death, 166; reasons for volunteering to fight, 63–64; reputation, 124; rise to presidency, 7; *The Rough Riders*, 82, 126, 151; Rough Riders' observations of, 106; speech at Naval War College (1897), 6, 41; on "strenuous life," 134–40, 164; as vice president, 157, 158; as vice presidential candidate, 148–52; view of America in 1890s, 5; view of Spain, 57; *The Winning of the West*, 5, 12, 25, 82
Roosevelt, Theodore, Sr., 11
Root, Elihu, 24, 154
Roughing It (Twain), 35
"Rough Riders" (entourages for TR during election campaign), 152
Rough Riders (First US Volunteer Regiment): accounts of Kettle Hill charge, 106–7; Arizona contingent, 84–85, 86; and boost in American morale, 129; composition of, 67–68, 76; creation of, 64; credit given to African American soldiers, 106, 108; demobilized at Camp Wyckoff, 126; doubted by regular military, 69–70; ethos, 82; example of qualities of American soldier, 128; expectations of eastern recruits, 77–78, 82; expectations of western recruits, 86; media accounts of, 98–99; principal weapon used, 91–92; public views of, 6, 69–70, 89; quarantine at Montauk Point, 126; recruitment of, 76–78; reunions of, 131, 160, 161; training in San Antonio, 66, 78–87; view that Americans would always prevail, 100
Rough Riders, The (TR), 82, 126, 151
Rowley, Alfred R., 79
Rustin, Henry, 156

Sagamore Hill, 104
Sagasta, Práxedes Mateo, government of, 48, 58
Salem, Oregon, 130
Sampson, William T., 90, 112, 124, 130, 145
San Antonio, Texas, 109; Rough Riders' training in, 66, 78–87
San Francisco, California, 29, 42, 80, 142
San Francisco Examiner, 85
San Juan Heights, 1, 2, 68, 91, 95, 101, 114; African American troops at, 131–32; casualties from, 111–12; Spain's loss of, 113; terrain of, 105. *See also* Kettle Hill; San Juan Hill

San Juan Hill: assault on, 101, 107, 110, 151, 165; dispute over credit for victory, 113; map of, 112; TR as "Hero of," 2, 132, 135, 158. *See also* "Battle of San Juan Hill"
Santiago, Cuba, 29, 88, 90, 112, 113, 114, 115
Sargent, Dudley A., 20
Schurz, Carl, 115
Scott, Winfield, 69
Sedgwick, John, 15
Shafter, William R., 90, 103, 105, 111; Cuban strategy, 91; leadership of Fifth Army Corps, 101, 114
Shaw, Robert Gould, 17, 106
Sherman, William T., 18, 24
Sigsbee, Charles B., 52, 53
Smith, Henry J., 14
smokeless powder (nitrocellulose-based), 91–92, 97
social Darwinism, 31, 140, 146
Somerset Club, 78, 80
South Dakota, state of, 73, 152
Spain: collapse of empire, 122, 141, 147; efforts at reform in Cuba, 50, 51; government of, 45, 50; influence on world stage, 141; peace treaty with United States, 128 (*see also* Treaty of Paris); rule in New World generally, 10, 88; suppression of Cuban rebellion, 44, 45, 48; vulnerability of, 10–11, 27–28, 33, 41
Spanish-American War, 3, 6, 7, 20, 29, 39, 47, 76, 122, 123, 145, 162; African American service in and aftermath, 132, 133; anti-imperialists' view of, 61, 89–90, 115; causes of American deaths in, 124; Congress declaring war on Spain, 33, 59, 77; fighting in South Pacific, 59–61, 140; fomented by media, 53; as "just" or "unjust" war, 61; McKinley's call for volunteers for, 71; and pride in American expansion, 123–24; US military preparedness for, 69; as "war of choice," 33, 61, 147
Spanish empire: as cautionary tale, 147; collapse of, 122, 147
Spooner, John, 153
Steffens, Lincoln, 78
Stevens, John L., 43

Stimson, Henry L., 24
Stoddard, Henry L., 16
Storey, Moorfield, 115
Strachey, John St. Loe, 163
Strong, Josiah, 25, 30; *Expansion, Under New-World Conditions*, 140–43; as expansionist, 22, 140; notion of Anglo-Saxon superiority, 23; and *Our Country: Its Possible Future and Its Present Crisis*, 22, 23, 140–42; as religious leader, 21–22
Student Volunteer Movement (YMCA), 23
Sumner, Samuel S., 103, 105
Sumner, William Graham, 146–47

Taft, William Howard, presidency of, 163
Tallman, George, 115
Tampa, Florida, 83, 84, 90, 118
Teller amendment, 58–59, 154
Tenth (US) Cavalry regiment, 88, 107, 133; in assault on Kettle Hill, 113; in assault on San Juan Hill, 110, 114; ignored by white Americans, 131–32, 160; praise of, by military historians, 115; praise of, by Rough Riders, 108
Texas, state of, 68, 72, 78
Texas Rangers, 73, 164
Third (US) Cavalry regiment, 113
Thirteenth Amendment, 133
Thomas, John R., 99
Topeka, Kansas, 157
Toral, José, 112, 113
Torrey, Jay L., 73, 74; rough rider outfit raised by, 83
TR. *See* Roosevelt, Theodore, Jr.
Tracy, Benjamin F., 29
transoceanic empire: answering need for regeneration, 25; United States as, 6, 25, 49, 135, 140, 143
Travis, Grant, 2
Treaty of Paris, 135, 137, 140, 146; anti-imperialist objection to, 123, 150; debate over, 123, 142
troop-raising: efforts by others, 73–74; TR's plan for, 73, 76
Tumulty, Joseph P., 165
Turner, Frederick Jackson, 24–25, 34

Twain, Mark, 14, 35; as anti-imperialist, 144–46
Twentieth Massachusetts Volunteer Infantry regiment, 14, 15
Twichell, Joseph H., 145

Union League, 80
United States: becoming world power, 153; as empire, 5, 11, 28, 31, 143; interests in China, 145–46; interests in Cuba, 43, 44, 47, 143, 154; interests in Guam, 123, 153, 155; interests in Puerto Rico, 123, 135, 136, 137, 154; interests in the Philippines, 60, 122, 123, 139, 140, 142, 143, 144, 146, 147, 151, 154; and Monroe Doctrine, 38, 41, 49, 61; overseas obligations of, 154; war in Philippines, 140; westward expansion in, 5, 29, 33, 35
urban life: "club" types, 80; as eroding traditional American virtues, 19, 21, 41
US Congress, 38, 47, 54, 56, 60, 71, 72, 111, 142; and annexation of Hawaii, 43, 50; declaring war on Germany, 165; declaring war on Spain, 33, 59, 77; McKinley's message to, 58, 66; and naval appropriations, 27, 29, 40, 41, 42; pressure on McKinley, 51, 58; support for citizen soldiers, 70; support for Pan-American Exposition, 155–56
US naval power, 122; enhanced, arguments for, 28, 29, 31, 39, 40, 41, 47; at Manila Bay, 59–60, 140, 145, 146; at Santiago, 90, 91, 112, 124, 145
US Naval War College, 6, 26, 41, 58
USS *Indiana*, 29
USS *Iowa*, 29
USS *Maine*, 33, 34, 49, 56, 58, 69, 74, 110, 118, 119; casualties from explosion of, 52–53; dispatched to Havana, 51; McKinley's response to disaster, 53–54; sinking of, 50–54, 65, 69
USS *Massachusetts*, 29
USS *Olympia*, 60
USS *Oregon*, 29
Utah: state, 152; territory, 35

Van Treese, Harry, 103
Vermont, state of, 58, 116, 157

Victor, Colorado, 151
Virginia, state of, 14, 15, 71, 72, 78
Virginian, The (Wister), 34–35
Virile Powers of Superb Manhood, The (Macfadden), 20
volunteers, motivations of, 76

Wadsworth, William Austin, 78
Walters, Frank M., 73
Warner, Charles Dudley, 14
"War Prayer, The" (Twain), 144–45
Warren, Francis E., 58
War Revenue Act, 71
Washington, Booker T., 132, 161
Washington, George, 5, 70, 125
Washington, state of, 152
Washington Post, 151
"Washington's Forgotten Maxim" (TR speech to Naval War College, 1897), 41–42
Watterson, Henry, 165
Weir, J. Alden, 55
West, American: appeal of, to easterners, 36, 89; in film, 159–60; in literature, 35–36, 85; mythological concepts of, 33–34, 85, 160; and notions of American identity, 33–34; qualities of character, as seen by TR, 82, 86; in Remington's art, 36–37, 55; representation of, in Rough Riders, 67, 68, 79, 80, 82, 109; romanticizing of, 36, 74–75; in Wild West shows, 34, 35, 131. *See also* cowboys
westward expansion, 5, 29, 33, 35; Turner on, 24–25, 34
Weyler, Valeriano, 45–46, 48, 57
What Social Classes Owe to Each Other (W. G. Sumner), 146
Wheeler, Joseph, 72, 84, 94, 98, 101, 130
White, Harry C., 100
Wild West shows, 34–35, 131
Wilkes-Barre Times, 126
Wilson, Woodrow, 163, 164, 165
Wilson-Gorman tariff, 44
Winning of the West, The (TR), 5, 12, 25, 82
Winthrop, John, 21
Wister, Owen, 12, 24, 34, 35–36, 37, 38, 55, 56, 122

210   Index

Wood, Leonard, 67, 74, 84, 86, 90, 91, 103; background before Spanish-American War, 76–77; as brigadier general, 101, 131; as governor general of Cuba, 131, 154; leadership at Las Guásimas, 96, 97, 98, 100; leading Rough Riders on foot, 90, 96; personality compared with TR's, 77, 79; recruiting volunteers in the West, 77; and training of Rough Riders, 82, 83
"Wood's Weary Walkers," 90

World's Columbian Exposition, 24, 75
World War I, 27, 162, 163
Wright, Horatio G., 15
Wyoming: state, 58, 73, 74, 152; territory, 35, 36

yellow fever, 93–94, 124, 153
yellow press in America, 46, 51, 57
YMCA, 20, 23
Young, Lafe, 131